GOODBYE LAKE HURON

Goodbye Lake Huron

A Pastor's Personal Struggle with Grief

For Marilyn Pike Nichols
Respected classmate + friend

A Memoir

by

Don Lichtenfelt

Don Lichtenfelt
8-26-14

WIND PUBLICATIONS

International Standard Book Number 1-978-936138-63-0
Library of Congress Control Number 2013945351

First edition

The cover photograph, a Lake Huron sunrise near Port Sanilac,
Michigan, was taken by the author.

Stories are the way we tell
each other who we are.

—Jane Gentry Vance

Acknowledgements

This book is the result of the contributions of many people—most of them associated with the Carnegie Center in Lexington, Kentucky, where writing classes and friendships have become the high-light of my retirement years.

Heartfelt thanks to my four teachers there (in order of their appearance in my life): Jan Eisenhour, Crystal Wilkinson, Phyllis MacAdam and Leatha Kendrick—each of whose encouragement and affirmation have kept me on the writing path. Had any of them frowned or rolled their eyes (in my presence) over my early efforts— had they said a discouraging word—I likely would have decided I was not a writer and called it quits.

Leatha Kendrick has been my teacher for the past several years. I do not have words to express my full appreciation for this lady—a master teacher who has generously shared her love for, and knowledge of, her subject with her many students. This book would not have happened without Leatha. Though circumstances forced me to miss some of her classes over the years, I never wanted to miss. I wanted to be in class.

Special thanks also to the classmates with whom I've been privileged to share Carnegie writing classes. Seemingly ordinary people before whose extraordinary life experiences and insights I have come to stand in awe. At the risk of slighting some deserving persons I extend special gratitude to certain long-time fellow class members whose careful reviews and feedback on my manuscripts provided insights, encouragement and improvement along the way. Especially: Georgia Green Stamper and Brenda Bartella Peterson (both of whom read and critiqued large portions of my manuscript), Alexander Hume, Pat Micheaux, Gail Koehler, Steve Rhodes, Jodaniel Swift, Flo Brumley, Janet Holloway, Doug Begley, Angela Anderson, Nora Burton, Davina Warner and others with whom I may have shared only one or two quarterly sessions.

Thanks to our special friends John Lynner Peterson and Brenda Bartella Peterson for their long-term interest and support for this project, their major investment of time and energy, their technical advice and help with my invincible ignorance of computers. John has prepared every photograph included in this book. Thanks for helping me look better than I am.

My appreciation to the parishioners in our several parishes—many of whom have not lived to see this book come to print. You live on in our hearts.

Major thanks to my wife, Vonda, who took less time to bring four children into the world than it has taken me to complete this book—and with greater ease and fewer tears. You have endured the birth-pangs of writing with me, and shed your tears along with me as we relived these stories.

It is my hope that my readers will appreciate—I'll not say enjoy—these memoirs in the same way I have appreciated my fellow class members' writing. Many chapters have been difficult to write and will be difficult to read—though I hope not unrewarding.

May you find that reading these stories adds to your insight into other people's lives, brings you a chuckle here and there, and helps you bear those difficult and dark times that come to each of us.

Contents

GOODBYE LAKE HURON

At the Cemetery

We do not believe in eternal life
because we can prove it, but we
are forever trying to prove it
because we can't help but believe it.
        — *James Martineau*

I give you broken shafts of sunlight
From fractured granite

I give you glaring sun
From polished stone

I give you engraved words
Far outlasting flesh

You may have the memory of smoke
Rising from blown-out altar candles

The honey smell of hot beeswax
Held in gleaming brass

You may have the hopes and tears
The silent fears that entangle
These death-impregnated moments

As we remind ourselves
In this multiplication of silence
This is a place of new beginnings.

— Don Lichtenfelt

Prologue

Memories Are All We Have

Life is all memory, except for the
one present moment that goes by so
quickly you hardly catch it going.
—*Tennessee Williams*

It's a sunny autumn afternoon in 1965 and Mom and I are sitting in the third floor patient lounge of Henry Ford Hospital in Detroit. Mom is sixty-one. I'm thirty-three.

The lounge is bright and cheerful except for our overpowering sense that death is not far away for her—maybe just outside in the hospital garden.

We hear the purring of surface traffic below us on West Grand Boulevard and the distant deep-throated sounds of trucks on the Davison Freeway running below ground level to our left. The sound is almost pleasant when muted by concrete canyon walls—like the sound of water flowing over rapids.

Mother's scalp glistens through her practically non-existent hair—the result of her chemotherapy. She has to place her finger over the opening in her tracheotomy tube to talk to me in short husky sentences. She knows her time is running out. Last month she had her tenth operation for the cancer that began in the large muscle of her thigh five years ago and then appeared in her lungs. Now it has her by the throat.

When Dr. Burroughs operated on Mom four weeks ago, he removed part of a tumor from her neck and inserted her trach tube. He looked like a badly beaten fighter when he came to the surgical lounge to speak to my sisters Lynda and Lorna (both nurses) and me. He slumped sideways in a chair next to us with his left leg over the arm. His hair disheveled, surgical mask wet and crumpled under his chin, exhaustion on his face—as he told us, "We nearly lost her several times. I think we made a mistake to operate but we have to

3

live with it now." Dr. Burroughs always leveled with us and we appreciated his candor.

Yesterday, when I was about to leave the hospital, Mom sat up in her bed and hugged me hard. I thought she'd never let me go. I felt as though I were in the grasp of a drowning person and about to be taken down myself. Thirty-three years as her son and hundreds of hours together in hospitals and we're still more like strangers than relatives to each other. It's as though, when I was born, there was a great rift between us which neither of us could close.

Here in the lounge a stray fly buzzes and bangs his head over and over on the plate glass window. At the same time mother, in her hospital robe, struggles with a pencil and half-sheet of paper. Now, with her brain starved for oxygen because of pressure on her carotid artery, this teacher who once had nearly perfect handwriting and printing sits and struggles to print something—to rescue her fading thoughts. I can read her first line. It says, "People I remember." She continues her list at a languid pace: Cary King—father, Velma King—mother, Richard Lichtenfelt—husband, Don—son, Lynda and Lorna—daughters. She includes her brother George and her sisters: Janet and Vera. That's all.

I watch her labor over her note. She adds a new heading: "Keep this for always." She *double* underlines her last words and slides the note toward me on the table. She looks me in the eyes and runs her finger along touching each individual word, "Keep—this—for—always," as though to underscore the importance of memory and things unmentioned—like our relationship that never bloomed.

* * *

Now, years after her death, I am keeping her note for as long as my "always" lasts. Some times I think memories are all we have. Memories are everything. Even the ones that never happened. Even the ones we wish had happened.

Introduction

Accidental Iowan

*Every man's life is a diary in which he intends to write
one thing, and is forced by circumstances to write another.*
—*Source Unknown*

Why would an old man, retired from the United Methodist
Ministry for over a dozen years, want to write about his life
experiences? Partly, I suppose, to see those years as a whole—in a
larger perspective. To relive satisfying times, and pay tribute to the
contribution that pain and struggle—in their odd way—make to life
and growth. Partly to answer the question of the aging WWII soldier
in the movie *Saving Private Ryan*, who—years after the war had
ended—knelt at the grave of his commanding officer in Normandy,
France and asked through trembling and tears, "Was I a good
soldier?"

I wonder what that soldier would have said if, upon rising from
his knees, someone had asked him, regarding his years in military
service, "Would you do it again?" I wonder, because shortly after I
met Susan, who is now our daughter-in-law, she asked me that
question regarding my years as a clergyman. "Would you do it
again?" She smiled and waited for my response.

I was surprised by her direct question. Maybe I should have
responded, "I don't answer hypothetical questions," or "hypothetical
questions get hypothetical answers," but that would have sounded
unfriendly. I hesitated, and then answered, "I don't know for sure.
Probably not."

I gave Susan my short answer. What I didn't tell her is that I'd be
reluctant to "do it again" for the same reason a soldier might not want
to reenlist after "doing his stint." While I regard the ministry as an

excellent way to be of service to others, I do not regard it as an easy life—and clergy don't always retire unscathed.

Sometimes, like a soldier, all a pastor can do is to stand with his people, share the pain, endure the sleepless nights, take the hits, and do one's best in a difficult situation. Sometimes, like a soldier, you might not feel like reenlisting—unless you could delete a chapter or two of your life—but that's another hypothetical, and leads to endless "what ifs?"

I gave no thought to entering the ministry until after my junior year in High School when I attended a church camp on Lake Huron near Lexington, Michigan. Dr. E. Wray Wilson, our District Superintendent, who had the body of an offensive tackle on the Detroit Lions, asked me on the final night during refreshments, "Don, have you ever considered the ministry?" I nearly strangled on my cookie and punch. When my coughing spasm ended, I allowed as to how I'd never given it a thought.

"Well, you ought to give it serious thought," he said, looking at me intently for a moment before he walked away to chat with other youth.

Several of my friends laughed too, when I told them about it. That confirmed my impression that it was a silly question to ask a teenager whose chief fantasy was to become the middleweight boxing champion of the world.

But the question would not go away. Dr. Wilson's words popped up again and again. "Have you considered the ministry, Don?" Part of me began feel it doesn't hurt to think about it. You know you'll never be a professional boxer—that's pure fantasy. *Yes, that's true, but I hate to give up on the idea.* So, what *do* you intend to do with your life? You want an occupation that's compatible with your Christian faith don't you? *Yes.* You want to do something to support people who are hurting and struggling. You want to be in a helping profession. *Yes, that's true.*

Gradually the commotion in my mind settled in favor of the pastoral ministry as a logical and valid choice, and that led me to assume the studies necessary for ordination in the Methodist—now United Methodist—Church. The belief that I was "called" carried me through many a difficult time where I could see no way through, but to trust God in the dark. For the better part of forty years I relied on the thought, "God has called me to this work, and God will see me through no matter what."

After I entered the ministry I recalled a bedtime conversation with my father. I was six or seven, and about the time I crawled into bed Dad asked me, "Donnie, what do you want to be when you grow up?"

I had a ready answer for that question: "A pilot, or a policeman, or a fireman." Then it occurred to me that my father might have some idea on the subject. I asked him, "What do you want me to be?"

"Well," he said, "I'd like to have one of my boys be a doctor, and for one to be a lawyer, and one to be a minister. Wendell is going to be a lawyer. Maybe you could be a minister."

I began to cry, and told him, "I don't want to be a minister." Just then someone on the porch twisted the rusty-throated doorbell on our front door. Dad shushed me, "Stop blubbering. You don't have to be a minister. You can be whatever you want to be."

I was several years into my life as a clergyman when I recalled that incident, and it made me wonder. Had God called me, or was I responding to my own deep-felt need to please a father who seemed almost beyond pleasing? Did God call me through my father? Or did I realize that the ministry was where human needs, and my interests and abilities crossed—or could be trained to cross?

I now toss those questions aside as unanswerable though I'm tempted to ponder them now and then. I acted on what I believed at the time. I completed a year at Central Michigan College at Mt. Pleasant—due mostly to my brother R.J.'s influence. He served as the director of food services and married student housing at Central. While I was at Mt. Pleasant, Dr. Charles Mackenzie pastor of First Methodist adopted me as student associate pastor. Reverend Mac was a short feisty gentleman and a former Golden Gloves Champion from New York. How many clergy are boxing champs? Maybe there's still hope for me.

I spent the balance of my college years at the conservative Asbury College (now Asbury University) in Wilmore, Kentucky, due to the influence of my pastor, Rev. Paul Pumphrey. Oddly, Paul graduated from the liberal Boston University School of Theology. But he served as a member of the Detroit Annual Conference Committee on Ministry. He said he didn't agree with everything they taught at Asbury, but he liked the deep earnestness Asburians displayed—their willingness to go anywhere they were sent and make a go of it. "As to any cockeyed ideas Asbury might teach—the world will knock that out of you soon enough," Paul said.

The best thing to happen to me at Asbury was meeting Vonda Anderson. We are different from each other in so many ways: she likes country music, I favor classical; she likes parties, I prefer smaller gatherings; she loves going to movies, I go only when dragged to them—unless it's a boxing movie. Vonda's an extrovert, I'm more into solitude. She devours novels; I read poetry and self-help books—to little avail Vonda tells me. She's a sweetheart; I'm somewhat of a curmudgeon. Still, we were married on September 3rd, 1953. Since then several friends have told us they felt sure our marriage would never last. Maybe not, but now we're in our sixty-first year and still counting.

As college graduation drew near classmates began to realize they may be seeing each other for the last time. A classmate asked me, "Where are you going for seminary?"

"Garrett in Evanston, Illinois."

He sucked in his breath with a quick hiss—surprised that I could "compromise" myself by going to a liberal seminary. I ran into the same response at Garrett when other students asked, "Where did you do your undergraduate work?"

Despite the disapproval on both ends, I'm glad I went to two quite different schools. I appreciated people and teachings in each school. I'm certain neither has a monopoly on truth. I was comfortable with the thought that "People don't care how much you know, until they know how much you care." I knew I needed love and understanding more than to have someone else's creed forced on me. I figured caring for others was more important than arriving at "final truth" through some supposed lofty omniscience.

With college behind us, Vonda and I turned our thoughts toward getting a student-pastorate in southwestern Michigan. That would give us a parsonage to live in, a modest income, and freedom to attend Garrett which was part of the Northwestern University Campus—all this while remaining in our home state of Michigan.

We announced our availability. No response. Weeks passed. Still no response. Time got tight. We needed housing and employment so we could get established before seminary began. We called a West Michigan District Superintendent. No current openings. Then we received a call from Dr. Glen Hartong, a District Superintendent in Iowa. The towns of Calamus and Grand Mound had had no resident pastor for three years. They would accept a student pastor. The annual salary was $3,000. No travel allowance, no heating allowance for the non-insulated hundred year old parsonage that gobbled up $500 a year in fuel back in the 1950s. It was 200 miles to seminary in Evanston, Illinois, but Calamus was on the Chicago and Northwestern Railroad. I could take the train in and back. The parsonage had a newly redecorated kitchen—the least I could do for Vonda. We accepted—sight unseen. The next day an offer came from Michigan. I wavered, but stuck with my commitment to Calamus. And that, as they say, has made all the difference.

Vonda and I headed for our student-pastoral appointment in our used blue Mercury that had logged over 117,000 miles. We had bought it from Professor Murphy for $1,000 just before graduation. The Mercury and a tiny rental trailer carried all our earthly possessions: wedding gifts, linens, clothing, my boxing gloves which I'd still be using, and an ugly green and white ceramic lamp that had belonged to Vonda's grandmother. For years I offered a five dollar reward to anyone who would "accidentally" break it. Vonda destroyed it herself, years later, when she moved the lamp table without unplugging the lamp.

With no Interstate expressways we drove through every town and city between my home town of Marlette, Michigan, and our new home in Calamus, Iowa. New friends—the salt of the earth—would be our mentors and companions for the next seven years. Under their patient tutelage we would learn about ministry, and about human caring. Here Vonda would begin her teaching career, become the mother of Colin, Lance and Lisa, and cover for me during my absence for parts of the next five years in seminary.

Here, over the next seven years, we would experience our earliest funerals, weddings, baptisms, murders, suicides and other human crises. Here we would initiate the building of a new church, and establish friendships that have nourished and sustained us well past fifty years—all because of a serendipitous moment that changed our plans and the course of our lives forever. I have wondered what if the Michigan superintendent had reached us a day earlier. Our lives would have been different in so many ways—but could there possibly have been a better beginning? I don't think so, but I'll never know because that was the road not taken.

Marlette Years
1932 – 1954

Home is where your story begins.
—Source unknown

The simplest questions are the most profound.
Where were you born? Where is your home?
Where are you going? What are you doing?
—Richard Bach

Family Portrait

No family can hang out the sign:
"Nothing the matter here."
—*Chinese Proverb*

*We are never done with thinking about our
parents, I suppose, and come to know them
better long after they are dead than we ever
did when they were alive.*
—May Sarton

A quarrel I'm still having with my dead parents centers on the apparent lack of wisdom in their decision to marry. Mine is not the only voice to be raised in protest. According to my Aunt Vera members of the Methodist Episcopal Church questioned Rev. Niemann's judgment in marrying Ruth King and Richard Lichtenfelt in 1931. So many that he felt compelled to make a public statement justifying his decision to marry a twenty-seven-year-old single woman and a forty-five-year-old divorced grocer who had sole responsibility for raising five of his seven children after his first wife, Susan, left him for another man.

In fairness to all, let's remember that 1931 was one of the worst years of the Great Depression, that divorce, or marriage to a divorced person was regarded as highly scandalous in those days. And that my "overly thirsty" grandfather Friederich Wilhelm Lichtenfeldt was a part of mother's newly acquired family.

Paradoxically, if this unlikely couple had not married, I would never have been born. For much of my childhood and youth that would have seemed acceptable because I spent a good deal of time reflecting on how I might exit this life, on the strong chance that it might improve my situation.

Around the middle of World War II, when I was about twelve my father took me to the Presbyterian Church for a supper and program—one of the rare times Dad took me somewhere. I had always wanted to attend the Presbyterian Church because some of my friends went there. It didn't happen. "Not as long as you put your feet under our dinner table," my parents laid down as law.

But, this evening Dad and I were in the Presbyterian Church for a supper, and afterward we would view display tables covered with many menacing war relics and souvenirs of war which local servicemen had sent home from the front. There were German and Japanese flags, numerous guns, knives, mortars, grenades, spent shells of all different sizes, and many other war items on display. Especially interesting to a boy like me who had three older brothers in military service—a boy who had no idea of the stress this put on his father.

Dad and I sat at the folding banquet table nearest the entrance. I was impressed with a colorful bouquet of flowers about eight inches high placed there as a centerpiece. Our whole family was big on flowers. I reached out with my right hand gently cupping the bouquet. "Look, Dad, aren't these pretty?" At once I felt a searing pain on my left thigh which brought tears to my eyes. Another of Dad's frequent and powerfully delivered pinches which he used in lieu of words to correct real, or supposed, social infractions.

I drew back my hand in a reflexive response, and sat there a few moments seeing only blurry people through my tears. I said nothing to Dad. He whispered through clenched teeth, "Don't touch!" As usual, I felt I'd not only done something terribly wrong but, worse still, I was what was wrong with his world.

I was terrified of my father. The slightest offense brought about severe punishment with whatever was handy: a hand, a belt, an oak yard stick, a razor strop, a wooden slat from a melon crate. I wasn't sure which hurt worse—the pain of being struck, or the fierce look of hostility on his face. Years of similar treatment led to my frequent fantasies of running away and living alone somewhere in the woods where nobody would mistreat me—not always tell me how bad I was. Often, in my growing hatred of all adults who abused their power and authority, I would dream of taking my own life. Then they'd wish they'd been nice to me, and I'd be free from further abuse and pain.

Mother seemed to agree with, or at least accept, Dad's methods. The closest I would get to support from her was, "Don't say anything. You'll only make it worse." I was further enraged at his excessive physical punishment of my younger sisters ... done in obvious hostility, and on bare flesh. Leaving welts up and down their legs.

I became convinced I was not really my parents' birth child or they would treat me better. Mother seemed shocked when I asked if I were adopted, and she was unable to comprehend my frequent suicidal talk. Her best counseling technique was, "Suicide is for cowards." I told her, "No! It takes courage to kill yourself, and when I get enough courage I'll do it." (I didn't know at the time that my sister, Clarice had already tried—twice.)

The log cabin where my father, the son of a German immigrant, was born on February 13, 1886, in Marlette, Michigan.

One bright sunshiny afternoon, when I was about ten, the world was looking dark and hopeless to me. I was alone in the house, and walked into my parent's bedroom. I opened the top drawer of their chest, and reached under Dad's clean white handkerchiefs. I lifted out his silver .32 revolver with the black knurled grip. I hefted it in my hand feeling its weight, and coolness. I turned the revolving cylinder. It was loaded, and ready for use. Slowly, I touched the tip of the cold barrel to my temple beside my right ear. I snugged my index finger against the trigger, drawing the hammer back slightly as I wondered what it would be like not to be.

15

I applied more pressure, felt the perspiration form on my forehead. Then, slowly released my hold and returned the gun to its hiding place beneath the white monogrammed handkerchiefs. I wasn't brave enough. I would have to wait until I had enough courage.

When my three brothers returned from World War II, my father became noticeably more relaxed—less angry. Business improved at the family store with the end of food rationing—though I gathered that Dad was still in debt. I was larger, and since I'd taken up boxing I got more respect from Dad.

Three years passed. I was sixteen. "Don't plan on going anywhere tonight," Mom notified me just before it was to happen, "We're going down to the Bloss Studio to have a family picture taken."

"Aw, Mom, I don't want to go," I said. "I was going over to Lee Osborn's. Anyway, we don't need a family picture. What good is it?"

Grudgingly I put on my only sports jacket—maroon corduroy—and my brother's flashy hand-painted tie with blue brush strokes. Not particularly appropriate. But I heard no complaints. Our family wasn't great on style.

Mr. Bloss arranged us for the family portrait. I was perched on a low stool. My sisters, Lynda and Lorna, eight and eleven years my juniors stood on either side of me. They wore identical cotton dresses. Mom and Dad stood behind us. Mother managed a half-smile, her thin lips pressed together above her triple strand of pearls. This woman who had married a man eighteen years her senior with a ready made family of five. How they happened to take the misguided—if it was that—step of marriage was beyond me. Perhaps it was a certain desperation on both their parts as they saw their chances slipping away—or a mutual need.

Dad's eyes were bright. His full smile makes me think Mr. Bloss had just said something amusing. Dad's Masonic pin gleamed on the lapel of his blue-gray suit. Not showing was the violent temper for which he was well known within our immediate family. Not showing was his own family history as the orphan son of German immigrants ... the perpetual grief of losing his first daughter, Virginia, in a gas heater explosion at age five ... the strain of having three sons in combat zones in World War II ... and so much more that he'd endured unknown to us.

My Father's Second Family —
L to R. — Lorna, Mom, Don, Dad, Lynda,

I sat front and center, staring into the lens of the camera. Mr. Bloss volunteered, "You can usually tell who's here under duress"— an obvious reference to me. He pushed the plunger with his right thumb, and we were frozen together in time in the only formal picture of my father's "second family." Frozen together in a closeness that belied the actual distance between us all.

* * *

Now, a lifetime later, and our parents both dead since 1965, I sit in our den with elbows resting on our oak desk—my head resting on my interlaced knuckles. My eyes climb diagonally up the left side of our picture wall to that same family portrait. Five people posing as a family. Appearing to be close when we weren't.

The sixteen-year-old boy in the maroon sports jacket stares at me with a look that says, "I'm not here because I want to be." And he still wonders, "Why couldn't we be a real family? Why couldn't we be close like other families? Why didn't we ever get to really know each other?"

I look back at the picture of the boy I was and say, "Maybe we had it better than we know—compared to the tough times they had to go through. Maybe we wouldn't have done as well as they did under their circumstances. Maybe there's no such thing as a perfect family."

And who knows, maybe someday I'll feel as helpless against suicide as my mother. Maybe I'll come to have more understanding of my parents' feelings.

Cleaning Fish

What is this life, if full of care,
We have no time to stand and stare?
— *William Henry Davies*

It is the summer of 1939. I am going on seven years old. Michigan and my parents are still feeling the effects of the Great Depression. Mother and father are deeply in debt with three children at home to feed. Happiness is scarce in our house. Smiles seem rare, and usually forced. My youngest half-brother is twelve years older than I. With older half brothers and sisters in—or coming to—our house now and then I have seven persons with parental authority to rule and overrule my life. But we didn't count "halves"—we just said "my brother" or "my sister."

I'm learning that life is grim, but here and there I find beauty— mostly in nature. Mostly when I'm alone. The butterflies and hummingbirds flitting in Mother's garden are my special friends, and the Jenny Wren that warbles outside my bedroom window to wake me each morning.

Today is Monday. I'm in the kitchen with Mother, when we hear the distant ringing of a bell. It's Emil Gish coming up Wilson Street with fish for sale. These days commercial fisheries are thriving on Lake Huron. Merchants buy fresh fish from the wharf in Bay City and peddle them on our streets in Marlette. Mr. Gish is moving up our dirt street driving his old chestnut horse, Bessie. After every sale he rings a bell mounted by the seat of his wooden wagon with wooden spoke wheels to let others know he's coming

Bessie is in no hurry. She moves with a rhythmical "clip, clop, clip, clop" stirring up miniature dust storms around her hooves. Mr. Gish slows down in front of our white clapboard house with a gentle "Whoa, Bessie," and a "Good morning, Mrs. Lichtenfelt." He slides the tops off flat crates made with clean white wood to show us his selection. I climb a wagon wheel with my feet on the horizontal spokes and gaze at these piscatorial wonders gleaming in summer sunshine in their bed of coarse cracked ice. "I've got Lake Perch, walleye, bass, and herring today." Their iridescent scales radiate glittering rainbow colors in the direct sun falling between our two maple trees. Their dark lifeless eyes ask unspoken questions.

Mother chooses herring—two for each of us. Mr. Gish weighs them in his battered suspension scale, and wraps them in newspaper. Mother pays him from a small leather change purse, and I get to carry them in past the climbing red roses on the south end of our porch, past the low red and black oriental poppies, and my favorites—the tall pink hollyhocks. We climb the unpainted steps into our rickety back shed, through the groaning screen door calling for oil, and into our unpretentious kitchen.

Mother takes the fish from me. She plops them down on an old copy of the *Port Huron Times Herald* spread on the mottled blue linoleum surface next to our long sink with its chipped white enamel. Our lone water faucet is mounted crudely on a galvanized pipe extending about a foot above the sink. There is a half-used bar of red Lifebuoy hand soap in the glass soap holder.

I pull up an old wire café chair that came from the little restaurant my father ran for a while before he became a grocer. Standing on the chair gives me a commanding view. Mother holds the first slippery herring down by the tail and strokes the scaler toward the head with a musical rasping sound. Scales fly like Christmas glitter. She beheads each fish with a sharp knife. She tosses the heads in the old triangular vegetable strainer in the corner of the sink. It is battered with use. She deftly inserts the knife inside the opening and slits a fish back to its anal orifice. All sorts of interesting things spill out on the newspaper. Mother holds the knife like a pointer. Her crooked thumb points away from her hand at a left angle—the result of a childhood operation which removed the extra thumb she was born with. She says, "See, these red things? They are gills. Fish don't have lungs like we do. Fish swallow water and the gills take oxygen out of the water so the fish can breathe. Fish drown in air, just like people can drown in water." She proceeds down the length of the small cluster of entrails using her knife pointer. "This is the heart that pumps blood around the fish's body. See this thing that looks like a little white balloon? That's the fish's air bladder. That keeps him from sinking to the bottom of the lake. The fish pushes himself through the water with his tail, and the other fins keep him going straight. This is his stomach—look here, it still has a minnow he ate for his last meal."

20

"Oh, oh, this is a mamma fish. See all these little yellow eggs? I'll fry them up special for you." And so the lesson goes on with her knife pointing out new things to my young eyes. Mother has done a few strange things in her life—like keep my dried up tonsils after Dr. Gift operated on me, and keeping my appendix (which turned out not to be the problem after all) in a tiny olive bottle with formaldehyde for preservative. Today she surprises me by giving me the little air bladder, and one of the herring's eyes for me to play with. The amazing little bladder floats entirely above water in the soup bowl mother gives me. I alternate between the wonders of my two new gifts. How do fish know to grow air bladders? How can flat black eyes take pictures like little cameras?

Mother proceeds to flour the fish in preparation for frying them in sizzling butter in her black iron skillet. Shortly the grand aroma of mild flaky fish frying will fill the room. We haven't even set the table yet and unbeknownst to me at the time mother has given me a special memory good for a lifetime.

Fishing with Dad

People forget years and
remember moments.
— *Ann Beattie*

My father loved fishing—no doubt about that. We have a number of pictures of him fishing in Otter Lake when he was a young married man. That was in the early 1900's when fishing was really good. One picture shows him trolling in a row boat in his white dress shirt and a tie tucked into his shirt half-way down. His sleeves are rolled up and he is wearing a farmer's straw hat. The combination is quite incongruous. Other pictures show him holding stringers full of good-sized pike. Another a single really large pike. I remember the way he lit up when he talked to me about those days, and how he would hold the line in his teeth as he rowed in anticipation of a strike.

You'd think anyone who liked fishing so much would go often. Not Dad. I don't know if it was his strong reluctance to work or play on the Sabbath ... if he was simply too exhausted from six long days of hard work in his grocery store ... or if the expense of driving the 80 mile round-trip to fish seemed prohibitive. Probably all three—plus his more advanced age and other confining factors.

Though he liked to fish, I often wondered why Dad didn't seem to like me. His grandchildren have told me they were frightened of him. I was more than frightened. I was terrified—as a therapist pointed out to me years later. From my adult perspective I can understand why a father who already had fathered seven children would not want another child. Especially in the midst of the Great Depression when he already had responsibility for five children from his first marriage, the youngest of which was twelve years older than I.

I'm sure I'd never have come into this world if there had been a reliable method of birth control available—short of abstinence. It's not difficult to believe my birth was an unwanted accident (a fact confirmed for me by my mother later on). What I don't comprehend to this day was the degree of hostility Dad seemed to direct at me as a child. I mention it here only because Dad and I had few relaxed and

22

Dad, Don, and spectator, fishing in Lake Huron from the
Lexington, Michigan, pier. Circa 1943

happy times together. One that stands out was the afternoon we went
fishing off the pier in Lexington, Michigan, on Lake Huron.

I can remember when there was commercial fishing on Lake
Huron, and there were fishing wharves at Lexington where fishermen
unloaded what their nets had taken. The fish were sorted, and put in
large flat crates filled with ice. You could buy fish right off the pier
then. Some of them were still flopping and twitching in the crates
before being sold or sent off to nearby markets. The marketing
portion of the wharves disappeared early in my childhood. I have a
vague unconfirmed memory of there having been a fire—coinciding
with the apparent demise of commercial fishing in Lake Huron at
Lexington.

The pilings and planking were still intact when we went fishing.
We fished up on the pier because Dad, being of necessity frugal, was
reluctant to rent a rowboat to fish on the lake. As a ten year old boy, it
seemed to me an awesome distance down to the water—maybe ten or

twelve feet. That was enough to scare me when the water was deep, there were no railings, and I didn't know how to swim and was afraid the fall alone might kill me.

We had dug earthworms from our back yard and baited our long shank hooks with all, or part of a worm. It depended on the size of the worm whether we used all of him at once, or broke him in half and used him twice. We dropped our lines over the edge from our fishing rods. No bobber. Just lowered the hook and sinker four or five feet down in the water and waited. I remember how good it felt that Dad and I were doing something together, and that he was teaching me something new. This seldom happened.

We waited a long time for the lake perch to discover our free meals. This gave me time to absorb the beauty of Lake Huron which stretched toward Canada further than the eye could see. What wonders—these gently undulating blue waves ... the pale blue sky with dozens of white gulls soaring overhead...other gulls walking the edge of the water looking for minnows...more gulls floating on the surface—rising and falling with the rhythm of the waves.

Those gulls with their raucous screeching...the bright sun warming my skin ... the slightly fishy smell of the cool breezes off Lake Huron worked their magic. This was a whole "nother" world to me, and Dad wasn't acting angry at me. He was almost like a friend.

"How do you know when you've got a fish," I wondered out loud.

"Oh, you'll know when it happens. Don't worry about that." Dad looked out over the water where huge ore boats plowed back and forth between Duluth and Detroit and Cleveland. The empty boats heading north rode high in the water. I remember how, to my child mind, the water seemed to be sloped upward toward the horizon, and how, in certain places, the boats could be seen from several miles inland at though they were perched high atop a long hill of blue water. In those early World War II days you could sometimes see twelve or fourteen ore boats all at the same time.

After a long wait, Dad's line suddenly took a dip and he announced he had one. He played the perch a bit until it tired, and then swung him up on top of the planks. Such a beautiful creature—fresh caught and shimmering in the sunlight, flopping vigorously, his scales—white and yellow and green—sparkling in the sunlight like jewels. Parts of him reflected the peacock colors of iridescence. It seemed a shame to end the life of so marvelous a creature. Dad put him on a stringer. He hadn't quieted down before I felt a strong tug on my line along with a kick of adrenaline as I hooked my first Lake perch ever. Both Dad's and mine were huskies over a foot long. They'd be equal to three or four average perch. It was hard to take my eyes off those beautiful creatures. They were bursting with life and energy in their last moments, looking out sideways from their heads with their large eyes. Their mouths opened and closed spasmodically as they gasped for oxygen… as though they were still in water. It was a shame to see them dying. I felt guilty and glad at the same time. I wouldn't want anyone to do that to me.

After a couple of hours we had enough to feed our family plus a mess for Grandma and Grandpa King. Then came the surprise—a large school of hungry perch had come under the pier as the sun neared the tops of the trees on the bank behind us. Dad and I, and a handful of other fishermen, began getting bites as fast as we could bait our hooks and drop them in the water. Soon townspeople and boat fishermen lined the entire perimeter of the pier. The fish seemed ravenously hungry and would take the bait as soon as it settled in the water.

Some fishermen had jigs that held a pair of hooks on their line. They were pulling perch in two at a time. Some found they didn't even have to bait their hooks. Just toss your line in, and the hungry critters would strike a bare hook.

As dusk fell, the number of fish being taken dwindled, and the people dispersed with large catches on stringers, in onion bags, in gunny sacks, and in pails. I never saw the likes of it again. Dad and I filled our laundry tub nearly full of perch, and gave away two or three dozen to other fishermen on the pier. We drove up the slope and through Lexington. We headed west on Highway 90 into the majesty of a marvelous sunset. Tired, and happy, and smelling of fish.

* * *

I've returned to that spot many times. The tremendous force of the waves and the scouring of the ice floes in springtime have erased those strong pilings. All that's left are a few big boulders that used to line the ramp up to the pier.

It's sort of a tradition for me now—to get out of the car and take a slow walk down to where the water cuddles the sand…to sit on those sun-warmed rocks and run my hands over their weathered surfaces…to remember how they were born in volcanoes in Canada millions of years ago and were carried to the shore of Lake Huron by glaciers thousands of years ago. I sense something of their great antiquity as I caress their surface and know that every atom of my body is as old as those granite boulders are. I look out over Lake Huron's deep blue water…up at her light blue sky with a mere handful of gulls soaring—quietly now—and remember one of the rare happy days my father and I spent together.

Model Child?

When I can no longer bear to think of
the victims of broken homes, I begin
to think of the victims of intact ones.
— Peter DeVries

It seems clear to me now that my parents had a special need for me to be a good child. Any child's behavior, good or bad, tends to reflect on parents. Especially so if a marriage seemed unwise to others from the start—unwise to certain members of the family, of the church and of the community.

My parents married in 1931. Mother was 27. Her first and only marriage. Dad was 45. He'd been previously married and was the father of seven children. He was responsible for five at the time since Virginia had died in a stove explosion at five years of age, and Janice lived with her mother from birth. In the midst of those, and other, built-in problems, my parents married during the Great Depression.

I believe it may have been as a consequence of public misgivings about their marriage that they made every effort that I, their first child, reflect well on them and their risky decision to marry. I felt the pressure to be a model child early on. I grew up afraid of snarling dogs, hissing cats and other natural dangers. I was also frightened of my father's leather belt and our oak yard stick, of wood slats from melon crates and words shouted at me with a snarl and looks from my father that seemed like they could kill me.

I was four years old, and a kindergartner when Nancy Smith—a member of my kindergarten class—was killed a short block from our house. She was struck and run over by a truck on Main Street near the Methodist Church. My parents took me to her little house down near the railroad tracks to see her body in state in the Smith's living room. They probably had their reasons—which, I'm sure, included sharing the pain of grieving parents—but today I wonder why parents would take a four year old into such a situation. Nancy in her little casket bore no resemblance to the bubbly, bright eyed little girl she was in kindergarten. Mom told me it was because the truck had run over her head and crushed her brains out, and that her head was stuffed with

27

cotton. I was invited to believe that would happen to me if I were not careful crossing the street. True, but the medicine was adult stuff and I was a child.

I grew up believing just about everything was dangerous and would harm me. That I dare not do anything without reference to my parents. I felt I was not entitled to have ideas of my own, or make my own decisions. I was almost always tense and uptight— ready to wince at the slightest suggestion of a blow coming in my direction from adults or other children.

As a married adult, I visited Niagara Falls for the second time. I looked down over the high railing and saw the small train carrying people down the slope to the Maid of the Mist—the boat that carried people by water to the base of the falls. Suddenly I was revisited by the sense of fear I'd had as a child when my father held me over that rail so I could

Don, long before he knew how to handle those gloves

see better, and then threatened to drop me. He was being playful, of course—but I wasn't sure. I felt I was a bother to him, and he would be glad not to have me around. It hurt to think I was nothing but a fly in other people's soup.

"Can't you do anything right?" Dad would growl at me. I became afraid to try because whatever I did was guaranteed to be wrong—or too expensive. Some of my "inconsequential" little habits were of major concern to him because of our shortage of money. "Don't scuff your heels when you walk. Shoes cost money you know." "Turn off the light when you're not in the room. You're running up the electric bill." "Turn the water clear off. If you let it drip, you waste gallons of water every day." Those complaints I could understand though I had a hard time remembering to do, or not to do them.

28

Dad never swore at me, but he when he became aggravated he often said a vociferous, "Blame you!" which you couldn't mistake for a blessing. (I never heard another person use "blame" that way and wondered if it were a German expression—since Dad spoke fluent German.) He often said—in a similar tone of voice—"You should be *ashamed* of yourself." I was—because he said I should be.

As in any child's growing up years there were occasional accidents, conflict and acts of violence in the community. There was no homecoming football game in our hometown of Marlette the year I turned ten. Ray Marcum our star half-back had been killed by a farmer's deer rifle. He had been part of a small group of teen-age boys who attempted to make off with watermelon from a farmer's field. It must have been near Halloween when boys felt such "pranks" were acceptable.

The frustrated farmer, wanting to protect his livelihood, scared them off and fired at the fleeing car with his high-powered rifle. He probably intended to puncture the car and leave the boys with some explaining to do. Instead his bullet passed directly through the trunk—and Ray's head—as he crouched in the back seat.

Early the next morning the death car was in Wilson's Chevy Garage directly across the street from my father's grocery store. Dad walked me over to look at the damaged car. He pointed through the right rear window where, in the morning light, I could see a giant patch of gore covering the center of the back seat. More of the same on the floor looking still damp and glistening, with particles of what I suppose was brain tissue splattered about the rear passenger space. I think Dad wanted me to know what the consequences of stealing could be. I was impressed. What ten-year old wouldn't be?

I believe my parents wanted me to be afraid of doing the wrong thing. Afraid to make mistakes that could be injurious, of course. But also afraid of stealing, and—above all—making mistakes that would disgrace the family. I feel that way because that's what he said to my sister Clarice when she left home on a train one time. "Don't disgrace the family," he told her. For much of our lives we lived with the fear that we might, and what could happen to us if we did. That, in brief, is how we were reared—and not all for the better.

A Boy's Eye View of World War II

Older men declare war. But it is the
youth who must fight and die.
— *Herbert Hoover*

There is many a boy here today who
looks on war as all glory, but boys,
it is all hell.
— *Gen. William T. Sherman*

I turned nine in November of 1941 and three weeks later, on Sunday afternoon December seven, I sat on our living room floor listening to my parents and my older brother R.J. talk. Our RCA table radio was playing in the background but nobody paid any attention.

Suddenly regular broadcasting was interrupted for a special announcement by President Franklin Delano Roosevelt and the four of us stopped to listen as he told of the Japanese attack on our naval fleet in Pearl Harbor. I heard him say "a state of war exists between the United States and Japan."

I doubt if any of us knew there was such a place as Pearl Harbor until that day and even so, they told me, Hawaii was in the middle of the Pacific Ocean thousands of miles way—and Japan was way beyond Hawaii. Still, my parents seemed worried for reasons I didn't understand and their apprehension spread over me the way a dark cloud passes over the sun and leaves you feeling chilly and susceptible to the unknown.

Not long afterward there were four red, white and blue service banners hanging in our front window. They signified that my three brothers: Wendell, R.J., Larry and my brother-in-law Lee Whaley (my sister, Clarice's husband) were in the military service of our nation. Soon pictures of those four brothers in uniform looked down at me from the top of our upright piano. I took time to look into each of their faces regularly. I tried to imagine where they were and what they were going through. Sometimes it scared me half to death as I tried to link them with newspaper and radio reports of battles going on around the globe—battles that are still active memories in our nation today.

Early in the World War II years my mother began a solo project which brought the war smack into my father's grocery store. Mom solicited snap-shots of all the service men and women from the Marlette area and posted those pictures and the soldier's address in several large blue wooden frames. She displayed them in the street-side windows of our family grocery store. She kept the addresses as current as possible so townspeople could write our warriors or send them care packages.

Soon Mom discovered she needed a way to indicate service people's status. She chose to use colored stars as symbols: Gold for killed in action, purple for wounded, white for missing in action, red for prisoner of war. It was no small task to keep the addresses and status up to date. Our store became a focal point for sharing information about the war, for public mourning for the wounded, the missing, and those killed in action. People would stand in front of the meat counter or near the check out and speculate about the progress of the war—and whose family members might be next to be sent into harm's way.

Often I stood by listening to adults share their fears, watching their silent tears and absorbing their sense of apprehension and grief. It seemed as if our community had suddenly become one large family and all those who went to war were our fathers, our brothers, our uncles and aunts.

* * *

Children could not escape the war at school. Even there we faced regular reminders. We pledged our allegiance to the flag on a daily basis. Every Monday morning children bought war stamps for ten cents each to support our country's war effort. When our book was filled with stamps we would take them to the Post Office or the Bank and have them converted into War Bonds. A $25.00 bond cost $18.00 and matured in ten years.

Day by day students shared any new information about their brothers or other relatives in the military. At first there was considerable rivalry between branches of the service. Music class created considerable competition to have your service man's military song sung first: *The Marine Hymn, Anchor's Aweigh* (Navy), *Off We Go Into the Wild Blue Yonder* (Air Force), *We're the Seabees of the Navy* (Naval Construction Battalion), *Over Hill, Over Dale* (Field Artillery) and so on.

Regular newsreels kept school children aware of the events of the war. I remember being terribly frightened by actual footage of the bombing of London with screaming sirens, burning and collapsing buildings, exploding bombs, anti-aircraft fire, and footage of the wounded and dead—most of them civilians. The films were black and white but they gave me Technicolor nightmares.

One grade competed with another in scrap drives to see which could collect the most scrap iron for making tanks, battle-ships, helmets, cannons, and the like. We helped collect scrap aluminum for warplanes. In the fall we took school-time and school busses to go into swampy areas in the country. There our school kids collected many dozens of burlap bagsful of milkweed seed pods. These provided kapok filling in life jackets for pilots downed at sea and for soldiers on troop transports. It felt good to think that what I was doing, as I stuffed dry milkweed seed pods into a gunny sack, might save a soldier or airman from drowning.

New stories of war circulated every day at school. I remember Steve Mateyak tearing up as he told how his brother in the air force had been badly wounded in the chest and would not fly again and how Johnnie and Anita Navarro were devastated when their brother Cecil was killed in Italy and hearing how David "Peanuts" Smith, fresh out of playing high school basketball had been killed in a Japanese air attack on his ship and, I think, he was buried at sea. I remember the day Junior Brown came to school and cried quietly for much of the day after he learned that his brother John had been killed in the Marine invasion of Iwo Jima. It seemed the mounting toll of death and destruction would never stop. I couldn't help but wonder if our family would be the next to hear that one of my brothers had been killed or wounded, maimed or blinded—or just disappear with nobody ever knowing the circumstances.

During the war years all my brothers were sent to major theaters of war. My oldest brother Wendell became an infantry captain in the Second Armored Division ("Hell on Wheels") under the command of legendary General George S. Patton. His infantry unit was one of several cut off in Belgium by the massive German counter-offensive known as the Battle of the Bulge. Our family knew from the news that his unit was surrounded, short of food, ammunition and warm clothing—and that a bitter winter blizzard prevented air drops to resupply them. His safety and survival became our main concern for weeks and made Christmas and New Year's Day somber reminders of the dangers he faced in Belgium.

My brother R.J. joined the navy and became second in command of LST 981 (Landing Ship Tank). His ship struck a mine in the English Channel during the invasion of Normandy and the crew thought they were going to the bottom. The Captain gave the order to abandon ship but the ship didn't sink. The mine damaged her propeller and steering mechanism and she remained dead in the water of the English Channel while the invasion continued. Later LST 981 and her crew were towed back to England and then all the way back to the United States for repairs. Following that, R.J. sailed on his repaired LST through the Panama Canal and across the Pacific for the invasion of Pacific Islands including the Japanese island of Okinawa, the fiercest battle in the Pacific.

My youngest brother Larry had been working for Lockheed Aircraft in California. They manufactured the twin-fuselage Lockheed Lightning P-38 fighters. Larry entered the army and was shipped to Calcutta, India for three years while the war ebbed and flowed in the CBI (China, Burma, and India) theater.

My brother-in-law Lee—a crack marksman—was an infantryman in the invasion of Normandy and beyond. He fought at San Lo in France where his unit was cut off by the Germans for some days. After it became history the newspapers carried an account of how those troops were without food and extremely short of ammunition. Some of them ate human flesh to survive and had to crawl out into no-man's-land to retrieve rifles and ammunition of dead soldiers in order to protect themselves from annihilation.

With few exceptions my brothers seldom spoke of their war experiences after returning home as was the case with most veterans.

LST 981

England
3 June 1944

Dear Dad, Ruth and Don:

When you read this, it will no longer have been news, but within a few
hours we will be moving out to take our place in the spearhead of the
Invasion. Will not have an opportunity to mail it until after the initial
thrusts, but will place them on my desk for someone to mail on the return.
Just wanted you to know that in these last hours before starting out I was
thinking of y ou. Try not to worry too much. At the moment I don't seem to be
nervous or afraid, however, there will be time for that later. The excitement
and last minute preparations may be responsible for that. Haven't time to
write the others so will leave that for y ou.

Hate to close with so little said, but time will not permit any more. Take
good care of yourself and send my love to the rest of the family. Will
always be thinking of you, and wish I could say something that might allay
your fears. Rather lonely, but you no doubt can imagine how I feel. Tell
Don to be a good boy for me, and to grow up to be the best of the Lichtenfelts.
We're all come a long way together, and I pray that we can soon b e with you again.

G'night Dad, Ruth, Don and the rest. My thoughts are of you all.

Your Son

My brother R.J.'s letter on the eve of the invasion of Normandy, France.

The Lichtenfelt
Brothers

Wendell

R.J.

Larry

War became the constant theme of conversation everywhere. Children's games and toys came to center on war. Metal was not available for toy guns but most every boy I knew had a hand-made wooden rifle and pistol and a hand-carved wooden knife for our backyard "attacks on the enemy." We wore whatever military surplus clothing we could get, and killed each other many times over in war games we would never have played had we known the true horrors of killing, wounding and maiming.

* * *

Our government urged every home to save kitchen grease from frying pans and roasts and turn it in for the manufacture of explosives. Most citizens planted "Victory Gardens" in their backyards so they wouldn't have to buy as much from stores and there would be more food available to send to our soldiers.

Coffee, tea, sugar, soap, butter and many other commodities were either not available at times or were in extremely short supply. My father went to his store under cover of darkness to grind what few pounds of coffee beans he received for his customers. Grinding coffee during business hours would have attracted too much attention. The noise of grinding and the conspicuous odor of fresh-ground coffee would have filled our small building in short order and word would have spread around town. After grinding coffee beans at night Dad bagged the coffee in plain brown sacks, tied them with string and set them under the counter for our regular customers. When regulars came in he'd simply sneak the coffee into their grocery bag and charge them for it. There would be no words spoken if other customers were nearby.

Often coffee wasn't available and we ground roasted soybeans as a substitute. I was too young to be drinking coffee, but I never heard anyone suggest that ground soybeans were anything but a sorry substitute for coffee.

When catalogs came to our home during the war many items were crossed out and marked "not available." This applied to items in most every category and it became obvious the war was changing the way we lived. To mend clothing and wear patches rather than to buy new was regarded as an act of patriotism. It made more clothing available for our soldiers.

Many other foods, gas, tires and other items were rationed in those days. We could not buy rationed items unless we had the appropriate government coupons or tokens. Even then we couldn't always get what we wanted. It was common practice for people to trade ration coupons with their family and friends to allow for people to get what each person needed the most.

Automobile production stopped during the war as factories in Detroit (then the automobile capital of the world) were converted to making military vehicles. Maintaining old cars became difficult as mechanics entered military service and replacement parts became hard to find or unavailable.

The federal government established a thirty-five mile per hour maximum speed limit in order to conserve gas for military use. Auto owners received little adhesive triangles to place on their speedometers at the thirty-five mark as a reminder to help in the war effort—and of course you could be fined for going faster. Only people providing vital services (like doctors, police, and volunteer firefighters) were given additional gas rationing coupons.

* * *

As in every war enemies demonized each other. Stories of the Bataan Death march circulated complete with reports of the bayoneting of those who could not continue. (Later I would have the funeral of a military doctor who was part of the death march.) We heard stories of Japanese soldiers tossing babies in the air and catching them on their bayonets, slashing open the bellies of pregnant women, torturing American prisoners, of tying American soldiers to trees, cutting off their penises and forcing the severed part into their mouths then gagging them and leaving them to die of their injuries. I couldn't help but form images generated by such stories—images of witnessing such brutality or of being the victim. I could not imagine—or maybe I could—such horrific acts of savagery. If I shuddered to *think* about these things, how much worse it would be to *witness* them in person…and how unbearable to be the *actual victim* of such atrocities.

Even regular radio broadcast stories became a part of rousing the American public with portrayals of the Japanese and Germans as cunning, treacherous, cruel, vicious, bloodthirsty people. It came as a shock to us later when we learned that, as might be expected in the heat of battle, our soldiers sometimes wreaked similar havoc upon our enemies. That was seen as justified by the extreme circumstances of war.

* * *

My father worked long hours in his grocery store because help was scarce with so many men gone to war or involved in work vital to the war effort. On many Sundays he joined other townsmen in donating his labor to the manufacture of military trailers as our local mobile home factories had been converted to military purposes.

In addition Dad spent certain nights serving as a volunteer air-raid warden. Citizens in Marlette were required to black out all lights in their homes when air-raid sirens went off. This was done so as not to aid the German Air Force if they decided to make suicide attacks on the tank and plane factories in Detroit using the polar route—the shortest most direct route from Germany to Detroit. Once Dad took me down to Kitley's Lumber Yard to spend the evening watching and listening for German Planes from a small lookout built on top of the roof. It contained posters with silhouettes of German planes and a phone to notify the authorities if we saw or heard anything. I conked out in the chair while Dad kept alert the whole midnight to six a.m. shift.

His volunteer work for the war effort proved draining for my father who had more service stars in his window than any other parent in the area. It frightened me to see him tired and worn—especially when he had one of his frequent "catch pains" which often caused him to cry out and drop to one knee. I felt certain one of those sharp pains would be his last and I'd have to report his death—or as the military might call it "collateral damage." I had no doubt his pains were real and possibly life-threatening. We had no way of knowing for sure since many doctors were called into military service and our two small-town doctors had little medical equipment and no hospital to work with.

* * *

Selfridge Air Force Base was located about sixty miles south of our town and often huge formations of B-17 Flying Fortresses woke us up in the morning. I felt awestruck as I looked out my bedroom window and saw hundreds of bombers going by in formation and heard the ominous roar of so many engines—four to each bomber.

In my youth I thought the Air Force was a good place to be if you had your choice of which military service you'd join. After all you flew your mission and came back. You had a clean, dry bed and good food and rest between missions. No crawling through the mud on your belly, no seeing the people you killed, no hand-to-hand combat.

I'm glad I didn't know at the time that most of those planes and their crews would not survive the war. They seemed such an over-powering force. How could an enemy stand up against such a mighty fleet of airships? Yet they did—with great ferocity.

Virgil Wilcox—who grew up in our town—piloted one of those B-17s. Once on a sunny summer afternoon—on a solo run—he buzzed our town several times with his *Flying Fortress*. The four engine plane made a horrendous roar as he flew over just above the treetops. I was cutting across Henry Fellows' back yard at the time and was so overwhelmed at the size of the plane (the biggest I'd ever seen) and its roar (the loudest I'd ever heard) and its closeness (it appeared as though it were falling on me as its shadow swept over me) that I sank to the ground in fright his first time around. Some days later I heard someone say that Virgil had been reprimanded for his unauthorized buzzing of his home town.

During the war Virgil's plane was shot down in France and he was listed as missing in action for some time. Our town breathed a collective sigh of relief when we learned that, though Virgil had been badly burned, the French underground rescued him and managed to return him to England. During his tour of duty in Europe he was awarded five Purple Hearts and promoted to Major.

I imagined myself as a crew member on Virgil's plane—facing anti-aircraft fire and German fighter planes. Felt the plane shudder and burst into flames. Felt it lurch out of formation. Wondered if we'd die of the flames before we crashed—or if we did survive the impact—if we'd be so horribly injured we'd just have to lie there in agony until German soldiers walked up to us and put a bullet through our brains, and our families would never know what happened to us in the end.

Major Virgil Wilcox (8th Air Force) and Sergeant John Brown (USMC) are among the military dead buried in the Marlette cemetery. When I visit my parents' grave site I usually visit Virgil's and John's graves as well. I stand beside their brass military plaques mounted flush with the ground and think of the day Virgil roared over Marlette in his B-17 and the day Junior Brown cried throughout the day after he learned his brother had been killed in one of the bloodiest Pacific island invasions of the war. I think of the horrors that men like them endured time and time again, and of their families who once wept over these graves…and are no longer here to weep.

Something holds me to places like this…some mysterious magnetism that makes me not want to leave … makes me want to just stand there in awe. I spend a while in silence and, before I leave, I always kneel to brush the debris off their brass memorial plates and pull any grass that is growing over them—as the small boy that is still in me attempts to honor their memory and regrets that they had to go through the insanity of war.

Maybe part of my fascination for places like this is the knowledge that someday someone may be looking down on my final resting place, reading my name and the years of my life and saying, "I remember … "

* * *

Toward the end of the war in the Pacific the Japanese discovered something our country didn't know about yet—the upper level jet stream. This knowledge allowed the Japanese to send balloon bombs from Japan to the US in 33 hours. Reports of fires and deaths caused by these bombs generated fear. One night as I lay half asleep in bed I thought I heard a thud and a dragging, scraping noise on the porch roof just outside my window. It had to be a Japanese balloon bomb—I'd been sensitized to expect it. I sat up with a jolt—my heart beating wildly—too frightened to get up and look out the window. Most likely the noise came from the wind blowing maple branches against our porch roof.

According to a TV documentary I saw recently the Japanese released about 9,000 such balloons. Three hundred have been accounted for in the US. Military men assume than many are still out there in wilderness areas of the American West. I've talked with enough family members of service men to know that there are countless "emotional bombs" left over after our country's wars and the casualties continue—even after "war's end."

* * *

When President Harry Truman ordered the dropping of the first atomic bombs on Hiroshima and Nagasaki, Japan, it seemed little thought was given to the morality of killing over 150,000 Japanese citizens. We thought only of the total number of people who would die in a land invasion of Japan—both American and Japanese, both civilian and military. Some argued that fewer would die from using Atomic bombs than in an invasion. Witness the fact that a total of nearly 250,000 persons (American and Japanese—including civilians) died in the battle of Okinawa alone. At that time it seemed that the Japanese had sowed the wind and were reaping the whirlwind. Only later did questions of massive destruction of civilian life, the thousands of living survivors seared by radiation, and the alteration of genetic life arise.

* * *

Upon discharge from service men were welcomed with parades, praise, and pride in their accomplishment. They began to take their place wherever there was an opening. Many took advantage of the GI Bill of Rights and got much of their college education at government expense as a partial recompense for their great sacrifice.

After the war our High School hired new teachers who'd known their share of horror. Neil Thompson, our new coach, had been in combat in Europe. Now he ran his teams as though other teams in the league were the enemy and he was the commanding officer. He was given to fits of hostility, swearing at team members and striking them on occasion. Because of his great bulk and unpredictable temper he sometimes frightened people in the community as well as players. On one occasion he publicly grabbed another man by the throat and pinned him on a table. We hadn't heard of PTSD (post traumatic stress disorder) in those days but it was there in disguise.

Dick Austin became our agriculture teacher. He left a large segment of his intestines in Italy after being shot in the abdomen in the invasion of Anzio. Cal Byers taught English and rented a room in the Fox residence next door to us. Cal was machine-gunned while escaping his disabled tank. He lost most of his left arm. Still he was cheerful any time I saw him—I have no idea what he went through in his alone times. He played catch with me on occasion. He'd wear the baseball glove on his only hand to make a catch, and then he'd flip the ball in the air, tuck the glove under the stump of his arm in time to retrieve the ball with his bare hand and make the return toss.

I felt strong respect and admiration for this young teacher/ neighbor who had gone thru hell ... yet whose face always seemed luminous with joy. I think it was because he came so close to death, and he was terribly glad to be alive.

* * *

To this day I am still horrified and fascinated by WWII documentaries and movies. As a boy I tried to imagine what our fighting men were experiencing in the rigors of training ... what it felt like to be on a bomber over Germany when casualties were over 100% in some units—when even replacements for the dead were being killed ... what were the feelings of those soldiers who were the first to hit the beach in an invasion carrying heavy loads of equipment through blood-reddened water up to their armpits all the time being fired upon by batteries on the shore ... what it felt like to be wounded, cold and alone in a muddy shell-crater in enemy territory ... what it was like to be wounded in the narrow hedgerow warfare in France and know you were about to be run over by one of your own tanks which had no alternative but to move over you ... .to be the victim of cruel torture inflicted by the enemy to gain vital information on troop movements ... what it was like to be captured and wonder if you'd live to become a prisoner of war ... or what it was like to be one of the first to liberate Nazi death camps with their stacks of rotting corpses which had to be bulldozed in mass into deep trenches. To the extent I entered those feelings I was horrified to the point of having to turn it off. Virtual reality is bad enough. What would it be like to be in such situations and have to put your own life on the line over and over again?

Bells, Bells, Bells, Bells, Bells

O peace! How many wars were
waged in [your] name.
—*Alexander Pope*

Victory is no longer a truth.
It is only a word to describe
who is left alive in the ruins.
—*Lyndon B. Johnson*

The first I knew about it was when the bells started ringing. Bells, bells, bells, bells, bells! It was an Edgar Allen Poe sort of day.

I was twelve at the time and we didn't have twenty-four-hour news stations back then. Commercial television hadn't come to our town yet. Many people in Marlette, Michigan didn't have telephones. We didn't have a phone. My father's grocery store didn't.

The sounds came from all over our little town. The Methodist Church across Wilson Street from us, with its slow, mellow bong...bong...bong! The Mennonite Church bell with its clang-clang, clang-clang; the Presbyterian bell with its slow dang...dang...dang; the Adventist Church three blocks south with its agitated clingity-clang...clingity-clang! Add the Marlette High School bell with its ominous ding...dong, ding...dong and you had a marvelous cacophony. Clingity-bong-clang-dong-bong-dang-ding-clang! They all rang at once making unplanned music the way an orchestra makes strangely beautiful music as individual musicians tune up—all at the same time.

The fifteenth of August, 1945, was a great day for ringing bells. The sounds flooded every space outside and in. You could not avoid hearing it. People tumbled out of houses, out of stores onto the street. "What's happening? Why are all the bells ringing?"

"The war's over! The war's over! Japan surrendered!"

People laughed through their tears and cried through their laughter. They hugged each other. They hooted and hollered. "The war's over. It's all over. At last! It's over! It's over!"

Then, as if for emphasis, the Marlette fire-siren began its mournful wailing, up and down its shrill arpeggios, screaming low and slow to

43

high and horrible. That siren always made my blood run cold and sent a shiver up my spine. It sounded like a dinosaur shrieking and roaring as he died.

Soon the steam whistle at Riley's Creamery joined in with its high-pitched scream, punctuated by whatever pauses the rope-puller chose to insert. People brought out every noise-maker they could get their hands on: pots and pans banged together like cymbals or thumped with serving spoons; whistles, duck calls, trumpets, trombones, bugles, automobile horns and shotguns—though ammunition was scarce and precious—whatever was at hand that made noise. Everyone of every age got in the act somehow.

Our high school marching band, in their red and white uniforms, led a spontaneous parade down Main Street that evening playing Sousa marches. Cars and trucks of many makes and models—up to 1941 when Detroit stopped making cars and turned out tanks, and trucks, and planes for war—all joined the parade with drivers waving, shouting, and honking their horns.

Our firefighters clung to the sides of their big tanker and sprayed water high in the air and every which way. People lining the streets got soaked, but didn't seem to mind. Our town's old antique fire truck—source of pride to old-time firefighters—chugged along coughing and sputtering until the hose man on the newer truck sprayed its engine with water and it stalled dead in its tracks. Its crew pushed the old truck to the curb so the parade could move on. Such a wonderful laughing/crying confusion.

Emerson Kitley drove his elegant Rolls Royce down the parade route. When Emerson blew his horn it was like a blast from the brass section of a symphony orchestra—mellow, and right on key! It was a stunning spectacle.

The noise continued well into the night. Two Methodist buddies and I took turns ringing our church bell. It was heavy and hard to get started. It took two of us youngsters to pull the rope down and get into a rhythm and when the rope went up it took a kid up in the air a few inches. We rang the bell so hard we turned it over. That meant no more ringing until some husky adult could climb up in the tower and right the bell again.

I walked alone down to Riley's Creamery where a drunken citizen was pulling the rope of the steam whistle. Finally he tired and I took over. After midnight the supply of steam expired. As I walked home down Wilson Street, revelers were still celebrating over on Main Street. In the relative quiet and dark, I thought of my three brothers whose military portraits lined the top of our piano. They would be coming home—alive! R.J. from having served in the naval invasion of Normandy and in the battle for Okinawa in the South Pacific, Larry from his three years of service in India, and Wendell from having served in the Battle of the Bulge—who was about to be shipped to the Pacific if the war had not ended when it did. We would see them again—unlike the family of hard-working young John Brown who was killed on the black and bloody coral sands of Iwo Jima or gangly red-headed "Peanuts" Smith who went from playing high school basketball to the Navy, and death at sea in the battle for Okinawa. These and too many others who went to war from Marlette would never be hearing a bell ring again.

Before long my mother would take down the snapshots of Marlette's service men and woman she kept posted in Dad's IGA grocery store window. She would take the military pictures out of their large frames and put them in her World War II scrapbooks along with the colored stars denoting wounded, prisoner of war, killed in action or missing in action.

As our warriors returned during and after the war, there were stories—most of them remained untold. But you couldn't help hearing about how Hugh Thompson felt compelled to sleep on the ground in his parents' back-yard after he came back from Guadalcanal with his nightmares of jungle combat with the Japanese. You couldn't help noticing Cal Byers had no left arm. He lost it to a German machine-gunner when he exited his burning tank. You couldn't help seeing Virgil Wilcox's facial scars from when the Flying Fortress he piloted went down in flames. So many stories— some told but most locked up in memory. So many stories of young warriors that would be sealed up until warriors became old and faded away.

But, for this day at least, it was a great horn-honking, bell-ringing, whistle-blowing, band-playing day. The war was over. Peace had come to Marlette and every town, city and village in the United States. Peace had come to Berlin and Cologne and Dresden—peace! For them it was the peace of the ashes.

There was peace in Hiroshima and Nagasaki—the peace of atomic obliteration. The only moving things there—the whispering winds of desolation as moving air shuffled radio-active dust this way and that. Another "war to end all wars" was over. "Never again," became our universal hope and expectation. But the seeds of other wars were sleeping in the dust waiting, waiting, waiting their time.

Winter Outing

A boy must be initiated into the world of men.
It doesn't happen by itself; it doesn't happen
just because he eats Wheaties.
And only men can do this work.
— *Robert Bly*

I am not a winter person. Though born in Michigan I've never gone overboard for winter sports—skiing, tobogganing, ice-fishing, winter camping—not even building snow forts and snow men when I was a child. My main recollection from such activities is of numbing cold, and red raw chapping on unprotected portions of my anatomy between gloves and sleeves, boots and pant cuffs and between scarf and hat. Our family didn't always have money for new clothes to keep the cold and snow out.

I'm not sure what pried me away from the comfort of my home to go for a winter hike and cook-out with some of our scout troop on one of the coldest days of the year—but there we were—six early-teenage boys stuffed in a Chevy station wagon and heading north to the river bridge at Deadwater. Mr. Reindel, our scoutmaster, must have had better things to do on such a cold day, but I'm glad he chose to take us places where our fathers didn't—or weren't free to take us. He parked his wagon on the squeaky snow at the shoulder of the road near the bridge. Snowplows had cleared a wide path there to limit the effect of drifting from blowing snow.

The six of us spilled out wrapped like mummies against the cold. Most of us wore long-johns, two pair of jeans, two pairs of wool socks, five-buckle rubber boots, two pair of gloves—one over the other, wool jackets over sweaters, and wool hats with bills and ear flaps, and scarves. We were cold-proofed and nearly immobilized in the process.

Still, we managed to scramble up the six foot ridge of compacted snow and ice left by the snowplow. We negotiated the far slope by digging in our heels as we descended and bounded toward the fence like huge living marshmallows. We held the strands of barbed wire fence apart for each other so as not to get hung-up on the barbs.

47

We paused to get directions from Mr. Reindel, and then proceeded to enter a winter wonderland unlike anything we'd ever seen before. Even in our rambunctious spirit of adventure we stood in awe with, "Wow! Look at that," and "Jeepers, I never saw anything like that before."

We stared at the bare tree limbs over our heads. They had been transformed into an ice crystal cathedral by the freezing of condensation on the branches. As we looked east toward the early morning sun each icy branch was lit with a magical radiance reflected in the hoarfrost. Here and there you could see rainbow colors gleaming from the branches where the ice acted as miniature prisms.

As we walked toward the river in this otherworldly beauty we discovered another surprise. Multiple layers of thin ice had formed when the river had overflowed into the marshland. It had formed one sheet of ice about a quarter of an inch thick which was held aloft by its attachment to reeds shrubs and tall dead grass. The water had dropped a couple of inches and formed another level of ice and another before receding within the banks of the river.

We stood there a moment awed by the reflected colors of the sun on the ice and the musical broken-glass-like sounds our feet made with each step we took on the brittle ice. It seemed a shame to mar anything so beautiful. If only we could preserve it forever for others to see—but ice comes and goes and this was ones of the few times we could break something to smithereens with complete impunity.

We struck out willy-nilly, each on our own irregular path. No other purpose than to shatter as much ice as we could. The sound was deafening and echoed in the hollow like some giant xylophone played by a musical madman.

We broke much of the available ice in our musical extravaganza, and moved on to slightly higher ground where my cousin Ivan discovered a set of rabbit tracks in the snow which entered a brush pile. Tom Rasmussen suggested that we try to catch it and add fresh grilled rabbit to our lunch menu. Mr. Reindel, who raised rabbits as a hobby seemed agreeable. We began dismantling the brush pile top to bottom in search of the furry critter.

I felt sure the usual menu of roasted hot-dogs would satisfy me. Besides, I thought it highly unlikely we'd capture anything as elusive as a rabbit. To my complete surprise we soon saw movement of fur and the boys managed to trap the rabbit by standing on branches which pinned it down until four gloved hands grabbed the rabbit's remarkably strong and kicking feet.

We stood in a tight circle looking down at our living meal. That poor rabbit knew it was a goner. To me there was something pathetic about a thing so wild and beautiful being held upside down with it heart thumping rapidly under its fur, and its panic-stricken eyes bouncing wildly in their sockets.

I was relieved when Mr. Reindel said, "Oops, we can't eat this one guys. She's female and she's pregnant.

The boys lowered her to the ground. We stood aside as they released her. She bounced pell-mell over the snow and into the safety of the woods as though she had wings. I wondered about her for several days. Did she miscarry or have her litter? How could her brood survive in such harsh conditions? Had we done great harm to a wild creature?

We found a spot on top of a slight rise that gave us a view of the wilderness landscape around us. We gathered dead wood and started a campfire. As the burning branches slumped into embers we roasted hot-dogs impaled on sharpened willow branches and ate pork and beans right out of the cans after heating them in the hot embers. This meal—along with carrot sticks and potato chips—tasted much better to me knowing we had let that poor rabbit go.

When we were full we huddled around our campfire and chatted and sang fun scout songs. We ended on a serious note singing *Trail the Eagle* (to the tune of *On Wisconsin*.) It reminded us that our goal was to persevere until we had achieved—what seemed unlikely to us at the time—the rank of Eagle Scout. It was a nice thought, but I doubted I'd ever come close to that rank. I struggled mightily just to reach First Class. Having to learn Morse code almost convinced me I wasn't cut out for scouting.

We sat there staring into the embers, and quietly dreaming for a moment—comfortably warm, well-filled, content and tired with our day's adventure. I wondered to myself if the other boys felt as I did—that a few friends, a kind scoutmaster, roasted hot dogs, baked beans, and a generous helping of natural beauty was just about all a boy needed. Just about all he could want for one day.

Little did I dream then that—with the help of caring scout leaders, merit badge counselors and scout camp experiences—I would become the first scout ever to earn all his awards for Eagle Scout in our little town of Marlette. I am forever grateful for the boost for living and serving that those special people gave this struggling Tenderfoot.

Practically Worthless Farm

No one has yet explained a blade of grass
or the haunting light of evening that falls
like a benediction upon us all. Yet we may
experience the meaning and wonder of it.
That is enough.
—*Richard Caniell*

I don't know what made my father buy that practically worthless forty-acre farm. Back in the 1940s family finances, and parental feelings were not subjects most parents discussed with their children—least of all *my* parents.

I overheard Dad telling Mother that Mr. Gorsline wanted $4,000 for it. Dad was going to offer $2,000. There may have been compromise. Anyway Mr. Gorsline accepted, and the land was "ours." It was three miles south and three miles east of town at the southwest corner of Montgomery and Gosline roads. About a mile from where Dad was born in a log cabin about sixty years earlier. Dad had his hands full as the father of three children still at home, serving as town clerk and running a grocery store. Buying the farm seemed pointless.

The buildings weren't much to look at. More of a liability than an asset. A barn that defied gravity, as it hung suspended on a crumbling foundation. Many of its boards were missing. It creaked ominously when the wind blew, like it was about to collapse. The house wasn't much better. No one had lived in it for years. Everything was old, gray, dusty, creaky, and worn. The roof of the porch hung precariously on the side of the house by whatever rusty nails held it. A family of skunks had taken up residence beneath the rickety floor. The chicken coop was in a state of collapse. The small granary was in the best condition of any of the buildings, but unlikely to be used again—ever.

To me the best part of this new/old forty acre world of ours was the land. With all its hills and marshes, it was untillable except for about eleven acres. The rest seemed fresh from the hand of the

Creator. Especially the seven acres of woodland on the south side where a little river flowed through it.

There was no practical reason to go there. Still it pulled me, much as a migratory bird might feel the urge to fly south during his first autumn—for reasons he could not explain.

While my parents struggled with the hopeless task of trying to make the house livable, and to wrest garden space away from the indestructible crabgrass, I sometimes escaped involuntary servitude, and headed on a nature trek. Out through the cool shadow of the barn where swallows swooped, and pigeons roosted. Past the old cow lot where you could always dig lively red earthworms for fishing. Through the edge of the spongy marsh where pheasants nested and muskrats built their watery houses, and frogs sang nocturnal choruses. Up the eroded gash in the side of the tallest hill, looking for pretty stones in the glacial gravel.

Once on top I could shout whatever I wanted at the barn, and it would echo my words back in loud multiples. As I walked down the pasture land toward the woods, I arrived at that steep slope which took me inside the woods, and into the shade of the tall maples, elms and under the big butternut tree where I could gather edible treasure in the fall, and get my hands stained greeny-black in the process.

Just beyond the butternut tree there was a narrow bend in the river where an elm tree, about ten inches in diameter, leaned low across the river. A wonderful perch for a young boy who loved to sit there listening to the river gurgle its water song, and toss bread crumbs to the hungry minnows. The woods were a place of deep wonder to me. Especially in the early spring when the warming air, and movement of water combined to weaken, crack, then shatter the ice on the river with a sound like a cannon shot.

Warmer spring weather brought the cleansing, life-giving rains— caused the woods to smell that rich earth smell of decaying vegetation which betokens fertility and growth. Then the pools in the lowest places of the woods became cradles of life. Water spiders walked across the water—their tiny legs making hardly a dent in the water ... but deep impressions upon my mind. Joyful singing sounds came from birds, and insects. Mating calls, frog choruses—magnificent musical improvisations. The chanting wind in the branches of the chokecherry trees rippled the surface of the pools. Surrounded by all this beauty, I felt at home with—at one with—the earth, the water, the music, and all living things—as though I was, or had been all these things myself.

On certain days I could spot a cluster of frog eggs entwined in twigs in the pool. Later I saw those wonder of wonders—polliwogs, like large black commas fluttering their tails intermittently, then sitting still in the water. Then, for a polliwog's own reason fluttering to another place looking for whatever it is polliwogs eat. No magic exceeds the wonder of polliwogs in pools. Polliwogs—water creatures sprouting tiny legs. Growing to be little frogs—amphibians equally at home on land or in water. To witness such a thing is to see the incredible, the unbelievable. It is to know a thing is true and still not believe it. Here wonders happened right before my eyes. The Morning Silverspots fluttering their airy dance and lighting on a sprig of goldenrod. I see these things with my eyes—sometimes even hold them in my hands—these tiny four-legged frogs, these butterflies. I see them around the life-giving pools. But I still can't believe my eyes.

I'm glad Dad bought that useless farm. I think maybe, in the back of his mind, my father knew, from when he was a boy living in a log cabin nearby, that there's a place in each of us that can't be filled with money or food, but only with pollywogs, and butterflies, and puddles and wonder.

Still Standing

Man is in love
And loves what vanishes;
What more is there to say?
—*W.B. Yeats*

As a barn it didn't amount to much—yet it was special to me. It sat on forty acres of hilly—mainly glacial gravel—land pockmarked with swales between the hills. Only ten or eleven acres were close enough to level to plow. It had roughly seven acres of woodland on the lower southeast corner. A small river curved through the woods and ran straight for about a hundred yards before exiting to the east. It held a strong attraction for my father whose business was his IGA grocery store, but whose pleasure was being outside in the warm embrace of nature.

So Dad finagled with the owner and we "inherited" this old, some would say good for nothing barn. I would guess it had been there close to eighty years with its solid hand-hewn beams, and hardwood pegs to hold its frame together. I doubt it had seen a new coat of paint or if it ever had one. In places the silver gray weathered barn-wood had been splintered off by forces unknown to me. There were dozens of small openings in the roof. The far end of the L was missing. Still dad was able to rent it out for storage of hay, and the lower level as a cow-barn for a couple of years. After that is just sat there empty and forlorn with no apparent reason for being. In 1953, when a monster tornado struck the city of Flint and killed 114 people, the tornado continued east across Michigan's thumb and carried a lot of Michigan debris all the way across Lake Huron to Canada. Dad thought sure the barn would have been flattened because the main area of the storm passed not too far to the south of town. As we drove out Montgomery road to check we saw several new barns destroyed and Cargill's large red barn twisted askew on its foundation. Not our barn. Apparently it had enough holes to let the wind blow through it like a sieve.

I became attached to the rickety old barn early on. For starters, it had a certain mystique when you stood inside on a bright day and could see many small shafts of sunlight piercing the roof, and the cracks in the side-walls. Dust motes danced in the bright light creating a sharp contrast with the mysterious shadows of the unlighted portions.

On windy days there was an eerie whining music resembling a bagpipe with its constant drone. Other times it had the electric hum of a mystical Aeolian harp. With variation of wind pressure its voice would shift from one of ecstasy to the moaning of a deep sorrow—as though it had human feelings.

Though badly broken down the barn was home for many chirping English sparrows with their little black kerchiefs around their neck. A few pigeons, short and chunky, bluish gray with two narrow black wing bands and iridescent necks and heads, had a fairly continuous soft guttural cooing, and sounded faintly like the echo of violin when they took flight. It seemed there was always at least one family of mourning doves with their soft sandy buff color, and their long pointed tails. Their low mournful coo-ah, coo, coo, coo sounded like a voice from another world.

In the lower level, still smelling of cow manure—a not unpleasant odor when well diluted—the barn swallows made their nests on the rafters, solid cups of mud reinforced with grass, lined with feathers and other soft materials. I have never been able to resist stopping and staring at those swift and graceful birds with their deeply forked tails. Dark steel blue in color, with their buff under parts, and rusty throat and forehead, they kept up a nearly constant liquid twittering and chattering—especially in the evening when they were on their final hunt and destroy missions in search of insects. Sometimes they would swerve close in their flights and you could hear the swoosh of their wings in the air as though some invisible entity were about to land on your shoulder.

I am not proud to say these were days I was fascinated with guns and felt compelled to shoot almost anything that moved. My twenty gauge bolt-action shotgun got a lot of use against starlings. When I could borrow my father's double barrel twelve-gauge I really felt omnipotent. Pheasant hunting was exciting, but so were frog hunting, snake hunting and crow hunting. Why I couldn't have been content simply to enjoy them as the miracles they are I don't know.

I was excited, when as a mid-teenager my parents permitted me to buy a Crossman .22 caliber pellet gun. It used compressed air rather than an explosive brass cartridge. It fired a small lead pellet that resembled a badminton birdie. The advertisement said that with eight or ten pumps of the lever you could fire a pellet through a one inch pine board. I tested it. True, you could splinter the wood with the pellet gun as well as with a standard .22. The gun had a tiny peep sight. I was impressed that if you had a small bird dead center in the sights up to 40 or 50 yards he was a goner. Looking back at those times I find it hard to believe I could have been so gun crazy. I have not owned a gun for nearly 60 years, and am opposed to the wanton destruction that seemed so socially acceptable in my days as a boy.

There were several times when my cousins and I shot squabs in the old barn, dressed them out, and roasted them on a spit over a small campfire. Good eating then, but it would be against my nature to do it today, unless it became necessary to survive.

Besides being a source of interesting otherworldly music, shifting patterns of light and shadow, a home for interesting birds, the barn was a great hideout for a coterie of kids playing hide and seek, or challenging each other to walk the full width of a barn beam with no support. I wonder that more kids don't come to an untimely end walking barn beams. My cousins, Ivan, Willard and Walter, who spent more time in barns than I, seemed to do it without fear. To me it was a death defying act. My heart would be thumping in my throat and my muscles tense and on the verge of spasm. I opted for the relative safety of boxing where you didn't have so far to fall.

Sometimes, my parents would bring my sister Lynda and me to the farm on a summer Sunday afternoon. Lynda and I enjoyed climbing the highest hill on the farm, which was immediately east of the barn. From there we would talk to the barn, and it would echo back our words almost as loud as we spoke them. "Hellooo!" *"Hellooo!"* "I love you!" *"I love you!"* You can appreciate that this old building was taking on a definite personality with me.

It took no time at all to discover that the best place in the world to dig for fishing worms was in the barnyard, right in the shadow of the barn. It took only three or four shovelfuls to half fill a tin can with lively red worms the fish couldn't resist.

All these childhood experiences were sixty-plus years ago, but I still have a special feeling for rickety old barns on the verge of collapse. When we pass one while driving through the country I will often say to Vonda, or think to myself, "Wow, what a good artist could do with that!" I'm not an artist, but I love the way artists can bring out dimensions of decrepit old buildings so it's almost as though they have a voice. As though at one and the same time you can visualize the barn during its glory days of usefulness, and its latter days of worn beauty and character ... hear the drone of wind through its boards, and hear the voice of long-dead farmers and their children reverberating in its echoes ... creating a permanence in the passing in our experience.

Our old barn wasn't much to look at, I know. But in other ways it was something really great. My dad sold the property to Ray Knaggs before he died. Ray's wife was Mr. Gorslin's (the previous owner's) daughter. Interesting how people get attached to land and welcome a chance to keep it in the family.

The barn has long since been removed, foundation and all. The earth around it has been bulldozed level and planted into grass. I don't know how it came to its end. It may have been burned. What I hope is that the barn boards and beams were saved and sold to people who would love and appreciate them—who would panel their den with the antique barn wood—would use segments of its beams as historic mantels on their fireplaces.

I'm saddened they took the old barn down. Even though I know nothing lasts forever I can't help wanting it to. If you were a newcomer to the area you'd never know there was once a barn there in that place. But I know, and the barn is still standing in my mind and it has a special place in my heart. There, I can still hear the wind whispering its mystery stories and the mourning doves cooing their low mournful coo-ah, coo, coo, coo in the rafters.

A Place without Time

There are no seven wonders of the world
in the eyes of a child. There are seven million.
—*Walt Streightiff*

Once in a lifetime, perhaps, one escapes the actual
confines of the flesh. Once in a lifetime, if one is lucky,
one so merges with sunlight and air and running water
that whole eons, the eons mountains and deserts know,
might pass in a single afternoon.
—*Loren Eisley*

I don't recall my Grandfather and Grandmother King telling me they loved me—ever. It wasn't necessary. Had they told me they didn't love me, I wouldn't have believed them. When I visited their home their love seemed to follow me everywhere—like soft music humming in my ears. As if they and I and the place were one while the music lasted.

When I was small Grandma took me on little excursions to explore the wonders of nature. "Look, Donald. Diamonds!" she said once, pointing between a spirea bush and the outside faucet. And together we admired a spider web—a thing of beauty in itself—but this one enhanced with beads of dew sparkling like diamonds in the morning sun.

On another day, after it had rained and the world had been washed, we walked down the driveway. Grandma stopped and pointed down, "Look, Donald, a rainbow." Those were days when cars leaked more oil than they do today and, sure enough, there was an iridescent oil slick on a puddle as spectacular as any rainbow." I never knew what we'd discover when we went out together—Grandma and I—but I knew it would be good and I felt closer to her than anybody else on earth.

Grandma and Grandpa's house sat on about ten acres of land at the very north edge of my hometown of Marlette, Michigan. Beside their two-story white clapboard house with attached garage, there was a small weathered cattle barn with a fun-to-play-in hayloft, a broken down corn crib and a small pasture with a pond on it. They called it Hanley's Pond after a previous owner.

It wasn't a natural pond. It was square. About 80 feet on a side, I'd guess. About four feet deep in the middle. It had been excavated in the 1800s—probably by one man with a horse and a two handled earth scoop—to be an ice pond. It helped supply local ice boxes all year. Even in summer the ice stayed frozen inside the ice house on the hottest days because it was insulated with layers of sawdust.

The ice house was gone years before I was born. Burned down. But the little pond was still there. Grandfather bought it around 1910. It was fed by a tiny creek which entered one corner and flowed out another. It was a great attraction to grandfather's cows, and to his inquisitive grandchildren. That pond held a lot more than water. It held beauty and wonder and mystery and magic.

As I approached the pond, alone or with my cousins, I'd often see a Great Blue Heron lift off—taking flight before pesky boys got too near. There were polliwogs galore and bullheads. Shiny frogs with protruding eyes leaped into the water with a splash from under our feet. Tenacious bloodsuckers sometimes attached to our legs when we waded in the water too long. Sometimes they tore skin away when we pulled them off. Crayfish scooted away from us traveling backwards like lightning as crayfish do. Clams navigated the bottom of the pond by sticking a white leg out of their shell and pushing themselves along, leaving a groove in the soft silt on the bottom of the pond.

We saw water spiders dimple the water with their near-weightless feet on the surface, green and yellow garter snakes, newts, and minnows and cattails waving in the warm breeze. We watched waterfowl bobbing for food, swimming underwater and coming up where we least expected them. In autumn Canada Geese in "V" formation flew overhead yawping in their raucous voices that go straight through you like a sudden outburst of bagpipe music…and maple leaves decorated the water like confetti.

Here we watched white clouds reflecting on the surface of the water in summer like a kaleidoscope changing with the wind. On autumn evenings, bonfire skies turned the water orange and crimson. We were hypnotized with an excess of beauty.

Michigan winters turned the water to ice, sometimes two feet thick. Grand for skating and sledding and sliding under each other like bowling balls. We built campfires from fallen limbs of maple trees and set them burning on the shore—just right for roasting marshmallows and hot-dogs, heating hot chocolate and warming numbed extremities.

My cousins and I rafted and swam in the summer—though I doubt the water would pass minimum standards of sanitation. We fished for bullheads and red horse and yellow and green striped perch. We would watch spellbound as a large dragonfly hovered near us with a buzzy clatter to his wings—then mysteriously reappeared in another spot without our seeing him move. And there was the music of the little stream gurgling between reeds and fallen branches. If you listened a while it put you in a trance. You'd forget where you were or that there was such a thing as time.

I went back to see the pond with all its marvel and mystery last June. It wasn't there. It had been filled in. Bulldozed flat. Covered with grass. Now it's the back yard picnic area for a little Pentecostal church. The tiny creek still trickled through the reeds and cattails on the north side. But there was no evidence that Hanley's Pond ever was—no sign saying "the place where you are standing is sacred to the memory of Don Lichtenfelt and his cousins."

It's a strange feeling when your special places dry up and disappear—fade out forever. When these places are erased, along with the people who surrounded them at one time it makes you feel like you're being erased too ... unless you're taking on new adventures and discovering new favorite spots and favorite people.

The only place my grandfather's pond exists anymore is in the memories of a small handful of people like me. That's why I write about it—so when I'm gone memories of his pond will be preserved in writing. So others can hear that mystical humming sound and maybe feel a grandmother's love again.

Before long I'll need to go back to Marlette and stand where our pond used to be—like a hummingbird climbing the air up and down in search of a feeding station that's been removed. As though expecting it to reappear because it belongs there. And I'll think back to when life was in its springtime...and all nature was singing for joy...and it seemed like nothing would ever be erased.

That Poor Boy Needs Help

A woman should be able to be both independent and
dependent, active and passive, relaxed and serious, practical
and romantic, tender and tough minded, thinking and feeling,
dominant and submissive. So, obviously, should a man.
— *Pierre Mornell*

Everything was peaceful in my life until that tall, blue-eyed blonde from Gaylord, Michigan, arrived for her freshman year on the Asbury Campus. I was coming off a failed romance at Central Michigan, and hadn't dated for a year. I hung out with several different girls being careful not to get too involved lest I get hurt again.

But, this new freshman, Vonda Anderson, was a real eye catcher. We both worked in the college cafeteria. You couldn't miss seeing her swishing around in her blue jersey dress, and hearing her laughter echoing from the hard walls of the kitchen where she worked at the dishwashing machine. She was obviously out of my class and destined for a better life than I could tempt her with. Still, I felt an obligation to myself to try to get her to date me. I'd kick myself forever if I made no attempt to date a catch like her. Lots of other guys would be eager to go after her if I didn't get the jump on them.

Using my best reverse psychology I approached Vonda in the crowded college dining hall as she ate dinner with a male student who I was afraid had similar designs. I interrupted their time together: "Excuse me; you wouldn't be interested in going to the Junior Class outing with me would you?"

She looked at me for a moment—I was expecting, and probably deserved, a turn-down—and after a brief appraisal she responded with a smile and a firm, "Sure!"

"You would?" I couldn't believe my good fortune. Suddenly I was in the same situation as a dog chasing a Cadillac, catching it, and not knowing what to do with it. This was too easy. She couldn't know what an unpromising person I was or she'd never have agreed to date me.

To throw further doubt on her competence, when she saw me coming up the dormitory walk to get her for our first date she said to her room mate, "Here comes the man I'm going to marry." I know it's true because (much later) she told me so, and she admitted that it was her maternal instincts that told her, "This poor boy needs help—bad!"

Several dates later she proposed to me—indirectly to be sure—but a proposal just the same. In the late hours of a late autumn day, when we were about to go each to our own dorm, she said, "Don, before you ask me to marry you, I'd appreciate it if you'd call my Daddy Lloyd (her step father) and ask his permission. It would mean a lot to him."

There was a prolonged silence on the line when I called Dad Lloyd, whom I'd met only once, and carried out Vonda's instructions. At first I thought we were disconnected, but then I heard, "Well, yes, I'd be pleased to have you as a son-in-law, Don." What else could he say in that situation?

Armed with Dad Lloyd's approval, I went with Vonda to the little frame building which was the original Asbury College. We went up the narrow wooden steps and into the small room set aside as a prayer chapel. We knelt together. I did not say, "Vonda, will you marry me." I said, "Vonda, will you be my *partner* in marriage." And she said, "Yes."

Next thing you know we were back in my hometown of Marlette, Michigan, for Christmas holiday. We're looking at engagement/ wedding rings at Hurlburt's Jewelry and Watch Repair. We bought a stunning diamond engagement ring (1/20th of a carat) in yellow gold with matching wedding ring for $67.00 plus tax. That was a major outlay for me in 1952 on a college student's budget.

I gave Vonda her ring onboard a Greyhound bus—parked at a gas station bus stop in Imlay City just north of the railroad overpass. We wouldn't bother telling our parents about our engagement until later. They had enough to worry about.

When we arrived at the Detroit bus terminal Vonda stood on the edge of a crowd, and said to me out of the side of her mouth, "Look at that man over there. He's staring at my ring." I knew he wasn't staring at the ring—he couldn't have seen it from that distance. He was staring at Vonda because she was mighty good to look at.

We didn't tell our parents about our plans at first. No need to add to their stress. We would write a full letter to justify our plans later when the time was right. That letter would become a great source of amusement in our family.

We chose September 3rd, 1953 as our wedding date—eight o'clock at the Marlette Methodist Church—my home church. Big mistake. It turns out to be one of the hottest days of the year. One hundred and three, with the humidity only slightly lower.

Don and Vonda, September 3, 1953

I'm standing in the church ante-room with my pastor, Rev. Paul Pumphrey and my brother Larry—my best man. Our clothes are already clinging to us as the result of perspiration in the heat and humidity. Before the evening is over the groomsmen's and my white dinner jackets will be soaked.

The clock points straight up—eight o'clock. Rev. Pumphrey turns to me, just before we enter the sanctuary, and says, "Well, Don, you're getting the hottest bride in town."

Once inside the sanctuary there's the awkward situation of Vonda's being given away by her step-father, while her mother—who abandoned her twice in childhood—and her third husband, Dick—sit directly behind Dad Lloyd. A little extra tension to liven the evening. But we forget that when Rev. Pumphrey starts the service, and Izzy Mitchell sings "Because," and the "Lord's Prayer." Turns out to be downright enjoyable, but too short. The service is over before we know it.

So the knot is tied, and in the reception line a friend says, only half in jest, "I give this marriage less than a year." Since then we've been told there were others who thought it would never last. Funny, but that thought never occurred to Vonda and me as a serious option—early or late in life. I don't know, but I suspect it was the strong belief that our promises were binding as long as we live—plus a lot of dumb luck which led to the celebration of our fiftieth wedding anniversary in September 2003.

When that first Golden Wedding anniversary card arrived we were both mildly stunned even though we knew it was about to happen. Is this really us—married fifty years? That only happens to old people—real old people who are decrepit. Couldn't be us because we feel like we've got a lot of living to do yet.

But, to be honest, I can see why some people felt the odds were against us. In a way, we're as surprised as the people who said it would never last. Vonda came from a twice-broken home, while I came from a supposedly stable Christian home—with a lot of hidden fractures. She's big city—I'm small town. She's lively, spontaneous and fun-loving—I tend to be more reserved. She loves country music—I'm inclined to classical and semi-classical. She loves to read novels—I could count all the novels I'd read on one hand when we married. She loves to dance—I prefer to canoe and to observe nature. She is a neatnik—I'm a clutterbug! She dreams of going to Paris—my motto has always been, "See Macomb county—or whatever county we're living in at the time—first." These things alone could have been the ruination of our marriage.

Add to that a dozen moves since our wedding, the stress of four building programs—one of which involved nearly sixty committee meetings in our parsonage home in the same year, the effects of thirty some deaths in the family (including one by murder and two by suicide), the discovery that our second son, Lance, was brain damaged as the result of encephalitis at age two, and Vonda's surgeries for cancer and we see how we could have fallen amongst the approximately eighty percent of all marriages which fail in circumstances like these.

Again, ignorance of the facts comes to our aid. We thought these sorts of things were reason for us to draw closer together and be mutually supportive.

Well, we made it. Here we are after sixty years of good times, tough times, laughing, grieving times, hoping, loving times. We're pleased to celebrate that we're still here—alive and in good health. We believe we've got a good thing going as we begin our second sixty years. And they thought it wouldn't last! Surprised? Me too! It helps not to know it can't be done.

Fight Night—Detroit

Boxing's dark fascination is as much
with failure, and the courage to forbear
failure, as it is with triumph.
— *Joyce Carol Oates*

"Ah, yes, boxing—the sport my wife loves to hate," I say, teasing Vonda.

Vonda shoots back with, "It's not a sport, Don. Boxing is brutality and it should be abolished." Then she nails me with a parting shot, "Besides, isn't there something incongruous about a seminarian loving boxing the way you do?" (All I can think of is St. Paul's saying, "Fight the good fight of faith," and that place where he says, "I'm no mere shadow boxer." But I keep it to myself.)

* * *

December of 1953, during the first year of our marriage. We stand in line entering the lobby of the Motor City Arena in Detroit. Vonda's step-father, Dad Lloyd, knows I'd rather box than eat. He bought three tickets—ringside seats, second row—and he's treating us—me at least—to "Fight Night—Detroit."

Inside the lobby two things stand out: the odors, and the posters on the wall. Odors from steaming hotdogs and draft beer, hot pretzels with mustard, heavy cigarette and cigar smoke, and whiffs of cheap perfume swirl around us—now and then a hint of body odor. We pass on the eats. We're already full.

Large posters of boxers in menacing poses grab my attention. Their intimidating "death stares" send a sharp feeling of excitement through me. Some posters are of greats like Joe Louis, former heavyweight champion of the world, a hometown Detroiter, Sugar Ray Robinson former middleweight champion—also born in Detroit—whose sheer grace in the ring made every fight part dance, and Willie Pep, former featherweight champion glaring from behind his bloodied face. When Pep fought you always knew there'd be blood because he cut so easily—had more stitches in his face than any other fighter in history.

The other posters promote upcoming fights and fighters. I imagine myself on a poster as we pass through: *Don Lichtenfelt, promising middleweight contender—ten rounds for the right to a title match.* I'll need to practice my "death stare" like General Paton practiced his "war face." I'm not likely to intimidate anyone with this tame face of mine.

We hand our tickets to the attendant, and pass down a dimly lit corridor into the arena. The spooky sloping hallway feels empty...lonely. Harsh echoes of raucous voices bounce off the bare walls. My imagination is at work. How would it feel to enter this arena as a boxer to fight a man I'd never seen in person? Gut check time. Do I really want to go through with this? Yes. Well, maybe not...but yes.

Another attendant checks our ticket stubs and points us toward the side of the ring we'll be on. He repeats, "Row B, seats 4, 5, and 6. Enjoy the fights!" We pass small groups, mostly men, in animated conversations—some in Spanish, some in Black English. The gathering crowd warms to the prospect of mortal combat. I feel hairs and goose bumps rising on my arms—as though I were charged with static electricity.

Our seats—made of hardwood and anchored in concrete, clatter as we lower them. Dad and Vonda share their thoughts about our surroundings. I stare at the ring: a large square platform about five feet tall, with four ring posts, and four tiers of ropes surrounding the empty space. A space lit with hot pitiless lights and surrounded by a restless sea of impatient fight-fans. Could this be an altar in disguise—one prepared for human sacrifice?

Vonda tugs at my sweater. "Check out the platinum blond in the clingy silver dress." With her is a short man wearing a dress suit and dress hat that stays on for the entire fight card. He sucks on one of the longest cigars I've ever seen, and creates a massive cloud of white smoke. I get the feeling he's not a business man in the usual sense.

Arena seats fill rapidly now. A man in borderline shabby clothes, who apparently drank his supper, settles in next to Vonda. He nods and smiles a rubbery alcoholic greeting. Before the fights are over he'll be resting his head on Vonda's shoulder. This is not your average Sunday go-to-church-crowd.

A large contingency of Hispanics congregate in the balcony. Many have brought brown bag lunches to go with their beer. Activity stirs in the ring now. The Cuban fans shout "Ariba! Ariba!" as their countryman climbs through the ropes for the first bout.

The harsh clanging of the ring bell "summons us to full wakefulness." The ring announcer steps up to do his thing. "Ladies and gentlemen…welcome to Motor City Arena's ... 'Fight Night—Detroit!' The first bout of the evening features two promising light heavyweights." He rattles on in his practiced cadence. "From Columbus, Ohio with a record of 14 wins—nine by knockout—and one loss, Bernie 'The Bull' Ostrander. Oooostraannder!" There is scattered applause. "In the opposite corner, fighting out of Miami, Florida, with a record of 12 wins, 7 by knockout, and one draw, Manuel "The man" Ortiz. Oooorrr-teeez!" His fans erupt filling the arena with raucous cheers, and more chants of "Ariba! Ariba!"

The ring announcer continues, "Refereeing tonight's fight—Mr. Hal Roach!" A smattering of boos and hisses rise to greet the ref. "The ringside physician—Dr. Paul Jarvis." I sense a noticeable non-response to the reminder that boxing can result in serious injury—even death.

The referee motions the fighters to the center of the ring and barks his instructions over the crowd noise. "Alright men, you know the rules. Watch the low blows. Break clean when I give the command. In the event of a knockdown, go to a neutral corner. Protect yourself at all times. Touch gloves, and let's have a good clean fight."

The clang of the opening bell energizes the crowd as well as the fighters as each moves out to establish dominance over the other. These fighters rank several cuts above the Golden Gloves Fighters we've witnessed before. They're superbly conditioned, highly skilled athletes.

To witness a fight at ringside feels entirely different from watching TV fights. In broadcast fights an announcer describes the action. Here it's just happening before your eyes—a story without words—more like dance or music than a broadcaster's narrative.

Now the preliminaries are over. Time for the main event. Two ranked middleweights square off against each other. Each fighter stands alone in the ring against a skilled opponent…each totally identified with his body…each revving up his ferocity…each focusing his gaze on the other like feral animals about to attack.

Of course there is the chance that all this could lead to what Mohammed Ali called "The nearest thing to death"…the symbolic death of knockout…which begins with that moment when one fighter loses control—can't keep up his defense.

This may be on the verge of happening in the ring just above us now as the third round winds down. One fighter, his face bloodied, and absorbing more head shots than is healthy, takes a vicious right hook to the face at the bell. It snaps his head hard to the right. Flecks of blood travel our way. Some spatter on Vonda's white blouse. She looks at me in disbelief. One more reason for her to hate boxing.

I sense myself uneasy in my love of boxing, though it became a controlling fantasy in my youth. I was the youngest and one of least socially mature members of my school class. An easy mark for anyone looking for someone to push around. The legitimate objects of my anger did not wear boxing gloves: the school bullies who felt they could punch me with their bare fists any time they wanted. Those who ridiculed me and called me all kinds of words that hurt. Those who tripped me into mud puddles, knocked my books out of my hands, and burned me with their lighted cigarettes. The excessive use of physical punishment by adults at school or parents at home using switches, paddles, belts, wooden slats from crates, oak yardsticks.

For several years I boxed wherever I could scare up an opponent (back yards, dormitory halls and basements, gyms, and the YMCA.) I realize that, for many fighters, it's basically about displaced anger—rage turned into art—what Joyce Carol Oates has called "ecstatic violence." I remember how it felt to be powerless and begin to feel a competence to stand up against tormenters. How fulfilling it feels to fight a good fight—win or lose—and not quit when your innards are screaming at you to quit—to think on your feet and improvise in mid-fight—to face a crisis without folding. I know how good it seems to confront your "enemy" (even if he's a substitute for someone else) and fight back as best you can. I know "boxing's dark fascination is as much about failure, and the courage to endure failure as it is about triumph." But I know too, how my own nightmare images were expelled after gaining a degree of competence in boxing.

All but the sharpest images of that night in Detroit have faded now. I suppose, in time, boxing may be abolished as Vonda feels it should be. But in 1980 our youngest son, Erich, took up boxing as a part of a High School martial arts course. Not as the obsession it was for me, but to fulfill a phys-ed requirement. Erich liked boxing, but had trouble with nose-bleeds which caused contests to stop. But, you know—despite her feelings about boxing—it was with Vonda's agreement that I sent a note to his coach. It read, *"Dear Coach Donley, as you know, our son Erich has a propensity to bleed when stuck on the nose while boxing. It is frustrating to him to have his fights stopped because of a minor bleeding. We would appreciate it if you would allow him to continue when this happens, and not award his opponent a Technical Knockout. Sincerely, Don and Vonda."*

Would I want my son to be a boxer? If he chose to be—but only in The Golden Gloves where referees are likely to end a fight too soon rather than let a fighter be pummeled. Professional boxing—definitely not. It can be brutal and certainly self-destructive. But for some of us boxing provides a way out of the ghetto we live in—whether poverty, abuse and neglect, or the prison of ridicule and low self esteem. Not the best solution, maybe, but one way—and sometimes we have to settle for second best.

First Blood

Yet it is reasonable to assume that
boxers fight one another because the
legitimate objects of their anger are
not accessible to them.
—*Joyce Carol Oates*

Last Summer I was in Dick's Sporting Goods looking for a floppy bush hat when I spied a well built young man in his thirties smacking a pair of new boxing gloves together. He flexed his arms and shoulders in a way that told me he knew how to use those gloves.

I waited for him to leave the area then walked over to where he had been. I slid out a box of twelve ounce gloves, opened one end and slipped a glove on my left hand. The rich smell of tanned cordovan leather flooded my senses. I ran my right hand over the curved face of the glove. Smooth as velvet. I resisted the urge to put the other glove on and do a little shuffle and shadow boxing.

Lest I appear like an old man trying to relive his youth, I pulled the glove off and was about to replace it when I spotted a little fabric tag on the cuff. I tilted the glove and read: "Warning: boxing can cause catastrophic injury."

Catastrophic injury. It seemed like I'd spent my first thirteen years trying to avoid that. My father often punished me for the slightest infraction using his doubled up leather belt, a shaving strop, a slat from a melon crate or whatever else was handy. As the youngest and one of the weakest members of my class at school I was an easy mark for anyone who chose to push me around. The slightest hostile gesture in my direction caused me to flinch. In their eyes, as well as my own, I was the class sissy with frightened eyes that seemed to say "hit me."

At times I came home from school in tears with torn or muddied clothes, a bleeding knee or cigarette burns on my arm. Mother would say, "Well, you'll just have to stay away from those boys." How was I to do that when these things happened on the way home from school?

Words seemed to hurt me as much as being hit: "Crybaby." "Coward." "Sissy." "Shithead." I felt powerless against the taunting, and my tears only made things worse.

Boxing was nowhere on my radar screen, until it occurred to me I might be able to inflict injury upon my tormenters. That revelation struck me one night at a Boy Scout meeting in the Marlette Town Hall. I had just bought a duck call for two dollars and something—a hefty sum in 1945 when I turned thirteen. I made the mistake of blowing it in Max Steele's ear. Max took exception, grabbed it from me and tossed my less-than-day-old duck caller in the burning coal stove which heated our cement floored meeting room. We began to scuffle and older scouts pulled us apart. They said, "If you're going to fight, do it right." They forced boxing gloves on our hands and pushed us toward each other from opposite corners of the room.

I'd never boxed in my life, and was sure this meant pain and humiliation for me. Max was older and heavier than I and he had a mean streak. I didn't know what to do as he charged toward me except to stick a stiff arm straight at him—more to fend him off than anything. Max ran into the clenched fist on the end of my rigid arm. Luck was with me. Max's nose began to bleed generously down his face and onto his shirt. The fight, if you can call it that—since I hadn't even thrown a punch—was over. I was an instant champion in my own eyes—or at least had the potential. My ten years as an amateur boxer had begun. I went home with visions of Max Steele's beautifully bloodied face permanently imprinted in my mental scrapbook.

I found ads in sporting magazines and sent away for several pamphlets on boxing. Following their instructions, I rigged up a heavy punching bag by filling a sea-bag with sawdust and sand. I bought a speed bag to develop timing, sawed off segments of lead pipe for shadow boxing, made a wall-mounted exerciser with bricks and pulleys and clothesline and bought several feet of half inch manila rope for skipping. I worked hard in my dank basement workout room. Finally I bought my first pair of boxing gloves at Piper's Sporting Goods.

I asked for help from two high school teachers who had been boxers. Ralph Jensen, our chemistry and physics teacher—a former coach and boxer—was willing to help. Ralph always impressed me the way he strode into a room exuding confidence. He had an aura of strength about him that said he didn't have to resort to violence—and you wouldn't be wise to pit yourself against him. Ed Huntoon, our shop teacher had fought a number of fights as a pro. He was glad to share his know-how with a neophyte. I tried to absorb and practice everything Ralph and Ed showed me about boxing.

It pleased me to learn that you didn't have to be the strongest boxer in order to win. Speed counted and movement, bobbing and weaving and feinting could neutralize the strength of a stronger opponent.

I loved boxing and sometimes postponed eating in order to box. The rata-tata-tata-tata, rata-tata-tata-tata of the speed bag was music to my ears. I liked the sound of the heavy bag as I pounded away using combinations—thunk-thunk-tha-thunk-thunk. I thrilled to the tick-tita-lick-tick, tick-tita-lick-tick of the skipping rope under my feet, and its whirring sound in my ear.

Every Friday night I'd lie on our living room carpet and listen to Gillette Fight Night on the radio. My heroes were the fighters I heard ringside announcers talk about: Joe Louis and Sugar Ray Robinson, Rocky Marciano and Willie Pep, Jersey Joe Walcott, Ezzard Charles, Rocky Graziano and Jake LaMotta. I pretended to be them as the crowd cheered, and the referee held up their gloved hands in victory.

I immersed myself in working out, visualized myself as a skillful boxer and challenged everyone I could—fellows of any age, any size. Returning service men, guys on the football team—anybody. If they were more skilled than I, I'd ask them to teach me what they knew.

Before long I experienced one of the most significant transformations of my life—from school coward and nobody to a person not to be meddled with. The turning point came late one afternoon as our football team came into the locker room after practice. Brad Maddox, a star on our football team, and one who had been particularly mean to me over some time, put me down in front of all the football team in the locker room. I don't remember what it was he said, but I remember how it made me feel—like a pile of manure. I felt my usual helpless rage—my inclination to swallow it and slink away. Until—the words came out of my mouth without my permission.

I could hardly believe it was my voice, but I heard myself saying, "Maddox, let's put the gloves on. I'll keep my right hand behind my back and I'll make mince meat out of you with my left." The guys on the football team looked up at him from the benches where they were taking their practice uniforms off and getting ready to shower. Brad glared at me with his usual surly look. I thought he might skip the gloves and attack me bare-fisted, but he didn't. He broke eye contact and went back to what he was doing without a word. The team took up their conversation again as though nothing had happened.

Nothing had happened really—it was a non-event—except for the big change in me. In a way I wish Brad had taken the challenge so I could settle some old scores. It would have felt good. But we didn't need

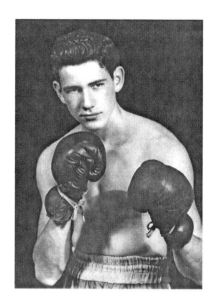

Don, sixteen years old

that. Maddox backed out. I was on the map at last. I felt I had become a somebody. Someone to be respected. Someone who felt a new confidence in himself.

During my freshman year at Central Michigan I worked in the college cafeteria. One day I saw a couple of upper class girls sitting at a table sipping cokes. They looked my way, giggled and whispered to each other—about me, I was pretty sure. As I cleared the table next to them, one of the girls said, "May we ask you a question?" Without waiting for an answer she asked in a condescending voice, "How *old* are you?"

"Seventeen," I said.

"We *thought* so," she said.

I felt like my baby-face was marking me for trouble again.

Ken Bradley and I lived on the second floor of Ronan Hall. Ken was into body building. He decided to throw a shoulder into me and drive me against the wall in the dorm hallway every so often—just for kicks. I put up with it as was my earlier habit.

I never knew boxing would help make friends, but it did. A group of students lined the walls in the dorm recreation room the night I

74

took on a Golden Gloves fighter from Saginaw. My opponent was well-muscled, but I had a reach advantage. Early on I tagged him with a combination—a double left jab to the face followed by a left hook and a straight right. His face was smeared with blood from his nose from then on. Nothing serious, but the bleeding was messy.

I caught a glimpse of Ken on the sidelines as we were mixing it up. He was obviously impressed and didn't want to be in there against me. Ken never threw another shoulder into me after that, and he dropped his surly attitude. Boxing is not without its social benefits.

In college at Central Michigan and at Asbury I fought several former Golden Glove boxers, and an ex-Navy man who had been middleweight champion of his ship. An upperclassman had fought a preliminary bout in Madison Square Garden. I wanted to learn all I could from better fighters than I—who, of course, did not take advantage of my novice status. Eventually, I reached a point where I felt comfortable with my skills. If I couldn't hold my own or defeat my opponent, at least my footwork, my bobbing and weaving, my slipping and blocking was good enough to avoid serious punishment.

During my student pastorate in Iowa, Terry Cooper, a former Golden Glover, and I boxed as part of a community benefit held at the high school. We had a sparring match the week before so we had a sense of each other's style. Neither of us wanted to embarrass ourselves, but either of us would have been glad to score a knock-down there on the basketball court.

Vonda was sitting next to Mae Wagner in the bleachers. When the match started Mae blurted out, "Oh, they really mean it."

I drew a minimal show of blood from Terry's nose. When the three rounds were over the referee held both our hands up and declared a draw. I took no small pleasure when a friend told me Terry had said of me, "That son of a gun can really hit."

In the interest of full disclosure, my ten years of boxing every time I could scare up an opponent did not include one sanctioned fight in a boxing ring. The matches were all in gyms, rec rooms, back yards, back alleys, dormitory basements and the like. I was knocked out (temporarily paralyzed, but not unconscious) once when I made the mistake of challenging Junior Brown before I had the necessary boxing skills. Junior was a tough, hard working farm kid and the fullback on our football team. He waded in and caught me with a hard right hook to the solar plexus. I stiffened like a board and saw the oak floor coming up to smack me. Later on I held my own with him as we did three rounds in the middle of Main Street during a home-town celebration.

There were times when I would have welcomed a full fledged black eye as a badge of honor, but it never happened. I sported a "mouse" (a small bruise) under an eye a few times. Boxing is as much about "being able to take it," as it is with "dishing it out."

My first and only fight in a boxing ring took place at the YMCA when I was in seminary in Evanston, Illinois. There were only three of us: a black semi-pro fighter, my boxing coach who knew us both, and me. It was a tune-up fight for my opponent. He had a look of invincibility about him, with arms and legs that looked like spring steel and the death-stare of a Joe Louis. Fortunately for me it was only a sparring match or I may have been "seriously killed"—as we said in those days.

In a miniscule but satisfying way, it was an historic evening for me: my first and only time in a ring, against the first black fighter to box at the Evanston YMCA—according to my coach.

As I drove back to my seminary dorm I heard an ominous electronic pinging sound on the radio that alarmed the entire United States. The sound of the Russian Sputnik—the first man-made satellite to circle the earth—made me feel a bit creepy, and afraid. Was Russia about to dominate the skies over us?

The next day newspapers reported a wave of near-hysteria in the American public. Ideas of US technical superiority over the Russians were shattered. October 4, 1957—the *space age* had begun, and the *space race* with Russia was on.

My private and insignificant little competition had been drowned out by a new international competition with frightening implications. The acceleration of the cold war with Russia made Americans shiver.

Calamus Years
1954 – 1961

You don't want to live in the past, but
it's okay to visit now and again.
— Mardy Grothe

What an interesting life I had, and how
I wish I had realized it sooner.
— Colette

Funny, You Don't Look Like a Minister.

All the world is a stage and most of us
are desperately unrehearsed.
—*Sean O'Casey*

I have sometimes wondered how many of me there are. Inside me is the little boy who cried when he thought he'd have to be a minister to please his father; the teen-ager who laughed when asked by a Methodist District Superintendent if he'd ever considered the ministry; the young man who thrives on the violence of boxing and fantasizes about becoming a middleweight champion.

Now, in July of 1954, I'm the college graduate leaving home in Michigan to become a student pastor in Iowa. Is there a softer "shepherd" side of me? You might question that. You might question my fitness for the ministry on many grounds—not least my immature twenty-one years of age, and being married for less than a year. My father even has to drive to Sandusky with me, and sign for me to get a wedding license because I was two months short of Michigan's legal age of twenty-one for males. More than a little humiliating. Vonda is nineteen and needs nobody's permission. Is that fair?

One of Vonda's friends, who was being only semi-facetious, asked Vonda, "Why on earth did you marry Don?" She responded, "Well, I took one look at him, and I said to myself, 'That poor boy needs help!'" That's a reference to when Vonda and I met while working in the college cafeteria. I was given to such avant-garde things as wearing checks and plaids together—ten years ahead of the then current styles. Vonda thought it strange, too, that I wore a pencil perched on my right ear as a sort of permanent fixture—an early habit developed in my father's grocery store in the days when you tallied up a customer's bill on the side of a paper bag. In addition to these and other quirks, Vonda thought I was a touch too sarcastic. Fortunately for me, Vonda took me on as a reclamation project.

Well, whether what we're doing is a good idea or not, we've passed the point of no return. We're leaving Michigan on the basis of a single phone call with the Davenport District Superintendent— whom we've never met; to serve two little rural churches in towns we've never seen; in the state of Iowa whose borders we've never crossed.

I'm unprepared for my father's tears as we leave. I didn't see him cry when his father died, though I was only four at the time. The only time I had ever seen him cry was when my brother R.J. left for military service in World War II. Dad is 68 now—with heart problems.

Were his tears because this may be our final goodbye? Were they for me because I had no idea what lay ahead of me? Could they be for Vonda because no young lady should have to begin a marriage in such uncertainty? Maybe all three reasons.

Once on the road I find that Dad's tears have triggered my own. I cry half-way to Flint—just as I cried all afternoon in school the day R.J. left for war when I was ten.

Tears past, we move on for Iowa in our used blue Mercury that had logged 117,000 miles. We're buying it from Professor Murphy for $1,000 with payments spread over two years. The Mercury and a tiny U-Haul rental trailer carries all our earthly possessions: wedding gifts, linens, clothing, a card table and two folding chairs, my boxing gloves which I'd still be using, and an ugly green and white ceramic lamp that had belonged to Vonda's Grandmother Lamb.

So here we are in our high-mileage old Mercury purring through shadowy woodlands, and sunlit fields. Our hearts blossom with exhilaration over the leap of faith we're taking together. New sights rush to meet our eyes: high sand dunes near the tip of Lake Michigan, the sprawling industrial wastelands of Gary, Indiana, and in Illinois we see gentle hills covered with nothing but cornfields—higher than a man's head, and greener than green.

Now we're approaching the Mississippi River—awesome to this small town boy who never dreamed he'd get to see it. Momentarily I'm back in Miss Adolph's third grade class. "Class, how do we spell Mississippi?" And we were singing back

"M-i-s-s / i-s-s / i-p-p-i!" But now, as we cross the bridge over those dark swirling waters and into Iowa, the spelling seems to be "R-u-b-i-c-o-n." Rubicon: irreversible commitment! On the Iowa side of the Mississippi, weathered old warehouses in Clinton greet us like friendly old ghosts from some unknown past. We are in our new home state. We are on our own.

* * *

We continue driving, and twenty-four miles west of Clinton we come to the village of Grand Mound, the outpoint of our new parish. We turn left off the highway and drive slowly through this little one-stoplight town where we would be spending so many hours and so much energy. Grand Mound appears neat and clean—even with its smattering of buildings from an earlier era. About sixteen small business places fan out from the traffic light. The white clapboard Methodist Church had been the former one-room school house in Grand Mound. It looked mighty fine to us.

A six-mile drive further west on US 30 and we're in Calamus—a town with no traffic light except the railroad flashers, and little concern for street numbers. Our arrival is less than triumphant. We pull off the highway, and drive past the Dosland Lumber Company, over the Chicago and Northwestern's double tracks, past Spider Shelton's Barber Shop, the yellow brick town hall, the rented post office on the opposite corner, Steffen's Tavern, the bank, and Huetter's IGA grocery—that's about it.

We spot a local at the next corner. We pull our Mercury over toward the curb to ask where the Methodist Church is. Ker-wham!! Our right front wheel drops into a storm-drain whose iron grid is missing. We're locked in place, and quickly draw a small crowd of curious people. Someone phones Carl Hansen, owner of the local farm implement shop. He drives down Main Street "high and lifted up" on a brand new Allis Chalmers tractor with front loader. He gets down. We shake hands and introduce ourselves. Carl tells me to leave the car in neutral. He hooks his front-end loader under our front bumper, lifts us up, and backs us away from the offending hole.

Our arrival is no longer a secret. Word spreads like fire crackling through a dry Christmas tree. I imagine someone saying, "I took one look at that new student pastor, and said to myself, 'That poor boy needs help. Better watch him, he might hurt himself.'"

Now we're standing in the hundred year old parsonage. It has been empty for three years. Smells dusty and musty—in need of serious cleaning. It is our "castle" with white asbestos shingles on the sides, an outside lift-up door to the basement, a coal furnace and no insulation. The second story bathroom is complete with free-standing claw-footed tub (holding the traditional glass balls) with many a chip in its porcelain—and linoleum floor covering with several worn spots.

There's a giant cottonwood tree growing off the front corner of the house. The living and dining rooms make us feel like we're in the middle of a magnolia grove with the large green, black and white magnolia blossom wallpaper—the most recent of five layers.

By way of compensation the congregation has just remodeled the kitchen. New paint, new wallpaper, new cabinets and sink, new floor covering. Next to the back door—and mounted on the wall—is an old-style phone. Oak wood cabinet with long speaker arm, a large handheld earpiece on a cord, a crank for calling the operator…and it's on a party line. We can forget about confidentiality on this phone line.

The solitary piece of furniture—in the whole house—is a green sofa bed which, when we open it, discharges a horde of centipedes. Vonda screams and heads for the stairs. I stomp and swat as many as I can. We do not enjoy our first night's sleep knowing that we are most likely sharing the bed with other critters.

Early next morning we locate our coffee pot, coffee, and dry cereal. We're eating breakfast at our card table in our pajamas, when Sylvia Hansen—church board member and president of the local school board—knocks on the front door. She is all business—too busy to pay much attention to our garb. She informs us that former pastors have paid scant attention to pastoral calling, and inquires whether we intend to call. Sylvia's hard grey eyes and firm-set lips—her barely detectable smile, elicit the mandatory "yes" she had come for. She gives us a list of shut-ins. We thank her and assure her they will not be neglected. Mission accomplished, she walks briskly back to her car. I'm glad I didn't know what she was thinking. I'm sure it was something like, "Why did they have to send us a boy to do a man's work?"

* * *

Today—true to my word and Sylvia's prodding—I'm out calling on members. I'm not by nature an extrovert, and any behavior resembling extroversion is an effort for me. Run into a little resistance and I feel rebuffed. When I knock on the door of the Ray Fisher home the first time, Ray appears at the door with a "Yes, and who might

82

you be?" look. I give him my name and say, "I'm the new pastor of the Methodist Church."

Ray bursts into laughter, and can't seem to stop. I'm thinking *what's so hilarious? Do I have a string of spinach between my teeth?* Ray tries to stop several times, but lapses back into laughter. When he finally regains his composure—his cheeks moist from tears—he says, "That's funny. You don't look the least bit like a minister!" (Turns out I've got a problem I didn't know I had. How is a minister supposed to look?)

About a year later, after I'm authorized to perform weddings, I'm robed and standing in the chancel of the Grand Mound Church waiting for the wedding party to process. I notice a dark-haired couple in the last row whispering and looking my way. After the wedding they come to where I am. The woman smiles and says, "You were probably wondering if we were talking about you. My husband and I are from Texas. We're Jewish, and I was just remarking that you look more like a rabbi than our rabbi." Well, if I don't look like a minister, at least I look more like a rabbi than a rabbi. Maybe that's close enough.

Our first invited guests in the parsonage are Richard and Melinda Eden. They live in a tall brick home about 150 yards southwest of us. Richard and his son-in-law, Harold Minor, farm together on a large scale. Both are members of the church board. Richard is on the short side, wiry with thinning hair that is almost always covered with a heavy red plaid cap. His complexion is ruddy from many hours in the sunlight on his tractor. His laughter flows easily. He has a mischievous side, and enjoys people. Melinda is taller than Richard, slender with blue eyes and a gracious smile. She has a regal bearing which stands in contrast with Richard's style.

One evening early on we invite Richard and Melinda over for cherry pie, coffee and conversation around the red Formica kitchen table which we bought in DeWitt at Bower's New and Used Furniture Store. (Mr. Bowers must have had a soft spot for young people just starting out. He supplied us with all the used furniture we needed for a hundred dollars. Of course you get what you pay for—from his stock of "turned-in" furniture.)

As the four of us sit in our kitchen talking, eating, and getting acquainted, Vonda is quick to acknowledge her ignorance of farm life. She tells Richard, "You know I'm a city girl, and I don't know a

Holstein from a heifer." Richard goes into a spasm, and starts choking on his pie. He shakes his head back and forth while laughing, then takes a swallow of coffee and wipes the cherry pie off his mouth with a napkin and says, "My dear, I guess you don't."

Vonda and I have a lot to learn about farm life—about everything to do with our new job. Our new parishioners—all of them in one way or another—will be our mentors and companions for the next seven years. Under their patient tutelage we will learn about ministry, and how love and caring are shared. Here Vonda will begin her teaching career, and we'll become the parents of Colin, Lance and Lisa. Here we'll experience our earliest funerals, weddings, baptisms, murders, suicides and other human crises. Here we'll initiate the building of a new church, and establish friendships that will nourish and sustain us well past fifty years—all because of a serendipitous phone call that changed our plans and the course of our lives completely.

I've wondered what if that Michigan District Superintendent had reached us a day earlier. Our lives would have been different in so many ways—but could it possibly have been a better beginning for us? I don't think so, but I'll never know because that was the road not taken. But I know there's a new person—a pastor—taking his place in my psyche along with the boy that cried, the teen-ager who laughed, and the youth who thrived on the violence of boxing.

Stale Donuts and Strong Coffee

When your parent dies you have lost
your past. When your child dies you
have lost your future.
— *Dr. Elliot Luby*

The function of [a pastor] is to be the
sounding board for grief.
— *Joshua Loth Liebman*

Frank Cowick startled me when he rapped on my dormitory door and stuck his head inside. "Don, you have a call from Vonda."

"Thanks, Frank," I said—not feeling overly thankful. Vonda seldom called me at seminary unless something serious happened. I pushed myself away from my desk feeling apprehensive as I walked down the empty hallway to the pay phone.

I traveled two hundred miles back and forth between Calamus, Iowa and Evanston, Illinois to attend Garrett Theological Seminary. School took six months of every year and that meant a return trip to Iowa each weekend to carry out my duties as a student pastor in two small-town churches: delivering sermons, personal conferences, visiting home-bound and hospitalized parishioners, weddings, baptisms and funerals.

Those responsibilities left precious little time to be a husband to Vonda—especially with our new church building program underway in Grand Mound. Vonda and I had planned some much needed time for ourselves this first weekend in June 1956. We'd put it on our calendar *in ink*—to insure that nothing took precedence: *Picnic at Maquoketa Caves State Park.* We looked forward to a quiet time together with Mother Nature alongside the Maquoketa River in the rolling hills of east Iowa.

I picked up the receiver and spoke a tentative, "Hi, Honey, what's up?"

"Hi, Don...I'm sorry to have to call you in the middle of the week like this but there's been a death—a little girl. You don't know her. Her parents asked for you to conduct her funeral."

When Vonda's call ended I hung up and slumped against the wall-phone feeling as though I had no control over my own life. Our plans were dashed again. There would be no picnic. There would be a funeral instead—the seventeenth since I'd started seminary last year. Several, like this one, took me home from school in mid-week and cancelled the precious time we'd planned together. I complained within myself—*God, give me a break. I have needs too.*

Death had intrigued me ever since I saw a dead squirrel on the road in front of our house as a child—even more after my grandfather died in the bedroom next to mine when I was four years old. I'd given Grandpa Fred a Smith Brothers Black Cough Drop to make him feel better but in the morning he was dead.

The funerals I'd been responsible for up to this point had seemed pretty equal in their sadness. I drew little distinction between the death of an aged grandparent and the death of a middle-aged parent, a spouse—they were all sad. This funeral was the first of many I would have for a child. Amy Goodell had died suddenly at age six of spinal meningitis.

Still, I fumed all the way home aboard the City of Denver. *We never have enough time together. Why does death always come at an inconvenient time? These people have attended church a few times but they aren't members. Why couldn't they ask another minister? Don't they understand I'm a* **student** *pastor?*

I worked myself into a full-blown snit by the time Vonda met me at the Chicago and Northwestern Station in Clinton and was in a black funk as we drove the thirty miles to our parish at Calamus. Not feeling the least ministerial. Feeling nothing but my own frustration and anger. I knew that with this mind-set, I was in no position to be helpful to Amy's parents.

I carried my suitcase, heavy with books, into the parsonage then showered and shaved and put on a dress suit and tie. Vonda prepared a light meal. I felt myself calming down somewhat as I ate and thought of how the Goodells were hurting. I knew I had to dismiss my frustration and focus on their feelings. As I drove our blue Chevy over the gravel road to their rented home on a farm north of town I prayed the words of the Psalmist, "God, put a new and right spirit within me."

A long uneven driveway led up to Goodell's side door. Hazel greeted me with red and swollen eyes and a wadded handkerchief in her hand. She continued to dab at her eyes and wipe her nose all evening.

Clarence sat on a worn sofa in the bare living room—his elbows on his knees, his head in his hands, facing the floor. As I entered he stood up and shook my hand, then threw his arms around me, clutched me and cried as though he were a child and I were his father—not a 23 year-old student pastor. I hugged him in return as he sobbed for what seemed an eternity. Finally, he released his grip and sat back on the worn sofa.

Their shabby furnishings told me these were not well-to-do people. Life had been hard for them. Though only in their mid-thirties they both looked much older—especially Hazel. Clarence worked as a custodian at the Calamus school. Hazel worked as a waitress down the road in DeWitt. They seemed to be losing ground rather than getting ahead.

Fortunately, for one so inexperienced, I didn't have to do much talking. Amy's parents were still in shock and disbelief as they told me about the onset of her illness and how—before they had any idea how serious it was—their only child was dead. By now I was thoroughly tuned in to their grief—attached to their nerve endings.

After they had poured out their grief for a time and we'd planned, as best we could for the funeral service, it was time for prayer and for me to head home to prepare for Amy's funeral. Clarence and Hazel sat side by side clutching each other as though they were drowning—as in fact they were—drowning in grief. I pulled a battered ottoman—no doubt one Amy had played on—to the sofa where they sat. We joined hands for prayer. I could think of nothing to say in the face of such overwhelming grief. I waited for words to come from somewhere. Words that might help and heal—if only a bit. As I took a deep breath and relaxed my body in order to be more receptive a strange thing happened that has occurred only two or three times since—and never so powerfully. It was as if the three of us, sitting there with eyes closed and hands joined, were visited by another Presence. As though together we were lifted upward to a high place in our minds… or as a kind of out-of-body travel.

My prayer was short. Mostly I repeated some of Clarence and Hazel's words. "God, we're hurting so. We don't know how we can live without Amy. We don't know how we're going to pay for her doctor bills or her funeral. We need your help real bad. Please help us get through her funeral and give us strength to go on in the days ahead." We prayed the Lord's Prayer together through tears and exchanged good-bye hugs.

As I drove home in the double darkness over the crunchy gravel road I knew clearly for the first time that it is not true, "A death is a death is a death." Some deaths are different—a lot different.

On the day of the funeral, bright sunlight—the kind that usually drives all gloom away—was scarcely noticed by the mourners who filled the small red-brick Methodist church. Many who entered found their tears near the surface. Those tears were released in torrents when Bev Scott sang Amy's favorite song, *Jesus Loves Me,* at her parent's request. I doubt that anyone remembered a thing about the service except the song, the tears and the hugging. Maybe that's all they needed to remember.

Smoke rose stiffly from freshly extinguished candles as we left in slow procession for the Calamus cemetery where we committed Amy's body to the ground in the hope of Resurrection. From now on Amy was a memory—a powerful memory.

* * *

A couple of weeks later I traveled to DeWitt, eleven miles down the Lincoln Highway to make hospital calls. During mid-afternoon, I dropped into the small café next to the Sunoco Station where Hazel worked as a waitress. I found it nearly empty. No music playing. Only two people sitting at a table in the corner by the front window.

I sat down on the second stool from the end of the counter next to Hazel. We had scarcely begun talking about how she and Clarence were doing when she sprang to her feet and served up a cup of coffee and a donut for each of us. She asked if I'd care to offer grace. We ate the donuts (which were stale) and drank the coffee (which tasted like the bitter Epsom salts my mother used to give me for constipation when I was a child) and we talked. We talked, sipped from the bitter cup and nibbled the bread of stale donuts. Thankfully, nobody came in while we hunched over the counter and Hazel talked of pain and loss, loneliness and hope, happy memories and sleepless nights. Under other circumstances I would never have drunk such bitter coffee or eaten such dried-out donuts. But I knew this was Hazel's gift of love to me and that time of sharing was one of the most powerful communions I've ever experienced.

* * *

I'm glad Hazel and I had that time together. It remains an indelible sacred time in my life as a pastor. Shortly afterward Clarence and Hazel moved away. I didn't see them again for about three years when Clarence called and asked if I would have Hazel's funeral. She had died of lung cancer at age thirty-nine. This time I felt no anger—only sorrow for Clarence who had lost his wife and his little Amy and sorrow for Hazel and Amy whose lives had ended far too soon.

All this happened many years ago now. Vonda and I still haven't made it to Maquoketa Caves State Park but I have revisited the Calamus cemetery. I can tell you there are now three red granite grave markers—each about the size of a man's shoe box—bearing the names and lifetimes of Amy, Hazel and Clarence. And I can tell you I still ponder their lives with the same sorrow I feel when I stand in a cemetery on an overcast day and hear the wind sighing in the fir trees.

In This Very Room

In three words I can sum up everything
I've learned about life. It goes on.
—Robert Frost

The Wapsipinicon River meanders 255 miles from its origin in Minnesota before it empties into the Mississippi River near Clinton, Iowa, and it drains the farmlands of some of the most special people I've ever met. Among them were Howard Anderson and George Wagner—boyhood friends who sustained their friendship over long lifetimes. They attended school together, fished for catfish and pike in the twists and turns of the Wapsi, speared carp (for smoking) in the backwaters of the Mississippi and hunted pheasants in the lush marshlands and pastures of their Clinton County farms. George and Howard bowled together at the DeWitt Lanes and thrived on each others company.

Our paths crossed when George and Howard were old enough to retire—but kept on farming—and I came as a student pastor to the little Methodist Church in the town of Calamus. The Wagners had been active in the life of that red brick church for decades and George—a lifelong artist—had painted the mural of Christ in the Garden of Gethsemane in the chancel.

The Anderson clan had attended the Norwegian Lutheran church in the open country outside Calamus—a picture-postcard church whose high steeple you could see from Highway 30 far to the north. Our church family was glad to have Howard, a Lutheran, attend with his Methodist wife Mary. Mary grew the largest patch of gladiolas in town. Often she gave free floral gifts to the church for its communion table and to hurting people who were sick or alone and lonely.

Howard and George invited me to join them on a trip to the backwaters of the Mississippi to spear carp and to bowl with them at the DeWitt Lanes—and though my lack of skill—in both spearing and bowling—had to be an embarrassment to them they didn't give up on me.

In the autumn they invited me to hunt pheasants with them on the Wagner farm. I felt more in my element while hunting. Early on I impressed them with a couple of lucky shots. One was a spooked pheasant in high flight—most likely pushing its top speed of sixty miles an hour. George and Howard thought it out of range and neither lifted his gun. I must have led the bird by ten feet. To their surprise the pheasant dropped about seventy yards away and George said, "I don't believe I've ever seen anyone bring a bird down from that high." Soon he was telling his friends in town what a great shot his new pastor was. I didn't mind the publicity a bit.

One day our talk turned to gun safety. George said, "Some hunters don't use their safety but I keep mine on full-time until I'm ready to shoot."

I said, "Well, I was taught not to rely on my safety—that the only way to be safe is keep your barrel pointed away from things you don't want to shoot at all times." George muttered something like, "Well, I suppose that's okay if you can do it but the idea of a hunter who's not using his safety makes me a bit uneasy."

Howard broke his silence, "Well, George, you and I have been hunting together for near sixty years and *I* never use *my* safety." All those years together and they were still learning about each other.

The time came when Howard's aging father fell ill. It didn't look like Henry would last the night. His Lutheran pastor had left for an out-of-state conference so the Andersons asked me to drop in for a pastoral visit and prayer. It was nearly dark as I drove our blue Chevy down the gravel road south of Calamus and turned into the Henry Anderson farm just where the road curves east before heading south again toward the Wapsi River Bridge.

Howard led me to his father's bedroom at the right rear of the house where Henry lay helpless in the last hours of his life. Pathetic to see this once husky farmer in his extremity—withered away, unconscious and struggling for breath. Made you not want to look at him out of respect—because who of us wants people staring at us when we're in that condition?

His wife Martha sat beside Henry holding his limp left hand in hers as he labored for breath. Tears stood motionless in her eyes as she fulfilled her "'til death do us part" vows after many decades of marriage. She said to me, "You know…Henry's father built this house when he came to Iowa as a homesteader…and he died in this very room. Henry was born in this room…now he's dying here. And I borned Howard in this room too." Howard—strong but gentle farmer that he was—stood somber and misty-eyed behind his mother, both his tanned and gnarled hands resting soft on her shoulders. She reached her right hand across her body and patted Howard's left hand, then looked back down at Henry.

It happened without warning. A heavy thud on the front of the house sent a shudder through the building. Then the sound of tires spinning in gravel as a vehicle sped away in the night. Momentarily stunned, we wondered what had happened. Howard left his wife, Mary at his mother's side and walked down the hall to the front door. I followed. He flicked on the porch light, and opened the door. We stepped out to see the shattered remains of a large pumpkin splattered against the front wall and over the porch. It missed the large picture window in the parlor by inches. Had that been the target?

Howard shook his head, more in sadness than anger, and moved back to the room where his father's death rattle was getting stronger as his body labored to take in enough air. "What happened?" his mother asked.

"Someone smashed a pumpkin against the house. Must've been their idea of a Halloween prank."

She shook her head and wondered out loud, "Why would a person want to do a thing like that?"

I stayed on with them, listening to their memories of family times past—both happy and sad. Before I left, Howard, his wife Mary and Howard's mother—the four of us—joined hands around Henry's hospital bed with two of us placing our free hand on Henry's shoulders. We repeated the Shepherd Psalm together as our affirmation of faith. I offered a short prayer of thanksgiving for Henry's life and the way some of God's best gifts come in the form of other people. We prayed the Lord's Prayer together then exchanged handshakes and hugs amidst tears. I took my leave around eleven that night.

I didn't go directly home but headed south to the Wapsi River Bridge. Maybe the Wapsi could help me think. I had the road all to myself, pulled to the side of the road and walked to the middle of the bridge with its see-through planking and rusty old frame and railing. I grasped the railing and felt surface rust crumbling loose in my hands, leaned over and stared into the dark water flowing by beneath my feet. The Wapsi gurgled along undisturbed by the events in peoples' lives. How could it be so indifferent … and so comforting at the same time?

The full moon reflected pale orange in the water—pumpkin like. Old Mrs. Anderson's question hung in my mind, "Why would a person do a thing like that?" My question as well. I doubt there was anything personal in tossing the pumpkin. Were they aiming for the big front window? Who knows? They say, "Boys will be boys," but that doesn't excuse malicious destruction or frightening people out of their wits—especially when someone is dying inside the house. Harsh and judgmental thoughts gathered in my mind waiting recognition.

But, I told myself *we don't always know what is going on in other people's lives when we say or do things that hit with a thud— like a thrown pumpkin.* Slightly chastened in my moral superiority, it occurred to me to wonder how often I'd said or done things that affected people in similar fashion. A couple of personal mistakes came to my mind unbidden—unwelcome. Like the time when I was a boy and aimed my BB gun at Mr. Fox's side window and pulled the trigger. Now I'm thinking how we all have a need to pray "forgive us our 'pumpkins,'" starting with me.

As I pushed guilt feelings aside and listened to the cleansing sound of the Wapsi I felt surprised to hear the voice of my father singing a snippet of one of his favorite songs: "Ol' man river, that ol' man river, he must know somthin', but don't say nothing', he just keeps rollin', he keeps on rollin' along. He don't plant 'taters, he don't plant cotton, and them that plants them is soon forgotten, but old man river, he just keeps rollin', he keeps on rollin' along."

Mortality—I was feeling it deep inside. Time seemed compressed. The old homesteader—gone. His farmer son—going. Who would the river of time sweep away next?

Henry died in the middle of that night. Next morning Harold cleaned off the side of the house and threw the pumpkin shards over the fence for the hungry pigs.

* * *

Years have passed since that night. You go down that country road now … you won't see Howard or George out working or hunting in the fields. You'll find them asleep in the village cemetery alongside their wives—Mary and Mae. You won't see old Henry's pigpen or his barn—not even the house his father built. All you'll see is that gentle rise on the south edge of the cornfield where an Iowa homesteader once chose to build a home for himself and his family. And if you drive a little further to the bridge you can stare down into the Wapsi and listen to her river music, and try to decipher her words for you.

Heading For Home

But in the night of death, hope sees
a star, and listening love can hear
the rustling of a wing.
— *Robert G. Ingersoll*

Extreme cold. Extreme silence. Extreme grief. Possibly the most I'd experienced of each up to that point in my early life as a clergyman.

David Davenport—dead at age twenty. Hit head-on by a truck late one winter night on Highway 30 in Clinton County, Iowa, as he returned home in the dark from his factory job in Davenport. Nobody knew for sure what happened. Did his car slip on glare ice on a curve? Did he drift into the oncoming lane because of a white-out from blowing snow? How it happened didn't seem to matter much at this point. Dave was dead—mourned by his pregnant wife, his mother and step-father, his younger brother Doug who idolized Dave, the church family of Wesley Methodist Church and the whole stunned village of Calamus.

Just last summer this tall, quiet, well-proportioned young man was scattering base hits all over the baseball diamond at the Calamus ball park ... and snagging long fly-balls that looked uncatchable. He had a phenomenal eye, good timing and power and—though not the fastest of runners—he had good base-running sense.

Dave applied himself to his studies, and seemed to give everything he did his best shot. His good looks seemed tinged with an unspoken sadness, through which he still smiled frequently. Altogether he was the kind of young man any parent would be pleased to call son. As a matter of fact most everyone in Calamus took pride in Dave, regarding him either as a son, or a brother.

I was in his home when his insurance agent delivered the $5,000 death benefit check to his young wife. Though at the time I had never seen a check that large, it seemed sadly deficient for what his young wife and unborn child would need in the days ahead. So much less than Dave would have brought home over years of full-employment. But death had dashed all dreams.

Now we were standing on the crest of a knoll in a new section of the Davenport, Iowa cemetery on the coldest morning of the year. Situation totally incongruous: twenty year old youth full of promise— dead. Weather equally incongruous: twenty-seven below zero with bright sunshine and absolutely no wind. As we followed Dave's casket through recently fallen snow it did not crunch beneath our feet. It squeaked like many extremely high-pitched flutes.

We were shallow breathing through gloves, scarves or sleeves because of the deep dull pain the Arctic air inflicted within our chests. The hairs in our nostrils froze together—feeling like frigid barbed wire. Small sluggish plumes of frozen breath escaped the fabric barriers we put over our mouths, did a slow coil upwards, and disappeared. The sun was as bright in the blue sky as the air was cold and motionless.

We had no sheltering tent on that little prominence, the ground being too cold to drive in stakes—even metal ones. Cemetery workers had heated the grave-site itself with a flaming gas-jet apparatus in order to thaw the frozen ground enough to carve out the new rectangular dwelling for Dave's body.

We huddled much closer than usual around the casket trying to draw some degree of shelter from the stinging cold by nestling against each other, like chickens under a mother hen.

As we clustered together in the oppressive silence just before the committal service, the words of one of Whittier's poems floated through my mind, "O Sabbath rest by Galilee, O calm of hills above, where Jesus knelt to share with thee, *the silence of eternity*, interpreted by love! Drop thy still dews of *quietness* 'till all our strivings cease. Take from our lives the strain and stress, and let our ordered lives confess the beauty of thy peace."

Extreme cold dictated that the graveside service be brief. Nor would there be any lingering for hugs, and condolences, and shared tears. We said our final farewell to Dave and simply turned our already numb bodies back to our waiting cars with their heaters which were not up to taming such cold as this.

So we turned our backs on the place where Dave would be buried in the cold heart of the earth as soon as we left the scene.

We turned our backs and walked in silent bewilderment—utterly incapable of assimilating death at such an early age. But, a strange thing happened as we headed back. I saw Dave in my mind's eye ... in the midst of a hotly contested ball game. He was rounding second base with his long fluid strides. He was looking to the third base coach for the signal to head for home.

You'll Never Find Me

As we acquire knowledge things do not become
more comprehensible, but more mysterious.
—*Will Durant*

Sylvia Hansen tried to launch me on the right foot as a new student pastor. She confronted me early on with: "Look, Don, we don't stand on ceremony here in Calamus, so stop calling everyone Mr. or Mrs. If you want to fit in you've got to call us by our first names." I noticed that seemed to apply to most everyone but Mr. Dillon. I didn't remember anyone calling him Otis. I never learned why.

Mr. Dillon was one of the better educated persons in the small rural town of Calamus, Iowa, yet he lived in a hovel with his wife Bertha. Their house reeked of age. Its gray and deeply weathered clapboards looked as though they'd never seen a coat of paint. Weeds grew knee deep in his corner lot, and the four posted front porch roof tilted precariously to the east. Made you want to tread easy on the porch for fear you'd bring the roof down on yourself.

Once you stepped inside things got worse. The living room was as cluttered as an antique shop after an earthquake. Bertha, aged eighty-four, was too sick to care. Mr. Dillon seemed not to notice. He heated their small single story home with a cast iron stove which doubled for cooking. He burned wood or coal—depending upon "availability." Most everything in the room was covered with dust and grime from coal smoke—walls, ceilings and furniture. You could write your name in it. Made you not want to sit down, but when you're a pastor you disregard such feelings and adapt to the situation.

Rumors circulated that Mr. Dillon sometimes treated other peoples' vegetable gardens as his own and sometimes raided the refuse pile behind the local grocery store for partially spoiled fruits and vegetables. Same thing with wood and coal piles—his "help myself to your firewood" became so predictable that one neighbor allegedly put a small explosive charge in his wood which blew the lids off the stove and filled the Dillon home with smoke.

Mr. Dillon's skin and clothing matched his house—greasy, grimy hands and face, as though he were a perpetual auto mechanic—except he had no car. Nails caked black with unknown material. Grey eyes matching his scraggly beard. Head topped with a crumpled and stained dress hat. Body odor? We never detected it, but that may have been because his clothes usually bore the pungent odor of smoke.

Once Mr. Dillon brought a quart of the most scrumptious blackberries Vonda had ever seen to our back door. Vonda thanked him profusely, but knowledge that he picked them with those filthy hands meant the blackberries never made it to our table.

In spite of the shabby impression he made on people, Mr. Dillon had graduated from college, and taught school before his mind went off on a tangent. I'll bet he was the only person in Calamus who owned an India paper edition of *The Encyclopedia Britannica*. Once, in a trusting mood, he pulled out a volume and showed me where he had stashed fifty and hundred dollar bills—many of each—between its pages.

Bertha Dillon died during my third year in Calamus. I conducted her funeral. Mr. Dillon continued to come to church—infrequently— and he continued to be unpredictable. Once Vonda sat by him in church. And in the midst of the Apostles Creed as the congregation was affirming belief in "the Resurrection of the body and the life everlasting," Mr. Dillon said in a loud whisper, "I don't believe that, do you?" Vonda held her finger to her lips and whispered, "We'll talk about it later."

Several months passed. Thoughts of Mr. Dillon receded as I continued my seminary program and helped lead in our new church building program in Grand Mound.

One Monday, I returned to seminary in Evanston, Illinois, and that night had a short but startling dream. My dream sequence started on the crest of Brady Street in Davenport, Iowa. At that spot St. John's Methodist church rises high on your left and the road drops sharply toward the Mississippi River. I saw the city with the Mississippi in the distance and the three bridges linking Iowa to Illinois. In my dream, I drove through the business district, down to the levee where the river muscled its way downstream as barges and ships plowed its waters. Darkness fell like a curtain on a stage and I felt myself to be part of a search party checking old warehouses along the river for someone—but for whom?

Then a voice startled me with its clarity. In sepulchral tones, I heard the words, "You'll never find me. You'll never find me." It was as though someone spoke them aloud in my ear. I sat up in bed startled and knew immediately that was Mr. Dillon's voice. But why would I dream of him, and what—if anything—did it mean? Next morning the dream was still with me. I told my roommate about it, and how it seemed an audible voice. It bothered me the rest of the week. I wondered if Mr. Dillon were okay.

Late that Friday, I arrived back in Calamus in time to check our mail at the Post Office. I thought of asking Mrs. Neff, our Post Master, about Mr. Dillon but told myself, *Forget it, Don, it was only a dream*. Our mailbox held a pink card notifying me I had a package. I presented the card at the window with, "Hi, Mrs. Neff!"

She said, "Hi, Don, have you heard anything more about Mr. Dillon?" The hairs stood up on my arms. Did I hear her right? I told her, "I haven't heard a thing—why, something the matter?" She said, "Well, he was down in Davenport at his daughter's house and came up missing. They're searching for him but so far as I know they haven't found him yet. They're afraid he may have drowned himself in the Mississippi."

"Wow! Sure hope they find him alive!" and I drove the two blocks home to tell Vonda about the dream and what Mrs. Neff said. Turns out they'd found Mr. Dillon alive a day or two before. But the fact remains that he went missing the night of my dream. He was in Davenport...on the waterfront. There was a search party and I was two hundred miles away from all this.

I've never quite known what to make of Mr. Dillon or that dream. But now, when I dream of people in trouble, I'm ill at ease until I've been reassured they're okay. Sometime my concern proves justified—more often it doesn't (unless people are covering up.) But I'm convinced there are extensions of our human minds whose mysteries will continue to haunt us.

The Chicken Coop in the Swamp

Change is inevitable except
from a vending machine.
— *Robert C. Gallagher*

A mind that is stretched by a
new experience can never go
back to its old dimensions.
— *Oliver Wendell Holmes*

Esther Henningson was old in body, but not in spirit, when I first met her as her student pastor back in the late fifties and early sixties. She lived in a small home with white siding and green shutters. Her dancing blue eyes still flashed from their deep sockets in her wrinkled and weathered face.

Everybody in the little town of Grand Mound, Iowa, knew Esther was one tough lady. Take that in the best sense of the word. Her stick-to-itiveness and bull-dog determination were legendary. Esther didn't take things sitting down and that feisty little woman was respected as widely as she was known.

To my best recollection people told how Esther and her husband started out early in life with big plans. They bought a big farm and a herd of cattle and a few hogs. As I recall they had four children—one of which died early in life. They had a large mortgage but they figured with hard work, a strong cattle and hog market in not too distant Chicago, they were poised for success. No reason to worry.

Except that Esther's husband had a hidden health problem nobody knew about until he dropped dead on the job one day. He left behind his reputation as a hard worker, his wife Esther, their four little ones, their herd, and a large mortgage.

People said that if Esther felt sorry for herself she didn't show it. She knew only one thing to do with adversity. Face it. Tackle it head-on. Don't even think about failing—and that's exactly what she did.

Early and late, summer and winter, springtime and fall, through rain, snow and mud, through sickness and aching muscles, this little wisp of a woman attacked her problem with the ferocity of a tiger. Esther barely topped five feet tall. I doubt if she weighed a hundred pounds soaking wet. She mothered her children, kept house, gardened and canned for the four of them. The rest of the time she helped her hired man slop the pigs, feed the herd, pitch manure and she became as physically strong as men her size—while working twice as hard.

The owner of the Mueller grain elevator in Grand Mound admired Esther because, though they had many customers who had their debt cancelled by bankruptcy during the Great Depression, Esther paid her debt in full though not legally required to do so.

Esther's toughest battles were behind her when we met. Still, her gnarled hands and tanned leathery face with deep crinkles bore mute witness to this woman's tenacity. She'd labored for years, and saw her brood raised to responsible adulthood and paid off the mortgage by sheer dint of will.

Like the bumble bee, which experts say cannot fly because of the laws of aerodynamics—its heavy body in relation to its stubby wings—Esther did not know she couldn't do it—so she went ahead and did it anyway.

Esther attended church as regular as clockwork when I first arrived. It didn't take me long to learn that her home was the ideal one to visit in mid-afternoon if I was feeling hungry while calling in Grand Mound. Or if I was coming home from hospital visits in DeWitt five miles further down Highway 30.

She'd open the door like an aged cheer leader. "Well, for goodness sake. Hello, Revner." (She always called me Revner—her word for Reverend which she felt compelled to use out of respect for the office regardless of my immaturity.) "Come on in." She'd clasp her hands together with a smack. "Can I getcha a glass of milk and a piece of raspberry pie?" Anybody who ever tasted Esther's raspberry pie—or cherry, rhubarb, pumpkin, apple or any other kind—knew they'd be foolish to turn down such a treat. What an ideal situation. Ester enjoyed baking pies, and I enjoyed eating her pie.

I made dozens of trips to her home over seven years—influenced, to no small degree by her expertise as a baker—but also because talking with Esther always gave me a lift. Being with her made me want to face my problems with a mind-set more like hers. She almost always greeted me with her, "Well, for goodness sakes. Hello, Revner. Come on in." And, as she opened the door for me to leave, she'd almost always quote a favorite saying of hers: "Remember, do thy duty that is best. Leave unto the Lord the rest." Esther exemplified duty with a capital D. She had earned the right to advise others.

Esther's church attendance started to sag when we entered our new church building program. The little old 114 year-old frame church that had been the first school house in Grand Mound was plenty good enough for her. No need to build new. I can understand her reluctance when so many events dear to her heart—baptisms, weddings, funerals and other shared experiences with dear friends—took place in that building which had grown sacred by association with people and events.

When the first unit of the new church was built, and we began worship services there, Esther stopped coming entirely. I continued my dessert visits and received Esther's customary greeting. We'd sit at her small drop-leaf table by the kitchen window overlooking her weed-free garden. She'd serve me a luscious piece of pie and a cold glass of milk beaded with condensation and begin her new lecture. "You know, Revner, I love you and Vonda, but why in the world did they have to build that chicken coop down in the swamp?"

The "loyal opposition" who were not thrilled with building a new church took delight in dubbing the first stage of construction as "the chicken coop in the swamp." Actually, its long rectangular shape and white vinyl siding did bear strong resemblance to a large chicken coop, and it was built in one of the lowest spots in town. So we had to chuckle along with them until the second stage of construction was completed with its stone façade and multi-colored stained glass windows.

I called on Esther several times after the second stage was completed. Got her usual treat, and the now customary, "You know, I love you, Revner but…" lecture. Finally I asked her, "Esther, have you been inside our new church yet?"

"No, I never set foot inside that chicken coop since they put it up."

"Well then, get your sweater on and let's go down for a look." I expected an immediate refusal. She hesitated, as though stunned by the thought, and then accepted my invitation. It may have been because she was taught to respect clergy from childhood. I'm sure she didn't want any of her loyal opposition friends to see her go inside "that chicken coop down in the swamp"—but she took the chance.

I unlocked the front double-doors and we walked through the entry hall into the spacious fellowship room which was flooded with bright sunshine. The well-appointed kitchen was visible through the open serving doors. "Ohhh, this is beautiful. I had no idea it looked this nice on the inside.

"Wait 'till you see the sanctuary, Esther." I pulled the double doors wide open. She stepped inside ahead of me. She took in the cherry-red dossal curtain with its distinctive yoked cross symbol, the red-cushioned seats and the hand-carved symbols on the chancel furniture and the communion rail. The swirly pastel colors in the stained-glass windows shown to good advantage—back lighted, as they were, by the late afternoon sun.

Esther—her mouth half open—was clearly astonished. "Whyyy, this is wonderful." She continued to drink in the unexpected beauty. She looked up to the stained-glass sanctuary lamps suspended from the ceiling and did a complete turn around to get the panoramic view. "Ohhh, this is sooo pretty." Then locking eyes with me she said, "You know what you need? You need a pipe organ in here. It needs a pipe organ." She nodded firmly, underscoring her words. The way she spoke with such conviction led me to believe the pipe organ might be about to become a reality.

Of course it didn't. It was just her nice way of saying that she'd changed her mind ... and she'd given her seal of approval to "the chicken coop in the swamp."

Get Me Out of Here

In the final analysis, the questions of why bad things
happen to good people transmutes itself into some very
different questions, no longer asking why something
happened, but asking how we will respond, what we
intend to do now that it happened.

—*Pierre Teilhard de Chardin*

The Chicago and Northwestern Railroad splits the little town of Calamus in two with a double set of tracks that carry cargo—both freight and passenger—between Chicago and the Pacific Ocean.

You had to pay attention to those tracks because you never knew if what was coming toward you was a slow freight train pulling upwards of 200 cars or a passenger train—maybe *The City of Denver* or *The City of Los Angeles*—going full speed across the Iowa prairie. And even after one train passed, you had to make sure another one wasn't about to blindside you on the opposite track.

One lazy summer afternoon, when all nature invited me slow down and smell the flowers, I approached the tracks on First Street just as the red warning lights began flashing and the bells began clanging in their panic voice. I looked left and saw a freight train well down the track but decided—in honor of my childhood days—to sit there in our '57 Chevy and watch the metal monster roar by as I loved to do as a child in my hometown in Michigan.

There's something about being near a moving train that's deep-down scary, and it makes you feel brave for having been close to something so large, so loud, so powerful and dangerous. You get a shot of adrenaline when you feel the earth shudder, the blasts of air being displaced by each car and the primal scream of the whistle.

So there I sat like a little kid in the midst of a sensory smorgasbord—the screaming, the loud clickety-clack of metal wheels on steel rails that flexed up and down under the weight of each car, the rush of warm air smelling of hot metal and grease, the quaking of the earth beneath me. I stopped too close to the train to count the cars as I often did but then I saw movement in my side view mirror—

something big coming toward me from behind at an angle. It was Chuck Nicely's gas truck backing away from the siding where he'd just filled up and now misjudged the space he thought was empty.

I laid on my horn but that was useless. Couldn't hear it over the roar of the train. I didn't want to move forward. Too close to the train. All I could do was push hard on the brake and hope Chuck wouldn't drive me into the train.

I felt the sickening crunch of metal buckling on my left rear quarter panel. The car skidded a few feet toward the train—then stopped just short of disaster. I was scared spitless. We both sat in our vehicles for a few moments to gather our wits as the long train continued to roar past us. Then Chuck pulled away and stopped. I got out first and walked toward his truck as he climbed down from his cab white-faced, trembling, and apologetic. "God, I didn't see you sitting there. I'm sorry." He told me not to worry—that his insurance company would take care of it. Then he added, "If you don't have a body shop, the Wheatland Body Shop does good work. Just a minute I'll give you my insurance company." His hands trembled as he handed me his insurance agent's card. I wasn't doing much better. He apologized again. I worried about his condition—hoped he didn't have a heart problem. There was no police report. We didn't have police to report to.

Fortunately my car was drivable. As I drove home over the tracks that were nearly my undoing I recalled that I'd heard rumors that Chuck was a mite too fond of alcohol and a little too fond of speeding for a man driving a gas truck. Some folks had expressed concern for the safety of his children when, at times, he'd take two or three of them riding in the cab with him. Whether he was impaired that day I don't know—could be. Anyway, that was the first and only time we met.

I couldn't imagine a man driving—of all things—a gas truck recklessly and I wondered what factors drove him to add other risk factors such as drinking and excessive speed to an already hazardous occupation. It seemed Chuck fit the proverbial "accident looking for someplace to happen" label. *Something, some intervention, may well be needed to prevent a disaster* I thought. Then I dismissed myself from responsibility. *You're a student pastor, Don. You don't have any leverage. Besides Chuck lives in Wheatland and he's not your parishioner.*

* * *

The following summer I was about to make a Sunday afternoon call at the home of Austin and Grace Briggs on Second Street. I was half way up their front steps when I heard the squeal of tires braking and a sharp blast on a car horn. I turned around to see Rod and Vickie Olsen in their red convertible. Rod shouted, "Don!" and motioned me to their car. "Hurry," he said. I knew by the angst in his voice and his distorted face that he had bad news.

He almost shouted, "Do you know Chuck Nicely?"

"We've met but I don't know him," I say knowing that he and Chuck are friends.

 Rod could barely blurt out, "He's burning up in his gas truck down by the Wapsi River Bridge—right now!"

"My God, what happened?" I felt paralyzed by his words—like a hard blow to the solar plexus stops you in your tracks and renders you temporarily inoperable.

"He tried to pass us on the highway. He clipped the bridge and rolled his truck. It caught on fire." Rod's lips were trembling as he talked. He fought back tears and said, "We stopped and ran over as close as we could get." He jerked his head back and forth as if trying to get the image out of his head. "Chuck was screaming, 'Help me you guys. Get me out of here' but..." Rod began sobbing and pounding his steering wheel.

Vickie took over in her choked, barely audible voice, "We couldn't get to him because of the flames. We just stood and watched. The Wheatland fire truck came. They couldn't do much either."

Rod recovered his voice long enough to say, "It was so horrible...we couldn't stand it...had to leave. We just came from there."

I put my hand on Rod's arm and gave him a long firm squeeze. There are times when you don't have words... or when the ones you have don't work. It's a frequent problem of mine.

* * *

Later that day the word spread that the fire was going so strong when the volunteer firefighters got there all they could do was direct water on the cab while the load of gas and oil burned itself out. They said all that was left of Chuck was half a man for his closed casket funeral in Wheatland where he'd lived with his wife and five little children.

His death was a ghastly semi-cremation of the involuntary sort—if you call driving a gas truck like a sports car "involuntary." Why do we take such risks with our lives? Squander life? Where is God in all this? Why must five children go through life absent the comfort of a caring father? How can God be good when he lets things like this happen—and far worse? Why do bad things happen to innocent people? Why didn't someone intervene? Why do so many questions have no satisfactory answers? Why? Why? Why?

Some people expect clergy to *provide* authoritative answers to questions like these and some clergy actually believe they *have* authoritative answers. All I can do is shake my head and live with the same questions as everyone else. The *"why"* questions have few certain answers. The *"how"* questions have more answers. How do we pick up the pieces and go on from here? How can we help Chuck's family?

* * *

Chuck's gruesome death shook the little town of Wheatland and all its near neighbors like a tsunami. His wife, his children, his friends, his customers, his church family, and many who never knew him must have shuddered to think about it. It became a focus of neighborhood talk but, as is usually the case with such events, talk of Chuck's death subsided after a while and gave way to other events that replaced it on center stage. My life went on too, but I seldom drove over that place on Second Street where Rod and Vickie stopped me without hearing Rod's voice sobbing, "He's burning up—right now!" And I seldom drove over the Wapsi River Bridge past that big scorched area—even after a new spring restored it to green—without hearing Chuck's desperate, "Help me, you guys. Get me out of here!"

Not Pictured

It's only when we truly know and understand that
we have a limited time on earth—and that we have
no way of knowing when out time is up—that we
will begin to live each day to the fullest, as if it
was the only one we had.
—*Elizabeth Kubler-Ross*

If the dead be truly dead, why should they
still be walking in my heart?
—*Winneap Shosone, medicine man*

The death of my oldest brother, Wendell, triggered nightmare times for our entire family that have lasted for years and whose residual effects are still with us.

It happened two weeks before Christmas in 1960—Vonda and I had just returned to our home in Calamus after the District Ministers' Christmas Celebration. Omar and Eve Petersen, a newly married clergy couple, had joined us for supper. We gathered in our kitchen. We were young. We laughed and enjoyed each other's company. Omar and Eve danced to Christmas music on the radio. Then the phone rang.

I had to shush the others and put a finger over one ear to hear my mother's call from Michigan. "I'm sorry Mom, I didn't hear you. What did you say?"

She repeated, "I said I have bad news."

I broke in with, "Is it Dad?' because he had experienced a stroke earlier and we had prepared ourselves for news of his death.

"No, it's Wendell. They found him dead of a gunshot wound in his office."

Wham—I wasn't prepared for that—couldn't assimilate it. I continued as if I were talking to someone I didn't know—about someone I didn't know. "Was it murder or suicide?" I asked knowing that attorneys often operate under immense stress and are not immune to either murder or suicide.

My mind was unable to assimilate this new reality.

"We don't know. That's all the information the police gave us. When can you leave for home?" Mother sounded in need of support. Though she didn't mention it, the shock of Wendell's death could easily precipitate Dad's death as well.

"We'll be on our way as soon as we can get packed and make arrangements with the churches. I'll need for someone to cover in my absence."

The shock of my brother Wendell's death made eating seem unimportant. He had been like a second father to the younger members of our family, and we feared for his wife and five children.

We loaded our luggage in the trunk of "Coralbelle," our 1957 Chevy. Our boys: Colin (4), and Lance (2) bedded down in the back seat. Vonda held our daughter Lisa, only six months old, as we drove off for Michigan in the dark.

We crossed the Michigan border about two in the morning and picked up a few details on WJR, "The Great Voice of the Great Lakes," on our car radio. Wendell had been killed by a berserk farmer, Joseph Austin. Wendell, as an attorney, had been representing Austin's wife in a divorce case involving cruel spousal abuse. In his paranoid state and angered at facing a court hearing as to why he failed to make payments to his wife, Austin had bludgeoned his wife to death with his fists, shot Wendell, then returned home and shot himself to death. We garnered few other details before arriving at my parents' home in Marlette.

Our grief was mixed with helpless rage and sorrow for Wendell's wife Lila and their five children: Richard (19) and in the Air Force), Barbara (15), Steve (13), Fred (12), and Mary (10). I recalled having crossed paths with Wendell at St. Joseph's Hospital one afternoon when he was calling on Mary. He said, "You know, you never know how much you love your kids until you hold them in your arms and wonder whether they're going to live or die."

Vonda and I, tired from thirty hours without rest, turned our children over to their grandparents and sacked out in the guest room. It was late afternoon and getting dark when we woke up for supper.

We wanted a newspaper for further news about Wendell so I drove the two miles into town in winter darkness to get one. The wind was cold and gusty and spitting snow as I parked in front of Robinson's Drug Store. I was almost alone on the street as I reached for a copy of the Port Huron Times Herald on the news stand. I hadn't anticipated the picture of Wendell lying on the floor of his office on the front page. I was glad it was dark so nobody could see my face and hands twitch and tremble and my eyes overflow with scalding tears.

I'm looking for a gentle way to introduce you to that photograph from the Michigan State Police Crime Lab. Thousands of people have seen it on the front page of the Detroit Free Press, The Detroit News, The Times Herald—hundreds have looked at it through their own tears—but I've shown this picture to fewer than a dozen people in the last fifty years.

So here you see my brother Wendell lying dead on the floor of his office with a pool of his own blood beneath his head. He's on his back in his business suit and directly in front of his desk. His desk is loaded with stacks of paper. His tie flopped into a curious hook shape against his white shirt when he fell. His dress coat and hat are hanging on the left wall; his diplomas from Eastern Michigan University and Detroit College of Law are hung high on the right wall. Five shelves of law books cover the first wall, with a smaller four tiered shelf the other wall.

This is not a posh office. In addition to the ordinary oak desk there is a matching desk chair, and two oak captain's chairs. You can see an eight inch pipe running across the ceiling above the large bookcase. The carpet is a deeply sculptured swirl design. To get to the office you have to climb a creaky wooden stairway over the Doggendorf Grocery Store. Wendell shared the upstairs with two dentists named Morrison—a father/son team. One of their receptionists discovered Wendell's body when she ducked into his office to say goodbye at the end of her work day.

Wendell had just returned from the County Court House in Mt. Clemens, fifteen miles away. He was going to finish some paperwork when—as police reconstruct it—Joseph Austin, the crazed husband of Wendell's client burst into the room. He fired three shots to the head with a forty-five and left Wendell's wife without a husband, his five young children without a father and the town of Armada without an attorney.

Another attorney, who knew that Austin had threatened Wendell several times, told the police of the threats. The Austin home was dark when the police arrived. They flooded the area with light, crept up and broke their way into the house stumbling over a pile of drapes which covered Mrs. Austin's body. She was battered beyond recognition—"looked like raw hamburger," Sheriff Almstadt told me later. It was such a gruesome sight they covered her up again. An officer who had gone upstairs shouted down, "There's another body up here." It was Joseph Austin, still in his overcoat—a picture of his daughter in his left hand (the face poked out) and a forty-five on the floor nearby.

Austin's rage had been monumental. Tests indicated he had pummeled his wife to death twelve or fourteen hours earlier, then took a pick axe to his house. He made kindling of tables and chairs, demolished the television, the banister leading upstairs, and the walls, as well as the furnace in the basement. He took photographs out of their frames, and pictures out of their albums, and poked out eyes and faces.

It has always struck me as bizarre that, sixteen Christmases earlier, Wendell had been an Infantry Captain in the Battle of the Bulge in which tens of thousands died. He came home safely—only to have this happen at the hands of a fellow citizen in a sleepy rural town where, as they mistakenly say, "Things like this never happen here." Wendell had taken this case as a favor to a friend. The caption under one of his pictures in the Detroit News read, "Slain trying to help."

Sometimes the effect of one person's life on the lives of others is not a ripple—it's a tidal wave … a tsunami. Joseph Austin's was. Sadly, he was in need of hospitalization for mental illness. Sadly, Austin chose to vent his rage on Wendell, and in doing so Wendell's family and the entire community of Armada. Sadly, he killed his wife, willed his two beautiful daughters one dollar each and the rest of his estate to two nephews in Lithuania.

At one point we consoled ourselves with, "Thank goodness none of Wendell's children were with him when this happened"—because we knew it was their habit to stop by after school to get a hug, some praise for school work or money for candy. Years later we heard family stories—now confirmed—that Wendell's then ten-year-old daughter Mary *had* been there—that Austin had pushed her aside to shoot her father.

112

Highly Respected Local Attorney Killed By Hate-Twisted Farmer After Hours of Brooding

Rampage Started With Wife, Ending By Taking Own Life

The Community of Armada paid their final respects on Monday, December 12 to one of its most respected citizens, Wendell H. Lichtenfelt, 46.

The full military honors concluded a weekend of hate, violence ending in a double murder and suicide, which the police estimated began its rampage on Thursday, December 8. Wendell Lichtenfelt, better known as "Dick," former Macomb county chief assistant prosecutor, was shot to death in his office, located in an upstairs office at 23062 Main street Friday afternoon by Joseph Austin, 67, a sort of Jekyl-Hyde character, but a crazed farmer with a fanatic hate blaming Lichtenfelt for the divorce action started two years ago by his wife.

Lichtenfelt's death climaxed a 15 hour period in which the beserk Austin had first bludgeoned his wife Tessie, 53, to death, on Thursday, December 8, ripped up their farm home, two miles north of Armada at 73160 North road, with a pick-axe,' then drove past Lichtenfelt's office several times, building up a warped hate that erupted into a violent death a second time, claiming the life of an innocent man late Friday afternoon, December 9.

Then Austin went home to his darkened farmhouse, walked through the kitchen where his

ATTORNEY WENDELL H. LICHTENFELT

would enter the bank and make false accusations; one time recently forcing the bank to go back over his account to 1957.

Austin, retained Frank E. Jeannette of Mt. Clemens as his attorney after being discontinued by Attorney Edward A. Jacob of Romeo in the earlier divorce suit, which discontinued on June 25, 1956.

Austin went to see Jeannette, early in August. He did not object to paying the $100 retainer fee. He seemed meek and mild, assuming a Jekyl-Hyde character.

had oredered him to pay Dick Lichtenfelt."

These series of events no doubt triggered the deaths of three persons — a mild mannered attorney, a mistreated farm wife and the enraged husband.

It is believed that in a fit of rage, Austin, described as a 5 foot 7 inch, 250 pounder with shoulders of a wrestler unmercifully pounded his wife with his fists beyond recognition after first using the butt of his gun. He then covered her body in the blood smeared kitchen with the drapes he tore from the window. There he must of sat down

One of many articles about Wendell's murder.
Armada Times, December 15, 1960

113

According to Barbara, Wendell's oldest daughter, Mary had run the three blocks home, and up to the bathroom with unexplained blood on her clothing. Barbara and brother Fred found her and helped clean her up. The murder had not yet been discovered. Mary appeared to be in shock and unable to answer questions. Her sister and brother disposed of the wash cloth they used to wipe blood off Mary before their mother could learn of it. As we learned later their mother, Lila, had been in fragile mental health and the children took care not to share things with her which might trigger an emotional episode—anything that might "set her off."

Wendell lay alone on the floor in the grisly police photo of his death, but there were other victims "not pictured" as photo captions sometimes say. Wendell's troubles were over. Lila's had been greatly exacerbated. She and her five children had been dealt enough traumas in an instant to last their entire lifetimes. The ripples of that horrific event continue to lap on the shores of the lives of all of us who knew and loved Wendell.

And so, other stories—almost as traumatic as the first—resulted from Wendell's murder, as well as the revelation of a hidden illness in the family.

We go through life, you and I, not knowing what we don't know. Not knowing the calamities others bear. Unaware of deep pain all around us in the lives of quiet people doing the best they can against heavy odds—and they're not even in the picture.

Sunshine in the Cemetery

This world is not conclusion;
A sequel stands beyond,
Invisible, as music.
But positive, as sound.
—*Emily Dickinson*

Those little towns of Calamus and Grand Mound, Iowa straddled the Lincoln Highway, the Chicago and Northwestern Railway, and our hearts. Vonda and I lived there seven years. She gave birth to Colin, Lance and Lisa while there. We completed a church building program I had initiated in Grand Mound. We felt we could have gone on living there for years, and were sad when it came time to return to Michigan. Time—because both my parents faced terminal illness and it seemed right to be near them.

Somehow my memories of Calamus involve constant sunshine, though I really know better. Our first winter there was a bright one and deposited little more snow than I could handle easily with a barn broom. Subsequent winters with howling blizzards erased any hope that was the norm. In summer the threat of tornadoes with mid-day skies that could turn green and black taught us to keep an eye on the sky. One ferocious storm put a large maple limb through our front window and soaked our carpet and furniture.

Still I think of our days there as bright with sunshine. I suppose that's because the people there were so friendly and patient with me as their new young pastor. I was only twenty-one when I arrived fresh from college. Vonda was twenty. The parishioners were glad to get what they could because the town was so small it was usually a student pastor or nothing.

It was in Calamus that I met my adopted mother, Anna Scott. She lived on a gravel road a short drive south of town; down near where the Wapsipinicon River meandered through fertile Iowa farmlands. Anna and Roy lived in a small home that had been built around the original log home built by Roy's father—not nearly as impressive as the homes of the "big" farmers who had large homes with impressive plantings. Roy was a bit of a curmudgeon, but he was aware of it, and

115

that made it okay. Anna was not a pretty woman except as a warm smile makes a person attractive—but Anna was the embodiment of maternal instincts. She extended her heart and made room for everyone. That made her beautiful.

Roy and Anna's home sat back from the road about sixty yards. The gravel drive was lined with tall cedars, and their kitchen area was smothered with trumpet vines that bloomed in magnificent prodigality in the spring, perfuming the air all around. The house was surrounded by flowering shrubs—spirea, mock orange, and beauty bushes. Vonda and I spent many a happy time in that home. The Scotts treated us like family and included us in family gatherings, birthdays and holidays. On occasion the family would disperse after dishes were done. Some played active games outside, others played cards or table games inside. If I were lucky Anna and I would go to the little sun room whose windows opened up on the stately cedars along the driveway, the Iowa farmland, and her bird feeders. Anna loved the birds and squirrels that came to her feeder. Loved to watch them, and admire colors, or laugh at their antics. Especially, she loved listening to the birds singing.

I loved talking with Anna—mostly about me—because that's the kind of person she was. She took interest in the details of other people's lives as though that were the most all-consuming aspect of her life. In addition we shared interest in gardening, music, poetry, birds and the church. But Anna and I didn't really need to be talking all the time. We were comfortable with long pauses and were content just to be in each other's presence.

Anna and her family became our family. It was a good feeling for two unusually young people trying to serve the Calamus and Grand Mound churches with no previous experience and minimal skills— and five hundred miles from our parental homes. But we felt accepted, and loved, and the people were patient with us as we learned. Accepted our shortcomings, and continued to support us with their affection—even when we blundered.

A number of the old people of Calamus died while we were there, altering the makeup of the town. Anna struggled with poor health, and finally died as the result of injuries suffered in an automobile accident.

I don't remember much about the funeral except that I was asked to officiate and I was numb with my own grief. It was a teary-joyous time for people who had been severed from a friend they loved—yet were so glad for the privilege of being Anna's friend for a time.

What stands out about that day for me was the committal at the Calamus cemetery. It was a great-to-be-alive kind of day as we stood on the slope of the hill. Bright sunshine. Warm breezes. A complete day. We had just committed Anna to the earth in the hope of the resurrection. I said "Amen" to the benediction, and at that exact moment a bird began warbling a most marvelous song. Everyone stood in stunned silence in the beauty of that moment. Several of Anna's friends in that gathering were avid birders. They began to ask, "What kind of bird was that?" Nobody knew.

I like to think of the beauty of that moment—the sunshine, the loving friends, the enchanting song from the throat of an unidentified bird—as God's visitation in one of God's many disguises.

Fraser Years
1961 – 1967

Whether it's the best of times or
the worst of times, it's the only
time we've got.
—*Art Buchwald*

Monument

There are things that we don't want to happen
but have to accept, things we don't want to
know but have to learn, and people we can't
live without but have to let go.
—*Source unknown*

My father and mother couldn't bring themselves to look at my oldest brother as he lay in his casket at the Tiffany-Young funeral home in Armada, Michigan. Gruesome stories surrounding the brutal double murder and suicide had circulated on page one of *The Detroit News* and *The Detroit Free Press*, as well as the *Port Huron Times Herald* and the *Mt. Clemens Daily Monitor Leader.* The horror stories were more than Dad and Mom could handle. They sat well back from the casket during visitation hours and none of their children remembers seeing them look toward the open casket during the entire funeral. One long look—close up—was enough for me.

Wendell's murder was more than Dale Young—Armada's funeral director—could cope with as well. Dale and Wendell were warm personal friends who lived just two doors apart. Dale left the reconstruction of Wendell's face to a mortician in another town after viewing the effects of multiple close-up gun shots. I wouldn't have known about the *other mortician* (Leroy Faulman) if he had not told me months later as we drove to the cemetery together for a burial service.

Frequent reminders of Wendell's death proved overpowering to me when I first moved back to Michigan after seven years as a pastor in Iowa. I had prepared to make the move before Wendell's death because my mother was in a losing battle with cancer, and Dad— eighteen years her senior—struggled with serious health issues as well. I had arranged with Bishop Ensley of the North Iowa Conference and Bishop Reed of the Detroit Annual Conference to transfer my clergy affiliation back to Michigan.

Four months after Wendell's death—while I was still living in Iowa—I had interviewed with Rev. Martin Stegal, District

Superintendent of the Port Huron District where I hoped to be located. Martin invited Vonda and me to join him and his wife Myra for supper at the Hi-Way Host Restaurant south of Marlette. Martin and Myra seemed warm and welcoming and after eating, getting acquainted and finishing our lemon meringue pie, Martin turned to business.

He pushed away from the table and tilted back in his chair as though giving me the floor. "Well, Don, you're coming back to Michigan and you'd like to serve a church fairly close to your family. Tell me what sort of church you had in mind." I felt as though he was opening the door of opportunity wide for me.

I welcomed the opportunity to have a voice in the decision as I remembered there was a day when Methodist clergy had no idea where they were going until they heard the Bishop read their assignments at Annual Conference. I told Martin, "What would appeal to me most right now is church in a rural community— possibly a county seat town—where I can settle down and exercise a ministry of pastoral care with people."

Martin surprised me with his quick—and I felt insensitive— response, "Well, I suppose that's okay if you don't have any ambition." I couldn't believe my ears. Surely this was an attempt at humor gone wrong. Who could deny that standing by troubled people—the lonely, the sick and dying, the grieving—was at the very heart of a pastor's calling?

I felt stung, and more than a little angry, at his assertion that a pastoral ministry to hurting people indicated a lack of ambition. However I tried not to show that I was nettled as I shared my "plan B" with him: "I'm also interested in the possibility of serving as an associate pastor in a larger church where I could learn from an experienced senior pastor." (I had inside information from friends in Port Huron First that my name had already been mentioned as a possible associate minister there.)

Martin lowered the front legs of his chair to the floor and rested his arms against the edge of the table. His second response was equally dismissive—equally discouraging: "Don, I don't know of a multiple ministry in Michigan where everyone's happy. If the associate pastor does a good job, the senior pastor gets all the credit.

122

If anything goes wrong the associate pastor gets all the blame." I felt disappointed that a man in Martin's office would make such a statement. I knew former associate pastors who revered their mentors—had an almost father/son relationship with them for life.

I didn't know how to respond to what seemed to me to be a blatant falsehood coming from a superior…and I didn't have a "plan C" to offer.

Then Martin leaned forward with his elbows on the table and his hands laced together. He flexed his fingers a couple of times and laid out *his* plan: "Now, *what I have in mind for you* is the mission congregation in Fraser. We've had three different ministers in there over the last five years. They started out in the VFW Hall, then they met in a hardware store and now they're meeting in a high school cafeteria. We're either going to get in there and make a go of it—or we're going to drop any plans for building a church there."

I felt a sinking feeling in my gut. Martin knew we had recently completed a church building project in Iowa, and seemed to be looking at me as a missing piece to his puzzle. It seemed Martin had no intention of taking *my* interests into consideration. He was herding me toward a place and into a situation I wanted to avoid. The door of opportunity seemed to be closing with me in the wrong pen. Was this going to be a "take it our leave it" offer?

I'd never heard of Fraser and had no interest in taking on the stress of another building program but, in order to buy time and come up with a way out of this predicament, I told Martin, "I'd still prefer my plan A or B, but I'll give it some thought and get back with you." I felt totally disheartened as we said our goodbyes.

All I knew about Fraser is what Martin had told me: it had been a small sleepy town overtaken by Detroit Metropolitan urban sprawl—now a bedroom community whose people, many of them engineer and educator types, worked in schools and industries in nearby cities. I was not attracted to suburban living but when I got home I took out a Michigan map to place Fraser in my mind. Wham! A revelation. Fraser is in Macomb County where my brother Wendell had lived and worked. In Macomb County and only five miles from Mt. Clemens where Wendell had served as Chief Assistant Prosecutor for five years prior to his death in the (then) second most populous county in

Michigan. I found myself torn between strong opposing feelings. Not wanting to live in suburbia and not wanting to go through another building program versus serving as a pastor in the same area where Wendell served as an attorney.

* * *

I recalled the day Wendell and his wife Lila had taken Vonda and me out to lunch in Mt. Clemens just before we moved to Iowa. We knew full-well that he did not have a universal high regard for all clergy types—nor did I—but, as we ate, he paused and said in a soft reflective voice, "You know, I can't imagine a more satisfying life than that of a *good* (his emphasis) clergyman. We'll do what we can to help you."

My brothers and sisters and I could always count on Wendell to be a source of warmth and encouragement—a sort of unofficial family cheer leader—a second father with more warmth than the first. Wendell took an immediate shine to Vonda upon meeting her and sent me a letter I treasure in response to my asking him to be an usher at our wedding. In it he acknowledged, "I know that Dad has some reservations about your getting married at this time," (since Vonda was nineteen and I was twenty—and both in college.) "But," he said, "It seems to me that you have made a fine catch. So I would advise you to marry her before she gets away."

Once we moved into our—hundred some year old—parsonage Wendell surprised me by shipping a two-drawer file and storage cabinet for my first office. Some time later he sent a copy of Life magazine's photo book *The Religions of the World*—probably to help me keep things in larger perspective. When, three months after arriving in Iowa, I had to have a kidney removed he sent me a series of cards and notes to encourage me during recuperation.

Several times I had consulted him over legalities of issues within our communities and he guided me through them. The first involved handling insinuations of incest in the congregation. The last issue involved a husband's sadistic treatment of his wife—his taking her out

124

WENDELL H. LICHTENFELT
ATTORNEY AT LAW
23062 MAIN STREET
ARMADA, MICHIGAN

July 11, 1953

Mr. Donald Lichtenfelt
Box 203
Marlette, Michigan

Dear Don:

I shall be very glad to be an usher at your wedding. Of course I do not have a cutaway coat or striped trousers, but perhaps you will dispense with those.

I have been intending to write you relative to your marriage, but as with everything else, I procrastinate. I know there is some doubt in Dad's mind as to the advisability of your getting married now.

The few minutes that I observed Vonda, she impressed me very favorably, and I daresay she will make a good wife and Mother. I presume you are in love with her. Therefore if you both feel the same way do not let anyone deter you from getting married. There is always a way to get along, and if you sincerely want to become a minister, the fact that you are married will be more of a help than a hindrance.

It seems to me that you have made a fine catch, so I would advise you to marry her before she gets away.

Lila and I shall be pleased to attend and participate in your marriage, and we hope that we shall be able to assist you in getting through college and starting on your chosen career.

Best of luck,

Dick & Lila

— Wendell's letter of support —

125

in the field and burning her repeatedly with cigarettes—which made front page news. Wendell's response —right or wrong—was, "Don't touch that kind of situation with a ten-foot pole. He likes to hurt her and she is willing to put up with being hurt. They'll likely turn on you and see you as the enemy." Only months later he failed to take his own advice in a similar situation and it led to his murder. As my friend Flo said, "He was protecting you—yet he did what he advised you not to do."

Our entire family took immense pride in Wendell whose accomplishments included putting Mafia members behind bars—in spite of threats on Wendell's life. In one case he had declined protection but law enforcement agents kept him under protective surveillance—without his knowledge—for nearly a year as he traveled home.

* * *

Even though agreeing to serve as a mission pastor in Fraser involved growing a congregation, major fundraising, building another new church and a new parsonage, I decided—for entirely emotional reasons—to accept. Even *insist* upon—the Fraser appointment—to carry on in Wendell's absence. I convinced myself that, if I could be half the minister that he was an attorney, it could be a tribute to him. I don't know whether it was a valid motive for such a choice. Maybe not.

I first discovered that my plan was flawed when I went to the Macomb County Building in Mt. Clemens to get a Michigan driver's license. Wendell had been in court in that building earlier on the day he was murdered. Its tall thirteen stories looked to me like a huge tombstone that blared out "DEATH!" like a stuck auto horn. I felt the irrational fear that it might fall and crush me. I had a panic attack when I walked into the County Clerk's office and couldn't find my voice—couldn't transact business there. Even the simple business of getting a Michigan driver's license. So I drove fifteen miles to the Utica county clerk's office where my application went smoothly. I experienced similar problems at the Art-O-Craft office supply directly across the street from the County Building. I stuttered and stammered and choked up as I ordered office supplies for the church.

The Macomb County Building, Mt. Clemens, Michigan

Similar things happened when I'd meet new people and they'd say, "Oh—Lichtenfelt, Lichtenfelt—are you any relation to the lawyer who was killed?" The tension was crippling me—shutting me down. Seven months after Wendell's death and I was in the midst of a new and unanticipated phase in my grief reaction. I would learn shortly that it takes eighteen to twenty-four months just to stabilize after the death of a family member—and *much longer* in cases involving violent death.

I knew this had serious implications for my work as a pastor. I shared my concern with Claire Wolf, an older minister whom I adopted as my "father confessor." Claire said, "Don, let me think about it for a while and see if I can come up with something that might help you." I thought the subject might never come up again, but the next time our paths crossed Claire motioned me aside—away from others—where we could talk. He said, "Don, you told me that when you saw the Macomb County Building it reminded you of a

127

huge tombstone and it was as if it were shouting 'DEATH.' I've been thinking about tombstones and why we have them. I wonder if—instead of seeing the County Building as a giant *tombstone*—you saw it as a *monument* to the things that were important to Wendell—a *memorial* to the things he stood for—if that might help you."

I felt glad Claire couldn't read my mind—though sometimes I thought he was the sort of person who could. I was thinking, *oh, for Pete's sake, Claire, what makes you think a simple thing like that would ever help?* But I didn't say that. I said, "I appreciate your giving it serious thought, Claire. I'll give it a try."

I did. Each time I went to Mt. Clemens—where you could see the County Building for blocks from any direction—I tried what Claire suggested. I'd try to dismiss the *tombstone/death* combination and think *"monument to the things Wendell stood for,"* and in a time so short it amazed me—and contrary to my expectations—it worked. It helped. I even found myself able to enter the Macomb County Building without feeling it would fall on me at any moment. Without choking up and losing my ability to speak. Without even thinking of death. I could even enter a courtroom and meet attorneys and other legal types who knew Wendell and hear them talk about his life, and death and their admiration for him—and it became helpful and healing to me. I began to think *maybe I am here for the right reasons* and the memory of Wendell's life helps me—and the Macomb County Building *is* *a monument* to important ideas of justice, and mercy, and kindness, and courage that we cannot let die. At last, I could bring myself to look at that *"tombstone"* and see it as a *monument* … and a friend.

Life in the Cement Mixer

In times like these it helps to recall that
there have always been times like these.
— *Paul Harvey*

"They've had three different pastors. They started meeting in a VFW hall, then moved to a hardware store, and now they're meeting in a school cafeteria. We're either going to *get in there and make a go of it, or we're going to pull out.*" Those words kept repeating in my mind.

The district superintendent of the Port Huron District of the Methodist church had just stated my assignment in clear and simple words, "Get in there and make a go of it." I had no way of knowing all that this new assignment would involve.

Fraser had been a sleepy village five miles north of Detroit, then got caught up in urban sprawl, and grew to a population of 30,000 and counting. It had become a bedroom community whose residents served corporations and institutions in the Greater Detroit area. At the time of my arrival the congregation was made up almost entirely of engineers, educators, and executive types—and a few blue collar workers. So far as I knew, all the residents of Fraser were white, as was our church. I had the feeling real estate agents were content with that arrangement. Later on, one real estate man pulled his daughter out of our Methodist Youth Fellowship because racially mixed groups met in the church.

In mid-June of 1961, Vonda and I, and our family of three young children moved into a small house on Beacon Lane which the Fraser congregation had rented for us.

As soon as we moved in, I took on regular pastoral duties with no church building and no office—except for a corner of our small house.

When we arrived, the building committee had been in place for several months. Members of the committee were responsible for locating and purchasing property, securing an architect and developing acceptable building plans, and overseeing construction. Along the way, our finance committee would need to secure

129

professional fund-raising assistance to underwrite the project from within the congregation. Our denomination provided some start-up financial assistance, but the bulk of the financing was up to us.

When we left Fraser six years later there was a new parsonage, new church building and a stable congregation with competent leadership—*but it was a bumpy ride—a lot like living in a cement mixer.* You expect roaring bulldozers, groaning gravel trucks, and the chatter of backhoes once the actual building process begins. You expect the clutter of equipment, mounds of earth, and pallets loaded with cement blocks, bricks and lumber. You expect the sound of hammers and circular saws and men shouting back and forth. That sort of chaos you expect—the creative kind that leads to a desirable goal. The other kinds of clutter, static, and chaos come as gate-crashers.

Words don't come to me in an orderly fashion when I try to write about our Fraser experience. For me, it's like trying to get a group of cats to line up single file—by name. The various parts of this story are not in exact sequence. Events seemed to compete with each other for our attention. In February of 1962 (eight months after we arrived in Fraser) Grandmother King— my major source of human warmth— died. I am not given to primal screams. Yet, when I visited her gravesite by the little West Berlin country church near Almont that summer, the screams exploded from me as I pounded the steering wheel in our Chevy and wept. I was totally surprised at my own reaction, and glad no one drove by to witness this uncharacteristic episode.

When I found that Fraser had no ministerial association, I solicited the cooperation of other clergy and together, in late 1962, we initiated the Fraser Ministerial Association. This voluntary association brought together clergy from Conservative Southern Baptist to Roman Catholic. This allowed all of us (including the five of us who were pastoring new start-up congregations) to share in what became a deeply caring fellowship, and to become involved in issues collectively. Monsignor Fred DeCneut told us, at the end of a long and harrowing personal experience, "It was the friendship and support of the protestant clergy that made it bearable for me." Then he wiped tears from his eyes with the back of his hand. Most of us shared similar statements at one point or another.

The 1960s were turbulent times—contentious times. The war in Vietnam touched every family in some way—always destructive. Three young men in our church family went to Vietnam. One was killed, one came back with severe post traumatic stress, another—who had been a helicopter pilot—died later from Agent Orange poisoning.

Protests against the war and against proliferation of nuclear weapons multiplied in cities and colleges nearby. Civil rights workers were being beaten and murdered. Demonstrations—both peaceful and violent—sprang up in major cities everywhere—including Detroit. Martin Luther King, Jr. gave his "I Have a Dream" speech in Washington, D.C., and assassinations seemed to be the order of the day.

In June of 1963, I drove to Detroit with our son Colin to join the Walk for Freedom and Peace lead by Dr. Martin Luther King. Colin was six at the time. Some in our congregation felt I might be putting the life of a small child at risk. (I couldn't help but think of all the black children—as well as adults—who had already been killed for no other reason than that they were black.) I felt there was little danger because the walkers were peaceful persons, and we were assured the police would be out in force. I felt taking Colin allowed him to witness and be a part of a movement that would change our country for the better.

The crowd that day was estimated at 125,000. National and state leaders who marched with Dr. King that day included United Auto Workers president Walter Reuther, a former Michigan governor, and the mayor of Detroit. They walked down Woodward Avenue singing "We Shall Overcome." The walk ended at Cobo Hall where Dr. King delivered his "I Have a Dream" speech for the *first* time. Later he shared it with the nation at the March on Washington.

My participation in the Macomb County Inter-Racial Association provided me with a high-point in my life: the privilege of meeting, and talking privately with Rosa Parks, "The mother of the civil rights movement." It strikes me as incredible that one so quiet and soft-spoken as Ms. Parks would be the one whose actions—her refusal to sit at the back of a bus in Montgomery, Alabama—initiated the bus boycott which ignited the nation-wide civil rights movement. As people said, "When Rosa Parks sat down the whole world stood up."

Had it not been for what *she* did, we might never have heard of the Rev. Dr. Martin Luther King, Jr.

On November 22, 1963 I pulled into our local Sunoco station. The owner rushed out, leaned in my open passenger window and said, "Don, have your heard? President Kennedy was shot." In February of 1965, Malcolm X, a nationally known Muslim minister and social worker, was killed. (His father had been killed by white supremacists before him, and his uncle had been lynched.)

* * *

In the wake of these national traumas, in May of 1965 my brother Larry found our father dead at home. At the same time, Mother was in intensive care at Henry Ford Hospital in Detroit and not expected to live. I drove there that night to tell Mom of Dad's death. Our family had debated whether to tell her at all, since the end of her life seemed immanent—but we knew she'd never forgive us if she lived and we hadn't told her. In spite of the shock, Mom—unable to attend Dad's funeral—lived a while longer.

* * *

Almost every day seemed to me like a failed attempt to juggle the different roles of a pastor: public worship, private conferences, weddings, and baptisms. Hospital calls, funerals, frequent committee meetings, the fund raising campaign, calling in homes and growing a church membership. Since we had no church secretary (or church office) at first, I became the editor of the church newsletter. In addition there were the usual concerns that—in one way or another—creates stress in every family.

In our case, a major stress involved our son Lance—who had had a serious bout with encephalitis when he was two. Vonda and I began to suspect lasting after-effects from his illness, but doctors had told us he was within the range of normal. We were not convinced and took him to Children's Hospital in Detroit for tests.

I recall Dr. Faigenbaum's brief remarks to me between tests, when we were alone. He said, "Well, Rev. Lichtenfelt, I suppose people will say the same thing about your children that they'll say about mine. If they do very well, people will say, 'What do you

132

expect? His father is a doctor—or his father is a minister. And if they turn out poorly, people will say the same thing. I think they'll pretty much do what they're going to do—regardless of their parents."

When all test results came in they confirmed our fears. Lance, the happiest and most joyful of our four children in childhood, had suffered brain damage. He would be entering special education and, most likely, living with us the rest of his life—or until the end of ours.

* * *

Meanwhile, the John Birch Society picketed our neighboring church (First Methodist in Mt. Clemens) before, during and after worship. They opposed the Methodist stance on civil rights, the peace movement, and in their anti-communist fervor seemed to see communists embedded in the church. Pastors would have been just as glad not to have all the attention—and false accusations.

Around this time I attended a Peace with Justice Seminar at Central Methodist in Lansing—practically in the shadow of the State Capitol. The program was about half over when Dr. Dwight Large, the senior pastor at Central, gently placed his hand on the speaker's shoulder and quietly announced to us that *we all needed to leave the building* and we were to walk directly to the steps of the Capitol.

As we left the building we saw several fire trucks with lights flashing, and learned there had been a bomb threat. After an abbreviated program on the capitol steps we—black and white—joined hands and swayed back and forth singing "We shall overcome" as was the custom in those days.

* * *

The new parsonage was completed, and we moved in (in January of 1962.) We hosted sixty meetings in the first year after it was built. Vonda gave birth to Erich, our fourth child, during April, 1962. Lisa, Lance and Colin were now two, four and six years of age.

We continued to hold worship services in the cafeteria of Richards Junior High. The new parsonage had more space than the rental house we'd been living in, and part of our living space became the church office. That meant that when Wanda Meeks came to our front door with fresh cuts and bruises on her face and two tiny children clutching her skirt out of fear of their father…when Matt

Bender came through our front door, threw himself down on a chair and began sobbing because his wife of thirty years had left him...when the Navy Chaplain came to our door in his crisp white uniform to request that I go with him to the Sanders home to tell Ted and Barb that their son had been decapitated inside a ship's gun mount firing at targets in Vietnam...our children were witnesses until Vonda could whisk them elsewhere in the house and calm their fears. The children learned, early on, that they were never to talk to others about things that happened in the parsonage.

* * *

Our congregation's hard work and generous giving led to the completion of our new church building. They chose a new name: Christ Methodist. On Sunday, January 25, 1964, Bishop Marshall Reed consecrated our church, and two other nearby new church start-ups which had been completed at the same time: Good Shepherd in St. Clair Shores and Wesley Methodist in Warren.

Our congregation celebrated their accomplishment, and relished having their own church home—especially those members who had endured the years of meeting in a VFW hall, a hardware store, and a school cafeteria. Vonda and I took delight that the church office was no longer in our home—though the church and the parsonage were now on contiguous lots. That made it easy for people to find a pastor when they wanted to—whether they were members or not—and many were not. It's just something people expect from churches...and pastors.

Martin Stegal, our district superintendent, sent me a letter of congratulation after Bishop Reed dedicated Christ Methodist. He wrote, "You have given leadership in what many people thought was an impossible task." I wondered if he might have been one of the "many"—I know there were times when I was. In his letter to the congregation Martin said, "There is a fine team spirit on the part of pastor and people that speaks well for the years ahead."

* * *

Harry Ostroski, as his name might lead you to believe, came from Polish ancestry. One of those "tough, but oh so gentle" types. One of the few American soldiers to fight the Japanese on US soil during

World War II on the Aleutians—that chain of islands strung southwest off Alaska.

About 5' 8" tall, a heavy smoker with a gravely voice, and all muscle, Harry wore wire-rimmed glasses and permanent 5 o'clock shadow.

Harry had experienced hardship as the child of immigrant parents and, as a blue-collar factory worker, he stood out in a congregation made up almost entirely of engineers and educators. He had had a life-changing experience which resulted in his being one of our most dedicated church workers and one of the nine members on the new Church Building Committee in Fraser.

Harry and I often voted on opposite sides of Building Committee issues. That hardly seemed worthy of notice because I never served on a committee with voters so evenly split—with most votes carrying by slim majorities. As far as I was concerned the voting made not a bit of difference in our friendship.

When the new parsonage was built Harry and his wife Wreatha hauled about forty trees and shrubs and planted them around the house—about a dozen sentinel cedars for the boundary, two sunburst locusts out front, along with a white birch and a flowering crab tree, plus several Sargent junipers and Rhododendrons next to the house. I helped dig and plant but couldn't keep up with Harry or Wreatha. They were strong, hard and willing workers.

Harry drove by our house on Garfield Road on his way home from work at a tool and die shop in Warren. He'd usually beep his horn and wave. I'd wave back. It was a little ritual that gave me pleasure. I felt pleased to be Harry's friend. Late one afternoon when I was mowing our lawn I happened to see Harry drive by with eyes fixed straight ahead. He seemed preoccupied. No honking. No wave in response to my wave. I recalled that was about the third time this had happened. I figured he had something troubling on his mind.

A few days later I drove to his home on Nunnely Road on Building Committee business. Harry, Wreatha, and their teen-aged daughter Andrea lived in a modest red brick bungalow with a large, well-groomed vegetable garden out back. There were five terra cotta flower pots by the side door—one was broken and collapsed within itself.

I attempted a little humor as I sat down in his living room. "Harry, I've got a bone to pick with you."

"Yeah, what's that?"

"You've been ignoring me as you drive by the house lately. You haven't given me the usual toot and wave."

"Well, now that you're here, I've got a bone to pick with you too." Harry wasn't being funny. I couldn't imagine what it was. He was plainly upset and reluctant to talk about the matter. Finally he got to the point. "Somebody told me that you said what we needed in this church was one less Polack on the board."

"Harry, I never said such a thing. That word's not in my vocabulary. Who told you I said that?"

"I'm not saying who said it."

"Well, I don't know how I can convince you I didn't say it but I'd sure like to go with you to the person who said that because it's a flat-out lie. You and I see things differently on the Building Committee but I've never once wished you weren't on the committee. I can't imagine why anyone would want to drive a wedge between us." Further attempts to get Harry to name the person proved futile but he seemed satisfied that I was willing to confront the individual in his presence.

Our friendship was back on track, but to this day I don't know who told that falsehood. I don't know if it was spoken carelessly, or as crude humor, or maliciously. But it almost wrecked a friendship. I'm glad Harry and I told each other we had a bone to pick. Otherwise our friendship would have been permanently soured and I wouldn't have known why.

It is not true—that old saying we used to chant in a sassy voice when we were kids: "Sticks and stones can break my bones but words will never hurt me." Words are as real and as powerful as stones— we've all experienced that one way or another. Words can break our hearts, and throw relationships into a tailspin. Words can destroy reputations and jobs and standards of living.

When we tell a lie it's like maliciously starting a fire. There's no telling where it will go, how far it will travel, how much damage it will do or how many innocent people suffer as a result.

My experience with Harry reminds me of the power of words both for good and for evil—how, as with gasoline, words need to be used with great caution. Even now, in most of our lives, there are painful situations that we're powerless to make right because we don't know what we don't know.

136

* * *

My memories of Fraser include the deaths of four infants and one toddler at whose funeral services I was asked to officiate. Each seemed sadder than the others. Julie Wilson, a sixteen month old toddler, remains etched in my mind. We cared for Julie several times in our home, so that her mother could go to the hospital for treatments. Our children delighted in this "new little sister," enjoyed playing with her and wondered "when can she come again?"

Julie was severely scalded in a bathtub accident, and rushed to St. Joseph Hospital in Mt. Clemens. I called on the family several times over the two weeks that she hovered between life and death.

One of the most haunting images imprinted on my memory came from the day before Julie died. I slipped into her hospital room, and saw her pediatrician standing alone by her bedside. His stethoscope hung around his neck. Tears streamed down his face as he looked down at her limp little body…feeling helpless against her burns.

* * *

In my Good Friday sermon that year I compared Jesus' "triumphal entry" into Jerusalem with current protest movements. I felt they both challenged the status quo, the centers of power, and abuse of power. It was a hot button issue, because the Rev. James Reeb, a Unitarian Minister and social worker, had just been bludgeoned to death by white supremacists in Selma, Alabama. A significant number of southern whites violently opposed civil rights workers who assisted black voter registration in their states.

Bob Turner, president of Macomb Community College, and a native of Louisiana, walked out in the middle of my sermon. Ouch. I figured we'd lost Bob permanently. When the service ended, I went to the front door to greet—thinking that Bob was long gone. He hadn't left. He was waiting at the door, not smiling but still friendly. He reached out and shook my hand, and said, "That's the best sermon I've ever heard you preach—and I disagree with you completely."

I appreciated his affirmation, and his candor. Bob remained with Christ Methodist church, and we remained good friends. I like it when things happen that way.

137

That afternoon I joined in a sympathy walk for Rev. James Reeb. Both blacks and whites had joined in to draw attention to his brutal murder and to indicate their unity with Reeb's cause. As we walked along Gratiot Avenue, we drew a few shouts of, "Go home, niggers!" and "Nigger lovers!" from people in passing cars, but for the most part the people were supportive. Some clapped to show their approval, others honked their car horns in support upon seeing our signs and banner.

For a time I walked beside an elderly African American man who turned toward me with tears glistening on his cheeks. He shook his head back and forth, and spoke in a strong rusty voice, "I never thought I'd live to see these days...but I have."

* * *

It may not have been the end of the world but it felt like the end of *my* world at the time—and just as I had begun to see the fruits of some pretty intense labors. Our congregation had completed the new parsonage and church building since we arrived. Membership showed growth. I felt good about my work and then a friend dropped the question, "Are you aware that Tom and Jenny Barrett are circulating a petition for your removal as pastor?"

I felt my brain short-circuit and spin into denial. *What?! Petition?! Why?! Methodists don't operate that way. We have a procedure to follow if there's a need. Barretts? No way. Tom and I played tennis down on the city courts. Jenny is secretary for our Building Committee. They wouldn't be people to go behind my back.*

In my head, I know it's expecting the impossible to have everyone love me...still I just hate it when not everyone does. I worked hard and felt loved and respected most of the time, and I didn't like feeling like a failure. This felt like my efforts were neither recognized nor appreciated.

As a young pastor in my first assignment following my student pastorate I didn't know how to handle this issue. Had I overlooked some obvious clues of trouble brewing? This was totally unexpected, and I barely slept or ate that weekend. I felt bewildered, betrayed and stigmatized. A pastor's reputation is about all he has to work with—if he doesn't have a good reputation no other church is going to want him. I felt someone had unfairly labeled me "fatally flawed." I kept asking myself where I'd failed to measure up.

On Monday morning, Helen, our church secretary informed me that our finance chairman had called and cancelled the evening committee meeting. An idea popped into my mind. Tom Barrett was on the finance committee. I asked Helen if she would notify everyone but Tom of the cancellation. There may have been better ways to deal with the situation but—right or wrong—I decided on direct confrontation. I was in the church office waiting as Tom arrived promptly at 7:30 PM, clean, scrubbed and sharply dressed after his day's work at General Motors. He seemed surprised to be the first one there.

"Hello, Don, where is everybody?"

I felt a rush of adrenaline as he took a chair opposite me. "Hi, Tom. Well… actually…our finance meeting has been cancelled—but I didn't tell you because I felt it was important that you and I talk."

"About what?" Tom seemed unperturbed. Had I received bad information?

"Tom, I've heard, in such a way as to believe it, that you and Jenny are circulating a petition for my removal." He said nothing, but his sheepish look and averted gaze—his lack of angry or puzzled response told me it was true.

I wish I knew how to finesse that situation. I wish now that I'd said something like, "I'd be interested in knowing why you felt the need to do that." But I didn't. I went on slowly, "Tom, I can understand that there may be times when people are not happy with me because sometimes I disappoint myself…I'm not a perfect pastor and there's not a congregation in the world that has one … and there are no perfect congregations either."

I paused, hoping Tom would open up. He didn't. He sat there staring just off my left shoulder. I continued, "If we got rid of our pastors or our church members every time we disappointed each other, soon there would be nobody left to be the church." I paused, inviting a response. Again, none. I said, "I don't believe our Christian faith makes us all think alike but it should help us respect our differences and try to live together as imperfect people—because that's the only kind of people there are."

Tom shifted his weight to another position—obviously intending to continue his stonewalling. I'd have felt more comfortable if he had spouted a litany of complaints so that we could talk about them. I had only his body language and his lack of denial to lead me to believe that the report of his activity was true. I have no recollection of anything he said before he left the office—unsmiling and with his head tilted down and shoulders drooping.

The next few months, we gave each other a wide berth. I was stung by the implied rejection of the petition—which apparently never reached our district superintendent or I would have heard from him. I hadn't a clue what motivated the petition or how many signatures were gathered, but the closer I got to the Barretts in a gathering of people the more ill at ease I felt. I resolved to be polite and friendly but felt reluctant to trust them.

Sometime the following year I went to their home on Beacon Lane and delivered some time-sensitive material. I would have avoided the trip if possible and my skin felt sort of creepy-crawly as I rang their doorbell. I planned to drop the materials off and make a hasty departure.

I'd called ahead to be sure someone would be there. Jenny answered the door and surprised me with, "Hi, Don. Do you have time to come in for a minute? Tom and I have something we'd like to talk to you about."

"Sure, Jenny," I said, wishing I had a reason *not* to stay. I followed Jenny into their living room as Tom joined us from the kitchen.

Tom smiled, greeted me with a, "Hi, Don," shook my hand and said, "Have a chair." We sat down—all three of us feeling ill-at-ease. Jenny led off, "As you well know, Don, we didn't feel you were the right man for the job a while back but we want you to know that we've changed our minds—and we're glad that Bishop Reed has appointed you to Fraser for another year."

Her words surprised me so that I barely knew what to say—so I responded with something like, "Well, Jenny, it means a lot to me to hear you say that...and it takes pretty big people to say what you did." There was no going into detail. Again, I had no recollection of Tom's saying anything—just a new sense of warmth and—I think— relief to have dealt with the issue. We chatted just a bit before I offered a brief prayer of thanksgiving—the three of us joining hands as we stood in the center of the living room as was my habit with our church family.

I drove off trying to digest what had just happened. Maybe the Barretts were bigger people than I because I was finding it hard to overlook the pain and loss of self-esteem this had caused Vonda and me. I still felt I'd been bushwhacked while giving a good effort in a demanding situation. Why did they put us through this? It didn't have to happen. They could have spoken to me—or the committee on pastor-parish relations—if there was a problem. Was this "reconciliation" for real or just a postponement until they would blindside me over another issue? I resolved to treat them as though the petition episode never happened—regardless of my residual feelings.

Another year slid by and the Barretts moved to Flint. Vonda and I were appointed to serve another parish and twelve years passed without our hearing about Tom and Jenny or crossing paths with them.

Then, late one July afternoon after I'd been hospital calling at St. Joseph's in Mt. Clemens, I returned home to Utica and Vonda met me at the door. "You'll never believe what happened. Jenny Barrett called to tell us that Tom died...*and* she wants you to have his funeral.

I was caught up in a swirl of uncomfortable feelings. Surprise at Tom's early death. Shock at being asked to conduct his funeral. Stirrings of painful past experience. I was back in Fraser reliving those days of hurt and uncertainty.

After a long pause, Vonda brought me back to the present. "Well, what will you tell her?"

I stared out the back window, took a deep breath and let it out. "I'll tell her 'yes, I'll do it.'"

Sometimes you have to do the right thing no matter how you feel about it. Will I never outgrow my need to pray that old prayer from the book of Psalms, "God, put a new and right spirit within me?"

To this day I wonder what prompted that petition, who actually initiated it and how many members may—or may not—have signed it. Obviously two people (by their own admission) felt I "was not the right man for the job"—a non-specific complaint. I'm far from omnicompetent, but we had a good track record of progress.

Most clergy learn early-on that they are going to catch flak from several sources—that they'll be criticized by some for being too liberal, and by others for being too conservative. It could have been my opposition to the Viet Nam war—a war which took the lives of two of our young men—which led at least one member to question

141

my patriotism. It could have been my stand on integration—my welcoming Afro-American speakers to the pulpit, the Macomb County Inter-Racial Association to meet in our space, and a talented Afro-American organist to cover in the absence of our regular organist. Maybe some folks believed the lie that was spoken of me—that I'd said regarding Harry Ostroski, "What this church needs is one less Polack on the board." That could have been justification, had it been true.

What happened to the petition? I don't know. My hunch is that it never gathered enough signatures to make it worth sending to my district superintendent or my bishop. Had they received it they would surely have taken the issue up with me—and quickly.

It's not likely I'll ever know the answer to that question. One more instance of, "We don't know what we don't know." Maybe it's true that "Other people's opinion of you is none of your business," though in this case I felt entitled to know. We seldom know when we've inadvertently given offense...and would want to apologize...or make amends...at the least, an explanation.

* * *

My mother lived another six months after Dad's death. She left us just after my thirty-third birthday, in November, 1965. The end came in a wild gush of blood—an oral hemorrhage that welled up and seemed to leap from her mouth like a geyser, covering her face and hospital gown with blood. My sisters Lynda and Lorna (both nurses) and I tried to clean up her blood before it spread further. When it was over, I rinsed my red hands in the hospital sink ... and watched the last of the pink water swirl ... and disappear down the drain.

I drove home alone just before midnight. Drove south on the Lodge freeway, and crossed over to eastbound Ford expressway at the interchange. I felt saddened, yet relieved that Mom's suffering was over. I drove only as far as the railroad overpass when, unexpectedly, a gush of scalding tears blinded me. I pulled over on the shoulder, and gave myself over to the sobs that shook me...not so much because of what had happened, as for *what had not happened between Mom and me*. I still wonder why we couldn't connect. Why we couldn't seem to get on the same wave length.

Several days after I officiated at Mom's funeral, Vonda and I knew we all needed relief—a getaway to something different. So, we took our four children to Cobo Hall in downtown Detroit to see the annual Christmas Wonderland that merchants provided for children. It offered music and costumed elves, all sorts of Santa's helpers, things kids could participate in—like a big snowman slide that swirled kids around on the way down. Just what we needed: a change, something different, something beautiful, and something fun.

I opened the door to the Cobo Hall auditorium. We were greeted with the sound of jaunty children's Christmas music, and squeals of delight and surprise from tiny kids. I followed my family inside, and looked up to see where the loud sounds of flowing water came from. It came from the first display on our right, which consisted of three giant fountains—each about ten feet tall and with three fluted tiers. They were filled with brightly dyed water—green, and blue, and nearest to us: red—"a fountain filled with blood" as the old gospel song says—splattering every which way. The sight of it and the powerful reminder of the way Mom died, provided me with months of Technicolor nightmares.

* * *

Two times my life was threatened at Fraser, and I did not take it lightly—especially since my brother had been threatened several times before his murder. Once a Vietnam veteran, suffering post traumatic stress promised to "get me." I have no idea what prompted his rage. I'm not sure he knew, but I made it a point not to stand with my back to doorways for some time after that.

In the second instance, Rose Dorsey told me, in her home, "You'd better get away from here quick, because Lou (her husband) told me he'd kill you if you ever came here."

"What? Why would he want to do that?" I asked—as I wondered why she hadn't spoken to me about this earlier.

"Because he heard you make nasty remarks about his Indian ancestry."

Rose, "I didn't know Lou *had* Indian ancestry. Even if I had known I wouldn't be making nasty remarks. I have Indian ancestry too, and it's a source of pride to me."

She said, "Well, I don't know what to say—except you'd better get out of the house before he comes home."

I didn't linger. I've learned to respect the power of deranged minds.

143

* * *

Well, that may not best place to end, but there you have it—a smattering of memories from our Fraser years. A sample of what it was like for one pastor serving in a church start-up situation in suburban Detroit in the 1960s. I'm glad I got out alive. Would I do it again? Once is probably enough.

Too much responsibility fell on Vonda, as my "unpaid assistant." She put herself into the project with a generous heart, but it wasn't fair of me to expect all she went through for me, and her beyond-the-call-of-duty efforts for the building program.

You remember how my district superintendent said, "We're either going to get in there and make a go of it, or we're pulling out." Well, we made a go of it—all of us working together. That was nearly fifty years ago now. That parsonage and church building have been a means of serving people in their need, their aspirations to learn and grow, and their desire to serve the world they live in all that time.

Were there happy times at Fraser? Yes, of course, and we took them wherever we could find them. But somehow, in the midst of so much grief, so much social and personal chaos, even the joy was tinged with sadness—much as two or three drops of food color can transform an entire glass of water.

Our family—plus Mary, my brother Wendell's daughter— left for my new appointment in Mayville in mid-June of 1967. Just before we left, I took a solo walk over to the new church, and took a last wander-through. Almost everything I laid eyes on triggered some sort of flashback of people involved in the building project, or building committee struggles to get it as right as we could with the money available.

I strolled to the rear of the chancel, placed my hands on the communion table and looked up at the cross—*remembering how I came to enter the ministry*. Then I stepped into the pulpit for the last time, and looked out over the empty pews. My God, I could see so many of the people of the congregation in my minds eye. Most of whom were still alive. Some who had moved and others whom death had taken during our years there. They took on life and movement in my memory.

Then, *remembering what brought me to Fraser*, I reached out, caressed the upper surfaces of the pulpit, and recalled the dedication of this our family's memorial gift to the church:

This Pulpit
Dedicated to the Glory of God
In Loving Memory of
Wendell H. Lichtenfelt
1914–1960

Mayville Years
1967 – 1970

I arise in the morning torn between a
desire to improve the world and a desire
to enjoy the world. This makes it hard
to plan the day.
— *E.B. White*

Pain in Paradise

Truths and roses have thorns about them.
— *Henry David Thoreau*

We must not confuse dissent with disloyalty.
— *Edward R. Murrow*

Sometimes dreams do come true. It was June, 1967, when Vonda and I first drove up Fulton Street in Mayville to see the church Bishop Loder had appointed us to serve. Vonda looked at the elegant Victorian home next to the church and said, "Ohhh, I hope that's the parsonage," but, of course, it wasn't.

When we moved into the small parsonage located on Main Street, there were eight of us: Vonda and I, our four children aged five, seven, nine and eleven, our niece Mary a seventeen year old high school senior—whose father had been murdered in December of 1960—and our silver and white schnauzer, Goober, who shared fourteen wonderful years of his life with our growing family.

A steady drizzle fell on moving day. The drizzle changed to a downpour as we squeezed our possessions into the small parsonage as best we could. Many boxes had to be stored in the basement. When I was called to the funeral home for the death of a local man that afternoon, I left in the midst of a cloudburst. Later, I returned home to a flooded basement. I found Al DeGrow, president of the trustees, standing there in his three-piece business suit—barefoot, trousers rolled up and calf-deep in water—muttering, "Can't understand it. This never happened before." Vonda's wedding dress was among the many casualties of the flood. Word spread that the new minister's wife was none too happy with the parsonage plumbing

In spite of a disastrous beginning, before the first month was over we felt fully embraced in the affection of this community, which was located in the rolling glacial hills of Michigan's "thumb." It began to feel as if we had always lived there, and were warmly accepted as family.

A year later the big house next to the church—the one Vonda wished was the parsonage—was purchased by the church for a surprisingly modest price. It would have cost many times what we paid back in the city. We found ourselves living in a dream house and we weren't dreaming. Clare Maiers, President of Maiers Motor Freight, and chair of the Pastor Parish Relations Committee smiled as he spoke to Vonda. "Vonda, this house is a wife killer. Why would you want to live here?"

Vonda lit up! "Oh, no, Clare, larger houses are easier to care for than cramped houses." Then she added, "Ministers may come and ministers may go, but I'm staying here forever." We all laughed at her declaration.

So we began adjusting to a strange anomaly. We were in one of the many small rural town parishes of the Methodist Church, but we were living in a parsonage better than most large city churches—maybe better than the Bishop's home. Well, we could handle that.

We delighted in the beauty of this marvelous old home. It had been built many years earlier by the wealthy owner of a birch products company—one that made toothpicks, tongue depressors, popsicle sticks, and who knows what all.

The tall house sat on top of a gentle hill in the middle of our small downtown—wonderful for viewing parades and keeping tabs on what was going on in town. The first two floors held six bedrooms, five baths, and a 420 square foot living room with a small music room off the north side. There was a built-in cedar closet in the upstairs hall. Every now and then I opened the doors to inhale that other-worldly cedar perfume that carried me into a cedar forest I keep deep in my mind.

The house had eleven-foot ceilings, a screened porch, a stainless steel kitchen, formal dining room with beveled glass French doors, and a chandelier. Double doors opened out on a patio. Just beyond the patio was a small, equally well-built play house, and the tattered remnants of what had been an elegant show garden. Out front there was a huge maple tree that became our "million dollar bouquet" when it turned bright orange and red in autumn

Here each member of our family had space to call his or her own. We settled down to make the most of it amongst the vicissitudes of small town life. We settled down to Colin's trombone practice, Lance's broken femur, Lisa's Brownie scouts, and Erich's first job shoveling snow at the furniture store at age six. Mary had graduated from high school moved back home to Armada. We missed her frequent drum recitals to the accompaniment of Tijuana Brass recordings—so did the neighborhood kids she attracted.

There were weddings and funerals, birthday parties, and the Tuscola County Harvest Festival with antique threshing machines and tractors. There were the ten foot Christmas trees we chopped down on Helen Higby's farm, there was sickness and there were accidents, and the three suicides in our communities. And, of course—this being the sixties—there was the Viet Nam War. We settled down to an uneasy truce between those who were for the war, and those who were opposed. Neutrality remained a difficult-to-maintain option.

There were uproariously funny Rotary Club meetings, and Rotary's long losing season on the blooper ball field—our only win coming in the last inning of the last game against the Mayville Firefighters. I was on second base when a squib hit trickled through the infield. The third base coach waved me home. I arrived a split second after the ball and collided with Len Cryderman, the catcher for the firefighters. He dropped the ball, and we won our first and only game to the sound of blaring car horns. The Rotarians carried me off the field on their shoulders singing "For He's a Jolly Good Fellow"—one of my very few (and very minor) sports "triumphs."

Laughter alternated with tears as a steady flow of people came and went from the parsonage, and the church office. Ray Galvin and Dale Kercheval, two young law students in our congregation faced the scorn of a hostile draft board. The board displayed strong resistance to issuing Conscientious Objector status, and seemed to impugn the patriotism of anyone who would apply for C.O. status. To my mind Dale and Ray had a moral courage equal to the physical courage of any warrior in Vietnam. I wrote the draft board defending their position, and saying we needed their kind of heroism too.

Later, a young soldier from our area was killed in the Tet offensive which began in late January, 1968. I was asked to have his funeral. I went to his home where his mother sat in stunned silence while his father took to angry words—words which could have been mine had it been my son. "Don't make him out to be a hero. Don't say he gave his life for his country. He didn't. It was taken from him! He was against the war. He wanted to join a peace academy, and help prevent wars from happening."

Later, at the cemetery, the American flag was taken from his casket, and folded. The uniformed military honor guard—a young combat veteran who had difficulty standing because of earlier wounds—hobbled to the parents, leaned over and presented the flag. The parents refused the flag. The young combat veteran was devastated. We all were. These were tense times in Mayville—tense times everywhere.

I regretted my anti-war sermon preached after the Me Lai Massacre in March of 1968. (Life magazine had printed color photos of some of the three to five hundred unarmed civilians murdered in the incident—including women and children.) Not that I felt in error, but I did not see the uniformed soldier home on leave from Vietnam. He was obscured by others as he entered late and sat in the rear pew. He trembled violently as he said upon leaving, "Sir, you just can't understand what it's like unless you're there." For his sake I wish I could have taken my words back. He didn't need more wounds. (The mass murder created global outrage, and increased citizen demonstrations against our country's involvement in the Vietnam War.)

* * *

And so our strangely brief three years in Mayville were filled with life and death, baptisms, weddings, and funerals, with graduations, and picnics…with local involvement in battles on the other side of the world, and grieving with the family who lost three members to carbon monoxide poisoning, and the three families who lost members to suicide…with laughing at Fred Moss's jokes, the warm fellowship of Rotarians, and the wonderful work of Mildred Holbrook and Nettie McNinch who ran the local thrift shop and gave thousands in dollars and goods to the needy in our area—and far beyond our horizons.

So many stories remain untold concerning these special people—their lives and their joys, their love and their silent tears, their laughter and their struggles—their demons and their heroism. I respect and honor these people. I salute them.

Somehow the house…and the town…and the people—the whole Mayville experience—seemed to melt into one. No, we didn't stay there forever—as Vonda insisted she would. But, yes, in a deep down way we have. In a way I don't fully understand we're still there. I can't bring myself to leave.

Fred Tinglan's Last Smile

No smile is as beautiful as the one
that struggles through the tears.

—Source unknown

The deep pain that is felt at the death of every
friendly soul arises from the feeling that there
is in every individual something which is
inexpressible, peculiar to him alone, and is
therefore, absolutely and *irretrievably* lost.

—Arthur Schopenhauer

I received word about Fred Tinglan's accident on a cold winter afternoon. He had put his extension ladder up to the hay loft of their small barn that morning for some reason. Apparently the ladder slipped from under him as he got near the top. He fell about twelve feet onto frozen ground and lay there for some time before his wife Clara found him and called for help.

As I headed for the Lapeer Hospital down M-24—with no idea of Fred's condition—I recalled what I knew about these church members. One thing I knew for sure was that one smile from Fred Tinglan could turn your whole day around. That man could light up a room and warm hearts and make people feel that no matter how bad things seemed—or actually were—they would be better soon.

Fred smiled a lot. Given his circumstances I could never figure out why but I'm glad he did. Maybe it was a carryover from happier times. But when Fred smiled you knew you were in the presence of a deep down loving person.

Fred and his wife Clara lived on a small farm west of Mayville on South Conrad Road. Their small home had seen better days—so had Fred and Clara. People told me Clara came from a good family and that she'd been a gifted pianist. She'd been an immaculate housekeeper who loved nice things…once…a long time ago. People said what changed her was the result of the difficult birth and early death of their only child. Whatever pushed her over that deep precipice in her mind, she was never the same again.

153

When I became their minister Clara hadn't played the piano in years though her grand piano still stood in her living room piled high with papers and magazines and general clutter. I doubt that her home had had a good cleaning in years. Tracked-in dirt marked traffic patterns through the house. Chairs, tables, the piano—everything—suffocated under a heavy accumulation of dust and piles of "stuff" most people would have discarded long ago.

It made you feel melancholy to be around Clara for long knowing what she had been…once…way back when. When I called in their home, no matter what the season, she wore men's work boots and baggy wool trousers whose frayed cuffs (several inches too long) brushed the floor. Often she wore one of Fred's old flannel work shirts. Over this she usually wore a soiled cotton print dress—and most days a baggy button-up man's sweater—also gray and grimy. In addition she often wore a pair of canvas gloves with the fingers and thumbs cut off at the knuckles—as though she were perpetually cold—even in summer. In winter her gloves and her face bore black smudges from feeding lumps of coal into the stove in their living room.

Clara's eyes were a misty blue above high cheek bones and hollow cheeks. Her mouth seemed slightly contorted as though by permanent sadness or by a stroke. Her long gray hair was soiled and matted in an upswept twist gathered high on the back of her head. Long tendrils dangled loose on either side of her head.

When I called on them, it seemed incongruous to have her serving me a cup of steaming hot tea in fine bone china while dressed like a bag lady. My inclination was to decline but I knew this was a time to forget about sanitation and accept Clara's gracious gesture with thanks.

Fred and Clara made the best of a bleak situation, working side by side on their small farm. I couldn't help feeling touched by the obvious affection and tenderness that passed between them—even in her pathetic mental state. They depended upon each other. They conferred dignity and honor upon each other with their smiles.

Once inside the city limits of Lapeer I pulled directly off the highway and into the hospital parking lot. Picking up Fred's room number at the desk, I headed to the second floor. I knocked gently on the open door of 238 and entered when a familiar male voice (not Fred's) said, "Come on in."

I felt relieved to find Fred propped up with pillows in bed and smiling his beatific smile. He'd suffered some broken ribs and had two bandages on his face. His left arm rested in a sling. Still, doctors had seen nothing life threatening and recovery seemed only a matter of time.

The "other voice" was that of Gordon Ewing, our High School principal (and fellow Methodist) who occupied the bed next to Fred. A bonus for me—two calls in one. I sat in the space between their beds and the three of us had a warm friendly chat. Both men were the kind who appreciated prayer so we joined hands as I offered a brief prayer—to which Gordon said, "Amen." Fred waved good-by with his free hand and gifted me with his glowing smile as I left.

I drove the twenty-five minute trip back to Mayville through gently rolling countryside with rich soil, scattered woodlands and attractive farm buildings dusted with snow. When the traffic thinned I slowed down and drank in the majesty of the scene. I felt woven into the beauty of the glacial landscape. The words of a song I'd learned in church youth camp floated back to me: "God who touchest earth with beauty, Make me lovely too, With thy Spirit recreate me, Make my heart anew." It felt good to be alive and good to be of some usefulness to hurting and lonely people.

My reverie was broken when I pulled into our driveway and Vonda came outside to meet me at the curb—sadness etched in her face. I stopped the car and got out where she stood in the cold. "Don, Gordon Ewing just called from the hospital. He said Fred died just moments after you left—that he just leaned back and stopped breathing—and he was still smiling." Vonda teared up. Tears puddled in my heart as well.

The days before Fred's funeral turned hectic. Clara was now alone in the world except for a brother who lived at a distance, and Clara didn't drive. Vonda used her considerable powers of persuasion to get Clara to stay with us so she'd be with friends and be near the funeral home for visitation.

Our four young children had never seen anyone dressed as strangely as Clara or as grimy as she. They stood on the sidelines and watched bug-eyed as Vonda went about the daunting task of getting Clara scrubbed up and dressed in woman's clothes for the funeral.

Clara had a near phobic reaction to water. She resisted at every turn and was afraid she'd catch a cold if she took a bath. Vonda told her, "I'll make the bathroom extra warm with the space heater and I'll put your bath towel in the clothes dryer so you can dry off with a nice warm towel." Clara remained hesitant. Vonda said, "Clara, you know you want to look nice for Fred."

Eventually Clara consented to Vonda's washing her hair—twice. Then Vonda left her alone with a tub of warm water perfumed with scented bath oil. The following day Vonda gave Clara a hair do and got her some ladies' dress clothes from the church thrift shop. Clara's friends were astonished at the transformation. Now we all glimpsed something of the beauty and dignity Fred must have seen in Clara at their beginning. Clara couldn't resist a pleasantly surprised smile as she looked at herself in the mirror.

Fred's funeral would be a simple service with few flowers, no special music and no lengthy obituary singing his praises. Every aspect would be plain and unadorned like his life. A few caring neighbors and friends would huddle together with their grief for Fred's death equaled by their sorrow for Clara's plight.

Surely Clara's grief was as deep as any freshly bereaved wife and she had fewer family members and friends to support her than most others. I wondered what would happen to Clara now—if Fred had *any* life insurance—let alone *enough*. I wondered how well her brother might be able to provide for her—how long caring neighbors would persist in lending emotional support.

I wanted the funeral service to be the best I could provide—the same as I'd want to do for the wealthiest most admired person in Tuscola County. I wanted the memory of this time to be healing and uplifting for Clara now and every time she called it back in memory.

I sat down alone at my desk in the church office—trying to remain open to any special insights which might be helpful in preparation for the service. I poured over poems and prayers in my files and jotted down ideas. I tried to recall the words of Fred's neighbors and church friends as a means of reflecting our common sense of sorrow.

When I was at seminary a guest speaker from the Baha'i tradition gave a definition of preaching I've never forgotten: "To express the inexpressible in words unforgettable." No matter how long I prepare, I never feel *ready* to deliver sermons of any kind—but at last you have to proceed with what you have—*ready or not.* You begin the task knowing that it's impossible and the ideal sermon floats out there far away in the atmosphere. When I rose to begin Fred's funeral, I knew that, as always, I was about to fall far short of the ideal.

Maybe that's why I felt mildly irked at the way Tubby Blackmore started funeral services at the Blackmore and Tubbs Funeral Home. He'd stand at the back of the room next to his tape player—one that had a continuous loop of funeral music—and when the grandfather clock struck the hour Tubby stopped the music instantly. No fadeout. No waiting until the end of a stanza. Then he'd point to me in a dramatic "you're on" gesture. I found it gauche and unprofessional but those in attendance must have felt too involved in their grief to notice.

And so I was "on" and proceeded with what I had to offer—ready or not. I noticed a neighbor of Fred and Clara's who seemed to be intent upon what I said. She nodded gently now and then and I felt affirmed.

Late in my reflection I saw through the side window that snow had begun to fall and I was reminded of an adventure I had with my grandmother when I was a child. I decided to share it with the small gathering:

"One Monday morning when I was small my Grandmother came to our home to do laundry with my mother as their custom was. She no more than stepped inside when she looked at me and said, 'Donald, get your coat on, we're going outside.' I had no idea what she had in mind but I knew whatever Grandma planned would be wonderful. So I got my brown mackinaw from behind the kitchen door and we walked outside together into one of the first snowfalls of the season."

"We stood in the driveway and Grandma said, 'Now hold out your arm like this and catch a snowflake.' She pointed her elbow straight out in front of her chin. I held my arm out like she showed me but I had trouble catching a snowflake because it was such a light snowfall. Finally I said, 'I got one, Grandma.'"

She stood close to me and said, "Now take a good look at that snowflake. See, it has six arms and every snowflake in the whole world has six arms but every snowflake is different from every other snowflake." Then she said, "People are like snowflakes. They look a lot alike but they're all different. No two are exactly alike." In that way she tried to teach each of her grandchildren that we were all unique, unrepeatable miracles of God."

I said to the little gathering, "Fred Tinglan was a unique, unrepeatable miracle of God. There was never anyone just like him before and there will never be another person just like him again—ever. You are a unique unrepeatable miracle of God, as is every one of God's children wherever they are. You and I beneficiaries of Fred's unique gifts which will go on giving to us as long as we live. His warmth and friendship, his humility and generosity, his smile which will light up our lives every time we recall his face."

Then I concluded the service with a benediction: "And now may the peace of God which passes all understanding, and the love of God, which never lets us go, enter into our hearts and lives and make them radiant in God's service as Fred did with his warm smile. Amen."

We followed Fred's casket out the door and drove in slow procession to the cemetery where we returned his body to the earth. After the committal service friends and neighbors embraced Clara. Some spoke words of appreciation for the kind of man Fred had been. Others insisted that Clara promise to call them whenever she needed help and said they'd drop in on her. I hoped they'd follow through. I hoped I would too—but I know how quickly good intentions fade out sometimes. Then the little band of friends and neighbors left for home leaving only Clara and her brother and his wife and me...and the cemetery crew waiting for us to move on so they could finish their work.

Clara said, "Well, I guess that's it." She smiled a teary smile as she took my hand and looked into my face. She said, "Thank you, I never knew something so sad could be so beautiful."

"Thank you," I said, and her brother helped Clara into his car and they drove off. I was left holding a clear image of Fred—that unique, unrepeatable miracle of God. He was smiling—glad to see Clara looking so nice again...just for him. Glad for friends who would stand by her...for him.

Empty Table

I have known days as lonely
as a soldier's empty sleeve.
—*Carl Sandburg*

The church is empty now. Phyl Moss our secretary locked the side entrance when she left for home two hours ago. I'm alone in the pastor's study finishing up on correspondence and it's past time for me to head home for dinner. I attach postage stamps, bind the short stack of business envelopes with a rubber band and stand up hoping to leave in time to beat Vonda's "Supper's ready, where are you?" call.

But then I glance out the office window and cannot take my eyes off what I see. I have a need for natural beauty that ranks near my need for air, water, food and exercise. This is one of those rare autumn days when the late afternoon sun slants through champagne colored air and the perfume of burning maple leaves drifts through the window screen like incense. Cars stir up a rustling wake of colored leaves with their passing and the aged maple beside the street lays its red leaves down on the cool grass. It's as though all nature is holding her breath in astonishment at her own beauty. I stare at this scene transfixed—unaware of myself. This panorama brings out the believer's unbelief in me. I see it. Yes. But I still can't believe it.

The desk phone shatters my reverie. I feel sure it's Vonda with her "Aren't you coming to dinner tonight?" But I resist the urge to answer right off, "I know, I'll be right there." It's best not to be flippant in a church office—you never know what the next caller has by way of surprise or shock. I use my formal voice.

"Mayville United Methodist, Don speaking." I feel silly being formal when I *know* it's Vonda.

It's *not* Vonda.

I recognize the husky authoritarian voice of my favorite church matriarch and she's in a hurry to blurt out an urgent message.

"Don, this is Helen Higby. Bad news. There was an explosion at the grain elevator in Saginaw this afternoon. Clifford Bolton was badly burned—may not make it. He's in St. Mary's Hospital. His son

159

called me from Ohio and wanted us to tell his mother before she sees it on TV. Can you drive out and break the news to Ann and take her to Saginaw?"

I don't want Helen's message to be true but I know it is. My immediate inner response is: *Oh, God, no. Isn't it enough that I just got back from a funeral home where a young father and his four year old son were laid side by side in their caskets—both victims of the father's handgun? How many gut punches can I absorb?*

I respond to her question, "No reason I can't Helen but, given Ann's precarious health, I'm not comfortable laying this on her without a doctor or nurse on hand."

Helen reassures me with, "Oh, I think she'll be okay. We don't have to tell her how bad the burns are. When she gets to the hospital and sees for herself there'll be medical personnel around."

"That's true," I say, feeling relieved that my words might not be the direct cause of Ann's death.

"If you don't mind, I could swing by after you've had a chance to tell Ann and the three of us could go to St. Mary's together." Helen had a way of directing people and making them feel it was their idea but, as usual, I welcomed her game plan.

"Good, I'd feel *much* better with you along."

"I'll give you a five minute head start and then I'll join you at Ann's house."

"Okay, I'll see you there."

I hang up like a dazed boxer trying to clear his head and call home to tell Vonda about Clifford—that I'll not be home for supper and that I have no idea when I'll be back. Vonda responds with an immediate, "Oh, no. Ann's so fragile. She doesn't need this on top of all her health problems."

I back our blue Chevy out the driveway stirring up my own wake of colored leaves and I stop for our town's only traffic light, turn left on green and head down West Saginaw Road. Fred Moss is locking up his Chevy dealership. He sees me, smiles and waves. I give him a little beep on the horn and wave back. I know Fred will feel terrible when he hears about Clifford.

I drop my visor to eliminate some of the sun's glare as it sags toward the horizon, feeling the sharp contrast between the incredible beauty of autumn in these gently rolling hills...and the horror of explosion, fire, and charred human flesh. How can such a terrible thing happen on a magnificent day as this?

I'm driving faster than usual as I leave town. Need to get to Ann before she gets the word on TV or from a neighbor. After fifteen years in the ministry I still detest this part of my work. I feel like an enemy—bringing people bad news and pain rather than comfort. *I'm admitting to myself that this sort of thing—on top of the recent deaths in our family—is getting to me. Didn't know I'd be spending so much of my time knee-deep in grief and I'm thinking maybe I need to bail out of the ministry before I crash.*

At the same time I'm seeing Clifford and Ann's faces—faces of aged people despite their mere sixty years. Clifford's eyes looking out from behind his dark tanned face with so many wrinkles. Ann, so frail, so slender and pale, with lighter blue eyes. Her worn face—framed in unruly gray hair—has the forlorn look of a person with nothing to look forward to. Helen Higby tells me Ann is on thirty-seven different over the counter and prescription medicines and she still finds herself slipping.

"That doctor should be in jail," Helen told me once. "But Ann trusts him and I can't get her to see another doctor." Helen was probably right. She had worked in her husband's drug store and pharmacy in Wyandotte for much of her life and had a feel for what was called for and what wasn't. Helen is in her eighties and in better health than Ann. I liked having Helen around. She let people know where she stood on issues—yet she did it with grace and a cynicism spiced with good humor.

I can see the Bolton home now, well back from the road on my right, under that tall cluster of Elm trees. It's seen better days—much better. And the small weathered barn to the left of the house seems to slump against some invisible prop. An artist could do great things with that old barn—make people feel good about the beauty of old age—about having character and the sheer endurance to hang tough in adversity.

I turn into the long dirt driveway that steers me left around the house, then curves right up to the back porch. I expect Ann to be nearby in the kitchen. Sure enough. As I climb the creaky steps I can see her inside through the screen door. She greets me at the door before I can knock.

161

"Oh, Don, I thought you were Clifford. I was expecting him before this. He's running late tonight."

As she lets me in I smell beef-stew cooking and see it simmering on the back burner of the gas stove. There's a card table covered with a white table cloth visible through the doorway to the living room. Two chairs. Eating utensils in place and the TV tuned to channel four where Detroit Tiger baseball has already started without Clifford.

"Can we sit down here at the kitchen table? There's something I need to tell you."

Ann's pale eyes grow larger. An involuntary twitch darts around her mouth. She seems to lose her balance for a moment before she sits down and waits apprehensively for my next words. I place my hand on hers.

"Ann, there was an explosion where Clifford works. He was hurt...pretty bad."

Ann wails a long, "Ohhh nooo!" and asks, "Is he going to be alright?"

"I don't know. Doctors say he's conscious and they're hoping for the best. They're treating him in the burn unit at St. Mary's Hospital."

Like clockwork Helen Higby appears. She lets herself in the back door of her friend's house and the two women hug—the friend who'd lost her husband a dozen years ago, and the one who might be about to lose hers.

Helen says, "Well, Honey, we'll take you to the hospital as soon as you can get ready."

Ann struggles to decide what she has to do before leaving. Eventually she visits the bathroom, tucks several medicines in her purse, turns Detroit Tiger baseball off, sets the evening meal off the burner, turns off the gas and pushes the lock button on the back door as we exit. I look back over my shoulder before closing the door. There's that card table, all set up with care, all ready for Clifford to sit down and enjoy his supper and Tiger baseball after a hard day's work. It has the look of an unclaimed sacrament. I feel a painful lump in my throat that wants to radiate through my entire body.

The forty minute ride to Saginaw is over good roads. Our Chevy glides along in near darkness as tires rippling over seams in the pavement induce a trancelike state in me. We're mostly silent, except for the two friends talking with each other in subdued tones now and then. "Do you think he'll be alright, Helen?"

Helen knows when to be hopeful and when to be realistic. I can tell by her voice that she is leaving the door open for hope without feeling hopeful. "I don't know, Honey, we'll have to wait and see what the doctors say. They can do wonderful things for burns now that they couldn't do just a few years ago."

As they talk I can't help but think of the obvious affection that passed between Clifford and Ann. He often referred to her as "Mother" and seemed to caress the word as he spoke it—reflecting a deep respect and appreciation. When they stood near each other in public, his arm was almost always around her waist. He was always "Clifford" to her but it sounded as though there was a "beloved" somewhere in there—even if you couldn't quite make it out.

After we arrive at the hospital I feel my apprehensions rise as we walk to the burn unit. What are we about to see? Can we control our reactions so Clifford won't lose hope for recovery? Is Ann likely to collapse on us?

A nurse guides us to Clifford's bedside. "You have company, Mr. Bolton." I linger just behind Ann as she walks up to him—in case she needs support. He turns his head toward her in obvious pain.

"Oh, Clifford," her tears begin to flow and her body trembles. I clasp her arm—just in case.

He speaks slowly through blistered lips, "I'm okay, Mother. I'll be alright." Ann can only touch his one hand. There is scarcely another spot that does not look red, blistered, or raw. Much of his body is covered with what looks like saran wrap—I suppose that's to limit the risk of infection and loss of lymph fluid.

We stay and keep up a minimal conversation. It isn't long until the nurse tells Ann, "Mrs. Bolton, we're going to give Clifford more pain medication now. It's best if you called it a day. You know, there could be many more days like this and you'll need your rest too."

Clifford survives less than a week. His IVs flow constantly in an attempt to replace fluids faster than they weep away. Lost fluids and rampant infection overwhelm all efforts to save him.

Three days later friends and relatives flock to Clifford's funeral. They enter the orangey-red Methodist Church whose bricks were made from local clay pits a hundred years ago. They come to stand by Ann and surround her with affection. To be a bulwark against the invasion of death. I try to remain open for thoughts that will make the family's grief more bearable and I focus on Clifford's words, "I'm okay, Mother. I'll be alright." That along with the words of Jesus, "I am the resurrection and the life; he who believes in me, though he die, yet shall he live, and whoever lives and believes in me shall never die."

Then—as much for myself as for others—a quote from the Roman Catholic writer, James Martineau, that has meant so much to me in my own struggles: "We do not believe in eternal life because we can prove it, but we are forever trying to prove it because we cannot help but believe it." I think people do not realize that pastors not only speak to grievers at funerals, they are often grievers themselves. I am today.

After the Blackmore and Tubbs hearse pulls away taking Clifford's body to a nearby cemetery; after we commit his body to its final resting place; after the church- sponsored luncheon is eaten and after the final farewells Ann returns to her home where she is surrounded by her four children for a time.

The church is empty again—except for a small clean-up crew in the kitchen. I go into my study. Alone. I pull my *Pastoral Record* from the shelf, sit down at my desk and fill in the first blank line under the heading of *Funerals: Date*, September 20, 1969. *Name,* Clifford Allen Bolton. *Age,* 61. *Member?* Yes. Then I take a deep breath, exhale, tilt back in my office chair and stare out the window as I had the day Helen called about the explosion. Now, just days later, the trees are nearly bare. The sodden leaves, plastered to the ground by a recent rain, still hold their color in the bright sunlight. I'm remembering that, in less than a year, those leaves completed their life-cycle from birth to death. There was a silent majesty about the whole process as, on occasion, there is in our lives.

Those leaves and those people still live in my memory and the image of that empty card table and two empty chairs is still part of the furniture of my mind. Still, on occasion, a source of near-tears.

* * *

You may wonder what became of Ann since so many of her friends—including myself—thought the shock of Clifford's death would claim her life in short order as well. You'll be pleased to learn that Ann went from looking like an ancient and feeble person to a stronger more energetic person in just four or five months—all thanks to Helen Higby. She finally succeeded in getting Ann to a different doctor who reviewed her situation, her symptoms and her medications. Her new doctor removed her from about half the thirty seven medications she'd been taking and her body made a good recovery.

Sometimes people snatch a victory from the jaws of tragedy.

Not always…but sometimes.

The South Fulton Street Tooth Factory
(A spoof on a friend.)

Humor is perhaps a sense of intellectual perspective:
an awareness that some things are really important,
others not; and that the two kinds are most oddly
jumbled in everyday affairs.
— *Christopher Morley*

Humor is the shock absorber of life;
it helps us take the blows.
— *Peggy Noonan*

Young Len Terkle was a swaggering, out-of-my-way, kind of guy—neither tall nor short—whose blond crew cut head, heavy jowls and short neck sat on a body whose contours somewhat resembled a bowling ball.

Len specialized in overheated rhetoric and snorted—actually snorted in disgust—at ideas foreign to his thinking. Like it or not Len was Mayville's only dentist. He was your man if you liked a steady dose of controversy along with your Novocain. Len relished pontificating on this or that hot issue while he had two fingers and a drill in your mouth—effectively stifling any rejoinder on your part.

Len was the catcher on our Rotary Club Blooper-Ball team. I'm not sure he was ever elected captain, but he barked out instructions to the rest of us like General Patton trying to shape up a bunch of incompetent recruits. It's no reflection on his competence, but we had a perfect losing season going into our last game with the Mayville Firefighters. We could hardly deny it—we were a poor excuse for a team. But, we snatched a three to two victory in the last inning with two outs and a man on second. I don't know if Len felt glad for the win or if he would rather that we had maintained our perfect record.

Len was only slightly less bumptious at Rotary Club meetings where he was somewhat offset by the dignity of Jerry Theines, Superintendent of Schools, George Sullivan, president of the

166

Mayville Bank, and Claire Maiers, president of Maiers Motor Freight. It's likely we'd all have taken secret delight if we could have deflated his bombast a bit.

An opportunity to do that dropped into our lap at the Annual Rotary Banquet at the Marlette Golf Course clubhouse that year. Rotary maintains strict prohibitions against advertising at its meetings. Therefore, before the banquet, I dropped into Len's office to chat with Amy, his receptionist. She was glad to provide me with a bunch of his business cards and promised to keep mum about it. I arrived early at the clubhouse and put a business card by each plate. As a consequence Len was fined thirty-two dollars for advertising at a meeting. Why not? He had the money and the fine went to charity.

Chuck Berry, editor of our newsletter, also nailed Len with a fake advertisement in the printed banquet program. It read: "The Terkle South Fulton Street Tooth Factory," with the sub-caption, "A good bite's no more'n right," followed by "Dr. Len Terkle, DDS." Len grumped a bit about paying two fines. Wouldn't be Len if he didn't grump. Grumping was his registered trademark, but he paid the fines in relative good humor.

That "South Fulton Street Tooth Factory" bit got me thinking. *Hmmm…what if we put up a sign like that over Len's exterior office door?* I bought a flawless pine board, one foot by six feet. I enlisted our son Colin, who has more artistic ability than I, to whip out the art work. Colin did a cartoonish script with no harsh angles, complete with a large petaled flower on each end. I delighted in painting the sign in fire-engine red, dandelion yellow, pea green and jet black. We put a screw hook near each end and waited for a chance to hang it under cover of darkness. We wanted to avoid being seen by anyone— especially Hilton Sarles our constable who patrolled Mayville at night.

It's dark and blustery and after midnight. Vonda—my willing accomplice—and I wait for Hilton Sarles to drive by on the lookout for "undesirables." We dash across Fulton Street with a short aluminum stepladder, the sign and our tools. We take refuge inside the recessed doorway to Len's office. We look both ways. The street is deserted. I mount the ladder with yardstick in hand and punch two small holes in the wood ceiling with a sharp awl. Vonda hands me two screw eyes which I insert—twisting them tight using a screwdriver for leverage. Ooops. Car lights coming from the south. We move the ladder back and flatten ourselves against the entrance.

Okay, all clear. Back up the ladder. Vonda hands me the sign. I hook it on and crimp the hooks with channel locks. Done. We chuckle to ourselves, check the street again and dart back across to our home and a curiously happy night's sleep.

Next morning we were up and looking to see how Len responded. As usual he walked to his office from his home two blocks away at around fifteen to nine. He looked up at his colorful new sign. "Hmmm, 'South Fulton Street Tooth Factory—a good bite's no more'n right.'" Len went inside. I half expected him to come back with a heavy broom or shovel and knock the sign to smithereens. Surprise—he didn't come out. He didn't bash it down. He didn't take it down with tools. It was still there Wednesday noon when the Rotary Club met for lunch.

"Okay, who's the wise guy who put the sign up?" Len demanded of his fellow Rotarians. Nobody could tell him because nobody knew. I hadn't told anyone and wasn't about to. Len had his suspicions but they didn't seem to include me. Everyone knows that clergy types don't do things like that.

The sign stayed up another two weeks or so and looked like it would be a permanent fixture on Fulton Street. Then one day it disappeared as mysteriously as it had appeared.

The explanation I heard at the next Rotary meeting was that a dentist from a nearby town saw the sign and felt that kind of sign didn't belong there. He called the State Dental Ethics Commission at the capital in Lansing. The State Dental Ethics Commissioner called Len and reminded him the sign was a violation of dental ethics. Len explained, "Well, I didn't put it up. My Rotary buddies put it up as a prank."

"It doesn't matter who put it up," the Commissioner told him, "The sign comes down post haste or you'll be stuck with a hefty fine." (Not to Rotary this time but to the State of Michigan.)

That was it. The sign came down. I've been told on good authority that Len took it home and gave it a place of honor over his fireplace. As far as I know Len is still scratching his head and wondering who put the sign up…and I still smile every time I recall the joy of being a secret troublemaker.

Author's note: This is to express my deep appreciation to those Rotarians, church members and townspeople of Mayville who brought me the gift of humor and laughter. You never knew it, but you were an island of joy in a sea of sadness for me during a difficult time in my life.

The Garage

> You cannot judge any man beyond
> your knowledge of him, and how
> small is your knowledge.
>
> *—Kahlil Gibran*

It's April 10, 1970 and spring is returning to Michigan. I hear birds singing their "glad-to-be-alive song," and the warm sun shines on moist soil and brings out the smell of new possibilities. I'm thinking *what a great day to be alive*—then my desk phone rings with a call from my cousin Willard. Something's up because Willard and I seldom have reason to talk.

"Don, I've got bad news," he says, "Grandpa King died this morning in his garage." Before I can respond he adds, "Under uncertain circumstances."

Half an hour later I find myself standing in that familiar double-car garage with heavy wooden doors that slid back and forth on a track—so hard for me to move when I was a child. Here we are, Willard and I, standing in the space where our grandfather died two hours earlier, on a still magnificent spring day. Everything appears pretty much as it had for the last ten, twenty…who know how many years? The only obvious difference in the garage is the potent reek of auto exhaust and a scorched area on the garage door just behind the tailpipe of Grandpa's car.

"They're pretty sure he died of carbon monoxide poisoning," Willard says, and the family agrees on that following medical tests. What they disagree on is just how it happened. Aunt Vera rules out suicide. "No, Dad would never do a thing like that," she says, "You know he had a slight stroke just two days ago. He must have experienced more trouble and got in the car to take himself to the hospital."

"Could be," we said, not wanting to coerce her out of her comfort zone by pointing out that the garage door was closed. Ultimately, she came to accept his death as a suicide saying, "Well, yes, it's true. Dad cared for his mother here in his home for a long time. He knew what an indignity a prolonged death could be—said he didn't want to go through the misery she did."

"Yes," we agreed, "he didn't want to be a burden to his family. At ninety-two and with chronic diseases Grandpa didn't have much to look forward to. It was his choice." Right or wrong, that's how I read it.

* * *

I do not recall a time when I was not glad so see my Grandfather, nor a time he didn't seem pleased to see me, though there surely must have been such times. Grandfather was warm but not effusive, and a man of few but gracious words. Capable at times of eloquence. He loved to quote from Thomas Gray's "Elegy Written in a Country Church-Yard." As a young man he had been a school teacher and then became a rural mail carrier and part-time farmer. In retirement, he served as church custodian at Marlette Methodist Church and as Justice of the Peace. He was always there if we needed him. He didn't intrude, but was like a mountain—a landmark—always visible on the near horizon. Now the mountain was gone but not the sense of his presence.

Here I am, back in his double car garage, where I loved to be as a curious child surveying his tools. I remember him using them. Not a new tool in sight. They're all old and worn but many are still shiny with frequent use. His garden spade and round nosed shovel. The scoop shovel I'd seen him use to clear away deep white snow in bitter Michigan winters and to shovel dark black coal for burning in his iron heating stove with isinglass windows. I see him now coming into the house dressed in his thick black corduroy coat with the fur collar and his fur hat. See him swing the hinged lid of the stove to his left and lift the coal scuttle up to his shoulders and empty the coal into the stove on top of the hot embers. Then there'd be a marvelous confusion as he swung the lid shut with a bang and moisture on the coal hissed and sputtered in protest and dark coal smoke rose above the stove and spread across the ceiling like a sudden storm. The frozen lumps of coal cracked and split against the hot embers. What could be more exciting to the eyes of a child than such wondrous chaos as this?

There, between the studs, you can see his garden rake, his scythe and sickle along with sharpening stones—all where he left them. Several flies and a honey bee hum their ancient incantations against the dusty window. Through the dust and cobwebs on the south window I see his vegetable garden. You could find him out there most summer days—hoeing away in his bib overalls, long-sleeved denim shirt, and battered straw hat stained with sweat. He enjoyed producing far more than he and grandmother needed and he delivered the extra vegetables to relatives and friends—usually persons he knew to be in need. In season, he gave away carrots, beets, tomatoes, kohlrabi and string beans along with lettuce, peas, radishes (both red and white) asparagus, currants, strawberries and sweet corn. The cornucopia of his generosity seemed as endless as I had thought the years of grandfather's life would be.

There is his well-used axe, his eight pound sledge, and the wedge he used for splitting of tree trunks for fuel. Every year he split a pile of maple—maybe eight feet high in the middle and fifteen feet in diameter. When that was all burned, he ordered coal from the local farmer's elevator. There, next to the back steps leading into the house, I see his battered and worn coal scuttle. Hanging by a nail on the wall—the ice tongs he bought around 1910 and used to carry blocks of ice up from his pond a football field's distance to the north. He placed those blocks of ice in his old oak icebox which was Grandmother's refrigerator for years.

There is his old horse collar hanging from the rafters along with a stiff and cracked leather harness. He probably couldn't bring himself to part with it after he no longer kept a horse for farming, and cows for milk and cream and butter. In my mind's eye, I see myself as a child standing beside him as he churns cream into butter in his two gallon Dazee butter churn. The gears are so worn he has to hold them together with a hardwood wedge. He lets me crank the churn until it gets too hard for me to turn and then he takes over again. Things like turning cream into butter are about all the magic a boy needs—and Grandpa was part of the magic.

Now, the mountain my grandfather had been to me is gone from the landscape forever. Still, as I shift my feet and hear the grating of pea gravel between my shoes and the cement floor, I feel comforted being in these sacred precincts—this dusty old shrine—with so many reminders of his life and work. It's as though I am a child again and see him on the other side of the room in church. I go to his side and receive the benediction of his smile and his hand resting on my shoulder.

And, no matter how he died, it's okay.

Holding Hands with Death

> Often the most loving thing we can do when a friend is
> in pain is to share the pain—to be there even when we
> have nothing to offer except our presence and even when
> being there is painful to ourselves.
> — *M. Scott Peck*

> …there is no more ridiculous custom than the one that makes
> you express sympathy once and for all on a given day to a
> person whose sorrow will endure as long as his life. Such
> grief, felt in such a way, is always "present," it is never too
> late to talk about it, never repetitious to mention it again.
> — *Marcel Proust*

Many of my family and friends still wonder why I left the ministry. If my memory is correct, only one friend has asked me straight out—with full expectation of a true and complete answer. I want this chapter to answer that question for those who wondered but hesitated to ask.

I'm not comfortable talking about why I left the ministry after sixteen years of service as a United Methodist Pastor—years that I considered reasonably successful. We (my wife Vonda supporting me each step of the way) were involved in three church building programs during those years. One that I initiated during my years as a student pastor in Grand Mound, Iowa; the second and third—the new parsonage and new church building completed during our next appointment to the mission congregation in Fraser—a northern suburb of Detroit.

I'm not comfortable with this issue because when someone leaves the local church ministry—unless it's to take up a related job as a chaplain or seminary professor or the like—it raises all sorts of questions in people's minds. I know, I've entertained the same questions when others have left the ministry. *Whoa. What prompted that decision? Had to be something serious. An affair with the organist or church secretary? Theft of church funds? Pending divorce? Maybe a complete loss of faith or serious physical or mental illness. Something serious—what else could it be?*

I'm feeling resistance toward the idea because it stirs up a number of painful memories I'd just as soon not relive. Yet, I'd want full disclosure if I were reading another person's story, so I'll open up as well. Besides, I probably need to take another stab at explaining it to myself. Identifying our motives can be tricky and motives are often mixed. Maybe I've deceived myself with my own explanation.

As a young student pastor at Garrett Theological Seminary in Evanston, Illinois, I took pastoral psychology courses under Dr. Carroll Wise who stressed the power and importance of human touch. Dr. Wise would say something like, "When we call on people in the hospital we sit down *beside* them so we're both on the same level. Nobody likes to have others stand over them and stare down on them. And sometime before we leave—during conversation or with prayer—it's good to rest our hand on their arm or clasp their hand and say something affirming like, 'Your friends are asking about you and hoping you recover soon.' There's magic, there's healing in human touch." I believed Dr. Wise and I tried to make touch and affirmation my practice when calling on the elderly, the sick and dying.

In retrospect, it may have been the memory of my grandmother's loving touch, and the difference it made to me as a lonely child, that made the healing power of touch as important as medicine.

Dr. Wise also emphasized the importance of *being present* when crisis comes—loss of job, illness, and death—whatever. "People will not likely remember what you said, but they will remember you stood by them. They will remember you shared their pain. They will remember how you made them feel." We knew when class ended that, "Being with" is as important as "doing for."

I remember the impact Dr. Edgar Jackson, a clergyman in New York City, made on me as he told a group of young ministers what helped him most following the deaths of his two sons. After his second son died as the result of a fall, a Presbyterian minister friend came to his home to offer sympathy and support. When Edgar opened the door his friend tried to speak, but choked up and couldn't say a word. Edgar invited him inside where the two sat down as his friend tried to compose himself. He made an effort to speak again and began sobbing. He shook his head and held his hands up in surrender. He stood, shook his head again in his impotence, embraced Jackson and walked out the door. And that—though entirely non-verbal—Jackson said was the most powerful message of comfort he received. That stuck with me. Even if helping people that way was all I could manage at times, I wanted to be that kind of minister.

A short time later, I had an interview with Dr. Richard Miller, my Church Administration Professor, who asked, "How are things going in your parish?"

"Busy—we've got a new church building program going but I'm spending more time calling on terminally ill and bereaved people than I thought I would. Sometimes it seems I'm hardly accomplishing a thing—like all I'm doing is holding hands with death."

Dr. Miller locked eyes with me and spoke slowly—deliberately, "I cannot imagine *anything* more important for a minister to be doing than to stand by his people when it's a matter of life and death." Dr. Miller had always impressed me as a sensitive, caring and humble person—and certainly a man with a pastor's heart. I chose to accept his gentle rebuke—or was it an affirmation?—and revise my priorities.

I'd been in my student parish about three years. One day, following a funeral at the Kelly Funeral Home in Grand Mound, Ray Kelly (the older of two brothers who jointly operated the home) stood by me as people filed past the casket and out the door. He said, "Beautiful service, Don. You won't be here long—you're too good. You'll go on to something bigger." I felt embarrassed by his sincere praise.

"Thanks, Ray, I appreciate those kind words; but I think they come from your warm heart—not your keen mind." I knew that flattery was like perfume—meant to be smelled, not swallowed. Yet, in my private thoughts, I allowed as to how I *did* feel particularly helpful at funerals. People told me I had a soothing voice that was a comfort in itself. One lady told me, "When you stood up to begin my mother's funeral, I felt as if I'd taken a tranquilizer because I knew we were about to be helped." Some said they liked the way I gathered up what friends of the deceased had been saying and reflected it back—the way I sized up a person's life and their contributions to the community. How I reminded them that some of God's greatest gifts come to us in the form of other people. But, in my naïveté, I persisted in believing that if I were helpful in grief situations, it was because if there was one article of faith I believed with "absolute certainty" it was eternal life.

Then the picture changed. The unthinkable—the impossible—what "only happens to other families" happened in our family.

Christmas time, 1960. Three shots to the head from a .45 and my oldest brother Wendell lay murdered on his office floor. His wife Lila lost her husband. His five young children lost a devoted father. The village of Armada, Michigan lost its only attorney. Devastation held sway in our family.

Ironically, the first funeral I had following my brother's murder was for a non-church-member named Joseph Austin—the same name as the man who murdered Wendell. What are the chances of that happening? How does one maintain an objective and detached professionalism in such a situation? With great difficulty.

The following summer, six years after I had entered the ministry and still unable to assimilate his death, I lingered at Wendell's gravesite in Armada's Willow Grove Cemetery then wandered aimlessly to the backside of the cemetery where I came across the cemetery dump. Rotting bouquets, once-used floral baskets and tangled ribbons—many with gold lettered words like *Husband, Father, Daddy, and Beloved Son ... **Brother**.*

Floral dump at Willow Grove Cenetery, Armada, Michigan

I stood still and stared. Bees by the dozens swarmed around the flowers and droned their buzzy mantras—lulling me into a trancelike state. Suddenly a distinct voice within me said, *Okay, Lichtenfelt, now is your moment of truth. Do you or don't you believe in eternal life? Is life a blown-out candle or does it continue in another dimension?*

At first I hesitated to respond—embarrassed, as though my answer might be overheard and be thought inappropriate for a clergyman. Then I answered silently and honestly. *I don't know. With my head I don't think so. With my heart I hope so.*

* * *

Late March, 1962. I expected my Grandmother King to go on living forever. She had to. She had been my emotional anchor as a child when it seemed hardly anyone else regarded me as worth their notice. I felt upbeat as I visited with her at the Marlette Hospital. I pulled a straight chair snug against her bed and we had a good talk. She held my left hand in hers and stroked the back of my hand gently with her right hand on and off during our visit—as she'd done so often in my childhood. Mostly she talked about her grandchildren and how they were getting along in life. She expressed her concern for their welfare and showed a crack in her conservative belief system as she told me she hoped *all* our family would be together in heaven, "Because I couldn't possibly enjoy heaven if all my family wasn't there."

At the end of our visit I offered a prayer while holding her hand. "…Amen. Well, Grandma, see you when you get home."

She looked startled—like I'd just pinched her. "You really mean it?" She sounded dubious. Like she knew something I didn't or like I was offering false hope. But I had no reason to believe we wouldn't see each other again.

"Of course I mean it. Be seeing you." I smiled and waved goodbye.

She breathed her last breath that night.

Later that week I conducted her funeral. We laid her body to rest in the old West Berlin Cemetery east of Almont beside the old white frame church she attended as a girl, and near her grandmother Marietta Standish Hulbert—a direct descendent of Captain Miles Standish, military leader of the Plymouth Colony. To me,

Grandmother's burial meant saying goodbye to a highly important part of my family history.

* * *

In 1960 when the berserk gunman murdered my brother Wendell, my mother had already been diagnosed with cancer with a prognosis—unknown to her—of two years to live. She gutted it out for five years through multiple chemo and radiation therapies and ten operations for cancer.

Mom occupied a bed in intensive care and was near death when my father died of heart failure in mid-May, 1965. Should we tell Mom about Dad's death since her doctors didn't expect her to leave her unit alive? My sisters and I agreed that if Mom lived longer and we hadn't told her about Dad she would feel great resentment. I broke the bad news to Mom as she lay hovering between life and death there at Henry Ford Hospital. We arranged for her nurse to give her a tranquilizer before I arrived to soften the jolt.

Mom lived another five months and died three days after my birthday in November of 1965. She experienced a raging oral hemorrhage that left her hospital gown more red than white. Now I had three powerful images competing for time in my Technicolor nightmares: *Wendell lying dead* in a pool of blood in his office as newspapers had shown him. *Mother drowning* in her own blood with her hospital gown thoroughly soaked with blood. *And my bloody hands* as I rinsed them off in the hospital sink—watching the last of the pink water swirl and disappear down the drain.

I had asked mother earlier if I might conduct her funeral. She agreed.

* * *

When Bishop Loder appointed me as pastor of the Mayville, Silverwood, Clifford parish in 1967, our district superintendent Tex Rickard said, "Don, I have only one word of advice for you. Relax and enjoy yourself at Mayville." Tex knew Vonda and I had been under more pressure than usual at our first two assignments. Not only were we serving churches in the ways most pastors do, but we gave major time and effort in bringing three building projects to completion. We had hosted sixty church meetings in the parsonage one year prior to the completion of the new Fraser church—while we met in the high school cafeteria for worship. During this time Vonda mothered four children under ten years old and frequently served as unpaid counselor to parishioners—putting her skills in guidance and counseling to good use.

After four church building projects, I know that feelings are seldom higher among church members than during building programs. Even if it's an exciting time it's demanding because everyone wants to see things done according to their own taste. Trying to reconcile irreconcilable differences is depleting. So when Tex said, "Relax, and enjoy yourself at Mayville," I planned to. I really did. But things rarely go according to plan.

Mid-June. 1967. On the day we moved into the small red brick parsonage in Mayville rain came down in buckets and thunder rumbled. The moving van was still half full when the phone rang.

"Is this Pastor Lichtenfelt?"

"Yes, sir."

"Hi, this is Vaughn Tubbs, Blackmore and Tubbs Funeral Home. I know you're just moving in but we have a family here who'd like to have the Methodist minister conduct their father's funeral. Could you break away long enough to come over and talk with them?"

"I'll be there as soon as I can, but they'll have to take me the way I am. My dress clothes are still packed."

I had no idea at the time that the next three years would be packed with the deaths and funerals of nearly a hundred persons: family, friends and parishioners—who in small towns with frequent association soon become friends.

The Mayville congregation held a reception for our family early in our first week. Our family now totaled seven persons. Vonda and I and our four children: Colin, Lance, Lisa and Erich—ranging in age between eleven and five and our niece Mary who had come to live with us during her senior year in high school. Mary, whose father, Wendell, had been murdered seven years earlier, now lived with us at the request of her sister Barbara and her aunt Charlene (her mother's sister) because Mary's mother had been showing serious signs of mental instability. Vonda and I didn't know at the time that Mary had been in her father's office when he was murdered and she still struggled with major emotional traumas. She would experience a catatonic episode during her first week at our home.

Our new assignment to Mayville also involved serving churches in Silverwood and Clifford. Each of the three small rural towns had a tight knit sense of community. Everyone pretty much knew everyone else. Townspeople saw pastors and priests as serving the entire community—sometimes as the poor person's psychologist. I'd already learned that "quiet small towns" are *not* quiet to small town pastors. And a pastor's "office" is wherever people happen to find you.

Extended personal conferences are as likely to happen on the street as anywhere else. I've no idea how many times someone— often a person with no church affiliation—stopped me in the aisles of the local IGA grocery store to pour out their concern over someone's accident or health problems or a child headed down the wrong path. Impromptu conferences popped up in the corner drug store, on the curb in front of the bank, on the bleachers at high school basketball games, between turns at our church bowling league at the Triangle Lanes, even as I tried to catch a snack at the Pink Poodle Restaurant or as I tried to mow our front yard or wash our front windows.

Among the first home calls I made was one to the Draper family whose nine-year-old daughter Carol was painfully deformed and rigid with multiple sclerosis. She found it difficult to talk and often whimpered in a way that broke your heart. Her entire family was absorbed in her misery which had become theirs as well. When death delivered Carol from her suffering, the entire community, including her new pastor, grieved for Carol and her exhausted and distraught family. I had learned early on that funerals for children do not go down easily. Children are supposed to bury parents and to reverse that order is contrary to nature—contrary to our emotions.

* * *

Not everyone understands that when a clergyperson conducts a funeral it involves far more than a service of memory. Often a single funeral means several, if not dozens of earlier visits to a dying person at their home or in a hospital. For me, preparing a meditation for a funeral involves upwards of two hours of conversation with the bereaved family as well as friends and relatives gathered at the funeral home. Being present as a pastor in the early hours following death serves both as a ceremonial presence to represent the church family and to gather information about people's feelings for the deceased. Those feelings can then be reflected in the funeral meditation to make it more personal. Often a pastor will make several home visits to the surviving family as they work through the early months of their grief. My experience is that a pastor and a grieving family develop a sense of being family as they go through the grief process together...from early knowledge of approaching death, through death, to some reasonable accommodation with that death.

I learned early on that death seldom quiets down after a burial and grief is often a long process—usually a couple of years at least—more if the death was sudden or violent.

Death was not quieting down for me. I found that deaths in my own family had been piling up on me—brother, father, mother, grandmother, and several dear friends and clergy brothers. I was unable to work through my grief over one death before the next death came and the next and the next. At the same time I had a constant responsibility for calling on *new* terminally ill persons and *families of newly deceased* persons. I found myself having to deal with multiple layers of death. The pain of grief grew crushing as it accumulated. Each new death in the parish stirred up sympathetic vibrations with previous losses and threatened to overwhelm me.

I began to experience a series of minor but pesky physical symptoms—including sleeplessness, a tendency to lose concentration and a touch of irritable bowel syndrome. I visited Dr. Parmalee, our family doctor who checked me over and found nothing of concern. Then he asked, "Have you been under any unusual stress lately?"

"No more than usual. Certainly not as much as you are under."

"I'm not so sure about that. I have a couple of big advantages over you. First, I make a lot more money than you do and I can take a vacation when things get to be too much. Second, I only deal with people who like me—the others don't come back. You have to accept whoever's in your congregation."

I got to thinking about that and how it's true that a pastor has to serve, as best he or she can, people that pastor might not have chosen as members of the congregation—just as certain individuals in a congregation often has to accept a pastor with a style and personality that does not appeal to them. (Much like any family-like constellation.) There is an endless list of issues that tend to divide. A pastor must serve people of all political persuasions—has to be careful not to represent his personal views as gospel in any final sense, nor to disrespect those whose opinions differ from his. During the 1960s, that meant serving people on both sides of the Viet Nam War, both sides of disputes over conscientious objection to the war, gay rights issues, women's rights issues, the Civil Rights Movement, racial violence, the impeachment of President Nixon—then in full swing, the Race Riots in Detroit that brought out the National Guard, left 47 dead, and where Vonda and I saw entire city blocks of Detroit in smoldering ruins. It was a minefield out there. So many people seemed to have a final irrevocable opinion on these issues. Yes, walking through a minefield is stressful.

I have no way of reconstructing the exact order of events in the Mayville parish. They seemed to spill across my path like a landslide over the three years we served there.

Within our first three months at the Mayville, Silverwood, and Clifford parish I was called upon to conduct the funerals of three men who took their own lives just weeks apart. I can still hear Ellen speaking of her fifty-two year old husband's death and saying, "People wonder why I'm not crying. Now at least I know where he is." Sometimes situations are made sadder because of complex grief reactions—an apparent lack of affection when there *is* affection. The apparent lack of grief when there *is* deep grief.

The second suicide—was it any less sad because an aged husband meant to conserve a small estate for his wife before it was eaten up by medical costs of his terminal illness? Might a death like this be included in Jesus' words, "Greater love has no man than this that he lay down his life for his friends?" Some even claim Jesus' death was a form of altruistic suicide.

Two more male suicides took place before my three years in Mayville were completed. Always jarring. Always the sleepless nights, the images and memories that refuse to go away.

* * *

Jennifer Parker, a top rank high school student who planned to become a doctor, fought a long heroic battle against leukemia. She and her parents rode the roller-coaster of highs and lows as hopes for recovery rose and fell—until death claimed her during our first winter in Mayville.

Where are the words to ease the pain of parents going through such dark times? They must be out there somewhere. I may seldom find them but I keep searching because I believe the right words can be a candle in the dark—and one lighted candle can relight other candles that been blown out.

* * *

Our friend Monsignor Ferdinand DeCneudt spoke to the Mayville congregation during our first Lent there. Fred spoke to us about Christians and Race Relations, referring to clergy involvement—both Catholic and Protestant—in the Selma, Alabama protest demonstrations. After his initial presentation he spoke off-the-cuff. With a catch in his voice and tears standing in his eyes he told how the Protestant clergy in Fraser stood by him in one of the most difficult times in his ministry.

We invited Ron and Ginny Krueger home for desert and conversation with Monsignor DeCneudt after the program. It seemed the Kruegers had barely left our place for their home when Ginny called to say Ron had collapsed on the kitchen floor. I got there quickly—before the doctor. Ron was not breathing and didn't start after I tried mouth-to-mouth resuscitation. I remember that overwhelming sense of helplessness as Ron lay dead on the kitchen floor and his two small children raced back and forth scared and shrieking like frightened little animals. One vomited under the stress. I was glad when a neighbor lady, a nurse, showed up at the back door, recoiled at seeing Ron's body on the kitchen floor, then gathered and hugged the children and Ginny.

As I conducted Ron's funeral a strong sense of unreality and denial held sway over his family and friends. How could this good and gracious man, in the prime of his life, be gone? Following the funeral I spent many listening sessions with Ginny as she felt her way through grief toward some sense of normalcy.

* * *

I know in my head that death is not necessarily closest to the oldest person in the community. It can strike anyone of any age at any time. Even thirty-eight seems far too young and Ivan, my cousin and best friend in childhood and companion in youth was thirty eight when he lost his bout with cancer in March of 1968. Cancer had left him paralyzed from the neck down. He displayed remarkable courage as he died a slow creeping death. As I spent time with Ivan and other dying friends close to my age, I felt acutely aware of my own mortality. There was always the thought *it could just as well have happened to me.* Would I accept almost total paralysis and impending death with the same grace and fortitude as Ivan? I'd like to think the answer is yes, but in my heart I know it's a lot to hope for.

Uncle George and Aunt Elsie asked me to conduct Ivan's funeral. What could I say? By this time I was accustomed to saying yes to relatives and could think of no honorable alternative. After all funerals are part of what pastors do and how could you say yes to one family member and no to another? I wished the deaths could be fewer and further between.

* * *

Cal Newman—a pleasant and laid back kind of fellow had driven a truck for Maiers Motor Freight for many years. One summer afternoon in June of 1968 television news told how Cal had stopped to assist a fellow driver on the expressway and was killed by another driver who failed to see him in time.

It was dusk when I arrived at the Newman home. Strangely Irene was alone—perhaps by choice. Her daughter Cheryl was not yet home from college and Irene, though in shock, revealed a tender and reflective mood.

We sat in her well-appointed living room with its handsome furniture and impressive drapes. No lamp was lit. Only faint light came through the window on the street. She daubed her eyes, and snuffed in her handkerchief now and then as she talked of how unreal everything seemed to her just then. How impossible for her to believe her husband of twenty-seven years was gone, and they would never touch again except in memory.

Then she surprised me by reciting a poem. It was almost as if I was not there and she was speaking into a vast empty void.

> Life is too brief ... between the budding
> And the falling leaf ... between the
> Seed time and the golden sheaf
> For hate and spite ... we have no time
> For malice and for greed...therefore,
> With love make beautiful the deed...
> Fast speeds the night.

She recited the entire three stanzas in her mellow voice and natural cadence. As she spoke, soft light from passing cars illumined her face—a face Cal would never see again. The poet and Irene are right—life is too brief. A songwriter's phrase flared in my mind: "Killing me softly with her song." If these stories are getting to you— if you're feeling dragged down to a hurting place you don't want to be in, but can't escape—then you're beginning to feel as I felt. Please bear with me. I too wanted relief from the ninety-some funerals scattered over those three years.

* * *

These are only a smattering of events. They leave out the story of the day I went to a funeral home and stood before two caskets: one large, one small. One holding the body of a young father, the other that of his four year old son—both victims of the father's handgun. Can you see how, in addition to the horror of the immediate situation, this would bring flashbacks of my brother's murder? How it might render a person almost incapable of carrying out a funeral—a grief ministry?

I'm leaving out extended reference to the afternoon my brother Larry and his wife Theda pulled up in front of our home. I'd been washing windows. Vonda was inside. I thought it strange that Theda remained in the car while Larry came to the house alone. Then saw that he was choked up and in shock—was barely able to tell us they'd received word from the military that their son Sid had been badly wounded in Vietnam. Surgeons had to amputate his leg, and he suffered from multiple shrapnel wounds. His other leg might have to be amputated also.

Vonda went out to talk to Theda, and said to me later, "I've never seen more pain on a person's face than on Theda's." Vonda still shudders when she thinks about it. Today Sid and his wife and parents live an alternate life to the one they'd anticipated. When lightning strikes the family tree the entire tree feels the shock.

* * *

When an assassin killed Dr. Martin Luther King, Jr. in Memphis it felt like another death in the family to us. We admired Dr. King for his peaceful protests carried out (we felt) with courage equal to that of a soldier on a battlefield. I'd met Dr. King, at a clergy gathering in Detroit. Our son Colin and I participated in the Walk for Peace and Freedom that he led in Detroit in 1963. I can still see Vonda's distorted and tear streaked face as she burst into an evening board meeting to announce, "Dr. King was just murdered in Memphis."

* * *

One warm and sunny afternoon in May of 1968, a Mr. Walter Gage—previously unknown to me—called to tell me of the death of his son Phil, a twenty-year old soldier who was killed in the Tet Offensive in Vietnam. He sounded like he was wound mighty tight as he asked if I'd be available for Phil's funeral services. As I entered their home I found Mr. Gage bristling with anger—much as I might have been had it been my son. Mrs. Gage did not feel like talking but sat off to one side. The slump of her body made her look like a wilted bouquet as she tended her tears with her apron. Mr. Gage gave me strict instructions about the funeral in his loud gruff voice, "Don't make him out to be a hero. He wasn't. And don't say he gave his life for his country. He didn't give his life. It was taken from him." He told how Phil had been opposed to the war and wanted to join a peace academy to study ways of preventing wars.

At the graveside service the wounded military honor guard who had escorted Phil's body home limped forward and joined in folding the American flag which had been draped on the casket. He hobbled to where the Gages sat beside the casket which held their son's shattered body. The honor guard bent over and spoke the words of formal presentation. Then he handed the flag to Mr. Gage. Mr. Gage—rigid and holding back tears—shook his head "no" and raised his open hands as a sign of refusal. The young soldier—taken completely off guard—swayed as though he were about to faint. The funeral director sprang to his side to give him support and escorted him to a seat.

If everyone at the graveside felt as I did, they were torn between wanting to put their arms around those grieving parents who had lost a son in battle and wanting embrace the young military escort who—limping from his wounds—was only trying to honor and comfort others.

* * *

186

May 27, 1969. The year after my cousin Ivan died, we were horrified to hear that my cousin Jim Luana was nearly decapitated in a workplace accident. Jim, a splendid human being—warm, outgoing, always wanting to be helpful—the kind of person this world needs more of—not fewer—dead at forty-three.

"Would you conduct his funeral, Don?"

"Of course, I'd be honored." But "honor" only takes any man so far. This "holding hands with death" was getting the best of me. Drowning in grief—that's how it felt and I wondered how much longer I could tread water before I went under.

* * *

Three months later the entire community of Fostoria was shocked when Randy and Ruth Mitchell were killed in a highway accident and left three small children behind. Relatives decided upon one service for the couple. At the cemetery, I stared into the two empty graves prepared for Ruth and Randy and thought of how the deaths of these parents had shattered the lives of those three children and dozens of others like a powerful tsunami.

Where do I find words that will even *begin* to comfort these people? This is the sort of situation that led one of my friends to say, "This makes me ask what happens when the rituals that are supposed to provide comfort break down." I'm thinking the best home remedy is drawing together as a community with lots of shared tears and hugs and large doses of practical help—over a long period of time. Our family circles may be broken by death. Still we're a circle—and we still include our deceased, but in a different way.

* * *

On the morning of April 13, 1970, as the sun shone like polished gold and birds were singing their glad-to-be-alive songs, I found myself standing inside my grandfather's garage and smelling the auto exhaust fumes which had scorched a spot on the garage door behind his tailpipe and killed him not many minutes earlier. My grandfather Cary King, 91, had apparently taken his own life. I believe it was to spare his family from having to care for him following his stroke, as he had found it necessary to do for his mother years earlier. To my mind, Grandfather was altruistic to the end.

I didn't officiate at his funeral. I wasn't asked—probably as a kindness to me. I wish I had though because he deserved so much more than the generic, one-fits-all, funeral sermon he got. It was one a minister could have used with almost anyone and tailored to nobody in particular. Guaranteed to be of scant comfort to anyone. I don't know if I could have done a satisfactory tribute to my grandfather. I'd like to have tried but I was running out of stamina for this sort of thing. I needed a vacation from death.

* * *

It didn't help that several church members and an older cousin for whom I had high regard had said to me, "When I die, I want you to have my funeral." I know they meant it as a sign of confidence and affirmation—even affection, but I couldn't bear the thought of one more family member or friend's dying before I did. Being a minister was proving to be too painful. My staying power was nearly depleted. Vonda labeled it "profound depression." I began to pray a short prayer I ran across somewhere: "Lord, please, either strengthen my back or lighten my load." Neither happened.

Simple daily tasks proved hard to handle. It seemed like I spent as much time longing for sleep as I spent sleeping. I'd sit in my office and stare at my bookshelves and beyond into empty space. Therapy didn't seem to be the answer. I needed a break. Something had to change—and soon. I had the feeling that something had to be me.

I shared my struggles with Ray Lamb, Vonda's uncle—a United Methodist minister and former district superintendent. "Ray, I just can't cope much longer. I'm thinking of surrendering my credentials—making a clean break—and calling it quits."

Ray shifted in his seat, leaned forward and looking at me with obvious concern, said, "Don, don't ever slam a door you may want to go through again. If you need to leave, then take a sabbatical. If you feel the same way after a year you can take honorable location"— which is sort of a United Methodist honorable discharge—"but you'll still have your credentials." At that moment I felt certain I'd never return to the pastoral ministry.

I felt tears in my heart as I pulled out two sheets of Mayville church stationery and wrote my district superintendent and my bishop requesting a change of ministerial status to sabbatical leave at our next Annual Conference in June of 1970.

I didn't understand. How could this be happening to me in the very place where we were feeling so at home, so loved and so useful? So surrounded by special people? Now I'd be an ordained minister without a church for a full year—probably for the rest of my life. How could I possibly be doing this to my family...to myself?

Shortly afterward, I found myself in Bishop Dwight Loder's office on the fifth floor of the Palms Building in downtown Detroit. To my surprise, the bishop had asked my district superintendent, Tex Rickard, to be present also. Bishop Loder had a policy never to let one of his clergy leave the ministry without an exit interview. I was not feeling up to spilling my innards to the bishop and Tex but I was surprised at what happened.

Bishop Loder had been told by doctors when he was a boy that he'd never walk again after his bout with polio. He wound up playing football for Nebraska Wesleyan. This special man came from behind his desk and drew up a chair near me with Tex somewhat removed. He said something like, "Would you care to tell me what's happening in your life?"

I only remember sharing my sense of inadequacy. My not having what it took to do the job—my inability to look upon suffering impassively. The uncertainties about my faith that I felt no good pastor should entertain.

Bishop Loder, in words I don't recall clearly, took each of my reasons for leaving and explained why they were qualities he looked for in clergy. He said he wasn't interested in pastors who were dead certain about everything, who didn't have a feel for the struggles others were going through. He said he wasn't interested in clergy who couldn't hold a hand and shed a tear and feel other people's pain and their sorrow...and their doubts.

I can't remember a time in my life when I felt more strongly affirmed or when any person gifted me with more sensitive understanding. Bishop Loder made me want to stay in the ministry. I *wanted* to stay in. But I knew I couldn't—not in my condition.

I was about to dissolve in tears as I left. I took the stairs down the five flights to the street lest I meet someone I knew on the elevator and lose my composure. I didn't want to leave this job, these people, but I knew I couldn't come out for the next round.

* * *

News that I planned to leave the ministry broke in a way I had not intended—at a hot-issue meeting of the Mayville school board with a larger than usual attendance. I had another commitment and could not be present that night. But I heard that a reporter from the Flint Journal was coming to cover the debate over whether the Mayville high school would continue Baccalaureate services on school premises or not.

Prior to the board meeting I had written the board saying I thought it best that Baccalaureate services be held in individual churches since there was considerable lack of unanimity between denominations. Wisconsin Synod Lutheran students were forbidden to attend as that would constitute joint worship with heretics. The pastor of Mills Memorial Baptist (and several open country churches) viewed Baccalaureate, as he put it, "Our last chance to get these kids saved." Father Tom of St. Joseph Catholic Church, a couple of other clergy, and I felt Baccalaureate should center on what all our traditions shared in common. We were uncomfortable with the Wisconsin Synod Lutherans excluding themselves—or were they excluding us?—and uncomfortable with the Baptist pastor (and others) wanting to treat it like the last day in a week of old fashioned revival services.

When my letter was read at the school board meeting, Becky Kelty, wife of Rev. Ed Kelty, pastor of Oxford Hill Church took the floor and said, "Why should Rev. Lichtenfelt have anything to say about it? He isn't even going to be here next year." So that's how the community—including four Methodist members of the school board—got word their pastor was leaving—all because of a broken confidence.

Several months earlier, following a meeting of the Mayville Ministerial Association in our home, Ed Kelty had lingered and asked me if I'd serve as president next year. I tried fogging, but Ed had pressed me with, "You *are* going to be here next year aren't you?" I wasn't prepared to answer that sort of direct question just yet.

"Ed, I'm asking you to keep what I tell you in strict confidence. Vonda and I will be leaving in June. I haven't told *anyone* in Mayville yet. It's important to me to break that information myself—at the right time, and in the right way."

190

"Oh, no, I won't tell a soul—not even Becky," Ed assured me, and I believed him. But he told Becky or she wouldn't have said what she did to the school board.

We learned of the leak when Beth Mitchell, our choir director, and her mother, Millie Doren, appeared at our front door around ten at night and Beth began to sing the opening words to, "Say it isn't so."

I knocked on Ed's front door at breakfast time the morning after the meeting. I'd never felt so betrayed by a fellow clergyman. I wasn't feeling forgiving. I wasn't feeling conciliatory. I was feeling confrontational.

When Ed opened the door I just looked him in the eye and said, "You Judas." He seemed surprised at my anger. After a little verbal exchange in the doorway he invited me in. Becky got up from the breakfast table and left the room without greeting me.

Ed and I continued our discussion in the discomfort of his living room. His basic stance was that the importance of continuing Baccalaureate in the public schools trumped the minor issue of breaking a personal confidence. We did not come to a meeting of the minds. That was the last time we saw each other.

Now Vonda and I would have to deal with this awkward situation. We had not told anyone of our plans—not our children, not our family, not our best friends. Now it had become public knowledge, and we had to respond under less than ideal circumstances.

* * *

When Tex Rickard announced my upcoming sabbatical leave at the Port Huron District Ministers Meeting, only two fellow clergy spoke to me about it with any specificity—probably out of the same caution I would have felt. What makes a man leave the ministry when he seems to belong there? Garrison Keillor said, in a *Prairie Home Companion* broadcast, "If a pastor allows that he's 'only human,' the first thing people think of is 'With whom and for how long?'" There's a lot of truth in that. People think *it's got to be something big— infidelity, mental illness, embezzlement or pending divorce.* Quite honestly, those would be my thoughts as well and I would not want to compel a friend to talk about such things against his will. I'd want my friend to *want to talk about it* and to take the initiative.

191

Of the two clergy who talked with me, one was young Brad Andrews who caught up to me in the hall. He was agitated and spoke through pursed lips. "I'm really mad at you. You *know* you belong in the ministry. I hope God smacks you good for this." Brad's outburst startled me and felt like the words of a stranger—not the words of the gracious person Brad had always been in my presence.

Shortly afterward he called me at home and apologized. "I didn't mean to be so harsh," he said, "I just felt so upset. You don't know it, but I used to come over to your services in Fraser, and leave during the last hymn. You're the reason I decided to enter the ministry. It's hard for me to understand your decision. But I wish you the best...and I'm sorry for what I said earlier."

Only minutes later, Bob Garrett, long time pastor at Port Austin, whose deep caring approach to ministry I admired, rang our doorbell and came inside with Charlene, his wife. They stayed and we two clergy couples talked freely as we shared a hastily-thrown-together dinner. Bob said, in response to my explanation, "I can understand why a man might have to leave the ministry because it hurts too much. I've considered leaving more than once." It felt good to hear someone else say that—someone I respected.

When Bob and Charlene left, our next step seemed a bigger leap of faith than when we first entered the ministry. We had little extra cash, and no job lined up. We needed to do some serious planning because in a few short weeks Bishop Loder would appoint another pastor to serve Mayville and "our" parsonage would become their home.

Mt. Clemens Years
1970 – 1974

I need make no excuses to anyone—not even
to myself—in taking time to let the depleted
wells of my energy fill up again.
—*Martha Whitmore Hickman*

You yourself, as much as anybody in the
universe, deserve your love and affection.
—*Buddha*

A Vacation from Death

Beyond his strength no man can fight,
although he be eager.
— *Homer*

I'd like to get away from earth for a while and
then come back to it and begin again.
— *Robert Frost*

My decision to leave the pastoral ministry after sixteen years of service might seem, to some people, to be the most foolish decision I ever made—but, for me, it was an absolute necessity. The combined deaths of my brother, mother, father, grandmother, grandfather, two cousins, and a close friend—in addition to the deaths of members and friends in the parish, and the constant calling on the dying and the grieving, became more than I could handle. I had not finished my grieving for one death before the next death, and the next. I felt like a battered boxer unable to come out for the next round.

We chose to move to Mt. Clemens because it was a fair-sized county seat town, and close to our former parish in Fraser where we knew a number of people. Mt. Clemens had a reputation for good schools—an important consideration if you have four children under age fifteen, as we did. People recognized the Lichtenfelt name in Macomb County. That's where my brother Wendell served as Chief Assistant Prosecutor when, during Christmas season 1960, he left the Macomb County Building and Joseph Austin ambushed and killed him in his Armada office.

Macomb County needed adult probation officers, and I counted on being one of them. But an economic downturn wiped out that possibility. Now the county was not only not hiring new officers, but had no plans to replace officers who retired, died, or moved. We discovered that situation about a month before our move.

So there we were with no home, no savings, no prospective employment, and a sagging economy. I don't know which best describes what happened to us after that— "There's no substitute for dumb luck," or "God takes care of those who can't take care of themselves."

With short weeks to go before we had to move out of our parsonage, we contacted a realtor and found a reasonably priced home available on land contract. It was a brick Tudor style—one of the least expensive homes on the edge of an affluent section of town. Our lack of standing with the bank became irrelevant when the realtor's fiancé, a friend of ours from earlier days, *volunteered* to provide a loan for the down payment. Whew! One big obstacle down.

Don, Vonda, Erich, Lisa, Colin, and Lance. Circa 1974.

We moved into 199 Moross with little more than the cash we received as a farewell gift when we left Mayville—enough to carry us maybe a month. Several promising job leads fizzled. Vonda lined up a job as director of Christ Lutheran's Pre-School, but that didn't begin for three months. We pared down our already modest lifestyle.

Powdered milk, pasta, and casseroles became the order of the day—the cheapest of everything.

In my six weeks of unemployment I learned that ex-clergymen who leave in mid-career have a lot in common with ex-convicts. People tend to regard you with suspicion and uncertainty. Some fidget and fumble for words in your presence and there is a degree of shunning.

I could sense people's unasked questions as to why I would leave my calling for other work. "What? Left the ministry? Whatever made him do that?" "Yes, you wonder what triggered such a decision." "One thing for sure, he's putting his family at risk—seems irresponsible to me." "It had to be something big. Who knows, maybe he cheated on his wife. Maybe he embezzled church funds. Maybe it's mental illness." Some people, who got their exercise jumping to conclusions, assumed the worst. I knew that from reports relayed to me by friends. I knew I'd have to live with people's unflattering estimates of me

With my back to the wall I could no longer be choosy. I scheduled an appointment with Al Ozias, a former church member in our Fraser parish, and an executive at Model Products—manufacturers of plastic model cars and planes. If I were going to provide for my family I might have to push a broom.

Al apologized. "Don, I'm sorry but we don't have any work worthy of your background."

"Al, I'm not looking for 'worthy.' I'm looking for a way to put food on the table for my family."

He paused, rubbed his chin, and then added, "The only opening we have is for assistant shipping and receiving foreman at our new Lionel Division if you were interested." Al just threw a life preserver to a drowning man. I grabbed it.

* * *

For sixteen years my work clothes were dress suits with white shirts and tie, and well-polished black shoes. At Lionel Division of Model Products they were blue jeans, t-shirts, and steel toed shoes. I sort of liked the new look. It seemed like a disguise, not the real me. I liked the idea of a strict forty hour week as opposed to my previous fifty-five to seventy hour week. I liked the absence of take home work, frequent calls at home, and frequent evening committee meetings. I liked the idea of no Saturday or Sunday work, no death or dying, no funerals, and no weddings or emergencies to cancel my days off. I liked having a happy wife again. As Vonda packed my lunch bucket she was ecstatic that her husband had a job.

I chose not to mention my previous occupation when I joined the staff at Lionel. I wanted to experience people as they really were, not as they often pretended to be in the presence of clergy. I didn't need friends like Henry Miller, my former barber, shouting, "Hi, Reverend!" to tip off his customers to watch their language when I came in his shop. (Although I preferred that they would chose appropriate language on their own.)

I had an inkling how a new immigrant might feel as I parked our blue Chevy station wagon at the corner of the factory where the famous Lionel model trains were now being built. I didn't know a soul in the building. I knew nothing about model trains. I'd always enjoyed watching them chug around on their tracks looking like a real train right down to the smallest detail including the authentic roar of their whistle. But I never had the urge to learn how they operated on electricity, or the names of all the parts that went into a train. I didn't speak the language.

I met Eddie, my new boss, inside the shipping/receiving office. Eddie was five inches shorter than I with a full crop of jet black hair, matching eyebrows and moustache, a slightly oversize nose and a wiry build. The irises of his intense blue eyes were rimmed with black flecks and gave me the impression that he could see right away I would not be a great asset to the company.

Eddie gave me a walking tour of the plant which was roughly the size of two football fields with assembly lines and main office on the north side. Storage for completed trains and accessories ready to be shipped out, tools and dies, four active truck wells, and our shipping/receiving office were on the south. My task, working alongside Eddie, was to oversee the loading and unloading of every truck in our wells, and to document everything coming in, and everything that we shipped out—often including heavy steel dies needing repair.

As it turned out, it wouldn't have helped me much if I knew the names of all the train parts because they didn't go by names— everything went by numbers. This was totally foreign to me. In my father's grocery store everything had a name: Del Monte Whole

Kernel Corn, Demming Red Salmon, Nabisco Shredded Wheat. In the ministry I learned people's names, relationships, and the streets where they lived. With my library it was a matter of knowing book titles and authors. But now I was going to have to learn a new language—a language of numbers. Each of the hundreds of parts went by a combination of initials and numbers. The people at Lionel threw part numbers around in a way that left me bewildered.

Lionel employees ran the gamut between the well educated, well dressed, white collar executives in the front office, through an assortment of whites, Afro-Americans, and a bus load of Indians from the Walpole Island Reservation in Lake St. Clair bordering Canada. With about a hundred employees on our shift I came to be on a first name basis with the majority of workers.

The day the Indian employees went on strike was a thriller—complete with war paint, feathered headgear, drums, chants, and war dances. I felt a bit unnerved, even though I knew it was mainly a drama to call attention to their concerns.

Uncertainty as to why I was there soon appeared on a wall in the men's room. Someone wrote with a broad black magic marker: "Don L. is a narc." (Narcotics officer.) I wish now that I had made it a point to remember the nicknames that flourished behind people's backs. The only two I remember are Jack and Sally—known behind their backs as "Dipstick Jack," and "Sally the whore."

"Dipstick Jack"—who was no dummy—apparently came by his nickname because of his inability to keep his hands of the women on the assembly line. You never knew what sort of mood he'd be in. When he chose to smile and turn on the charm he became charismatic. At other times Jack operated on the verge of rage—as on the day when he burst into our office (with five people present) swearing about something, brushing the paperwork off two desks, and kicking a swivel chair across the room. The chair slammed into my shins, and stung me big time. Jack wasn't the least apologetic.

My ministerial background prompted me to refrain from any immediate physical response. However, being relieved of some ministerial inhibitions, I said, "Jack, you're spoiling for a fight. Let's you and I go down to the Y and put the gloves on. I'll keep my right hand behind my back and cut you to ribbons with my left."

Jack stood and glowered. Terry, from quality control, spoke up. "Well, Jack, you heard what he said. Put up or shut up." Jack hesitated, and then walked off without a word. Our relationship improved significantly after that. I was glad I could tap resources that were not available to me as a pastor.

"Sally the whore"—I never asked how she came by her nickname—sometimes stopped to talk with me during lulls, and eventually learned I was a clergy type. It was she who informed me that the passage in Genesis, "Thou shalt not eat of the tree that is in the center of the garden," was a prohibition against oral sex. That was news to me, but who knows for sure? When I left Lionel at the end of two years, Sally helped throw a farewell party for me with cake and ice cream, and gifts: a radio, cash, and tears—including Sally's.

The novelty of going to work with a lunch bucket, driving a beat-up Volkswagen (so Vonda could drive our Chevy), and coming home grimy had worn thin during my second year. Furthermore, hemorrhoid problems convinced me that lifting heavy steel dies wasn't in my best interest. I put out feelers for another job and came up empty. I turned to an employment agency in Detroit to see if we could link my background experience to a new job. I overheard the manager call a secretary over, point to a letter she had just typed, and ask in an abrasive tone, "What is the function of this comma?" He sent her back to do it over. Sheeesh! I was glad I didn't have her job, or her boss. I had no clue I was about to link up with New York Life, and a general manager who was equally a stickler for detail.

The Grosse Point Office of the New York Life Insurance Company was not in upper crust Grosse Pointe. It was in the more blue-collar East Detroit (now Eastpointe) just across Eight Mile Road from Detroit. But the Grosse Pointe name carried a certain prestige as did the mahogany paneled office of Curtis Vreeland, General Manager. Curt, a Dutch Reformed Conservative Christian and Right Wing Republican wanted Vonda present for our initial interview. After opening pleasantries, Curt demonstrated for us how a sales presentation might proceed—complete with the customer signing on the dotted line. "Now, Don, if you can do that, and sell just three $25,000.00 Whole Life policies a month you can double your previous year's income with Lionel!"

I smiled a smile so big I thought my face would split, and signed up as a New York Life Agent with training to begin immediately. Here I could render a valuable service and, according to Curt, make a comfortable living to boot. With my name recognition as a former pastor in the area I had a backlog of people who would surely turn to me every time a family member was married and needed life insurance for their new spouse—who would surely turn to me every time someone bought a house and needed mortgage insurance to protect their family—who surely would call me for life insurance every time a new child was born.

I sent printed letters to everyone I knew offering my services complete with a list of impressive references including Monsignor Ferdinand D'Cneudt, Methodist Bishop Dwight Loder, Leo Cooney President of Master Card in Detroit, plus seventeen other presidents of corporations, and doctors. All I had to do: sit back and wait for the phone to ring. Wrong again, Donald!

Unlike the pastoral ministry where my phone rang all hours of the day and well into most evenings, I hardly needed a phone. The New York Life training manual was right, "Life insurance is not bought—life insurance is sold."

There I was with thirty-one other New York Life agents, three assistant managers, our general manager, and six secretaries. Many were persons whose names sounded strange to my rural Michigan ears: DiLorenzo, Massad, Iacona, Serapiglia, and Monacelli. Olivaries, Sherba, Sjolander, Zielinski, and Keersmacher. We were all part of the team—or as it sometimes seemed—the zoo.

One bright afternoon I was heading down the long hall toward the men's room when Luther Rogers, a steady producer—in spite of, or perhaps because of his pronounced limp—called me to his desk where he was completing an application form. "Hey, Don, how do you spell cyanide?"

"Cyanide? What happened? Somebody poisoned?"

Utterly serious, Luther said, "No, he was in Cyanide Hospital for surgery." I explained that it was not Cyanide Hospital, but Sinai. The New York Life training manual was right—there is such a thing as a sympathy factor when people buy insurance.

One afternoon, Curt, our general manager, stepped into my windowless office to introduce Dave Vanover as a new agent who would share office space with me. Dave was an ex-Detroit Cop. He left the force after the 1967 race riots that lasted five days and left forty-seven dead, and entire blocks of Detroit smoldering for days with National Guard Tanks patrolling the streets.

As we shook hands Dave's trained eyes noticed I had a client's check with a large peace sign on it. His first words to me were, "Oohhh, the sign of the American Chicken!" This from an officer who had just joined the white flight from Detroit.

I bristled. "Oh, you mean the peace sign. Dave, if anyone has a right to that symbol it's the young man who wrote that check. He just came home from Viet Nam where he was a helicopter evacuation pilot. He's no chicken. He's one of the most courageous men you'd ever meet." And so Dave and I—the conservative Baptist hawk, and the United Methodist dove—developed a warm, but adversarial friendship until Dave's death after his retirement from New York Life.

Usually, I kept a low profile so as not to antagonize my General Manager on whose good graces I depended for my employment. But Curt loved to ask probing questions to smoke out dissidents with opposing views to his own. Once in a group training session Curt asked me right out, "Well, Mr. Lichtenfelt, what do you think of President Nixon's decision to bomb Cambodia? Do you think he made the right decision?"

I was surrounded by pro Viet Nam war advocates and Nixon loyalists. I responded, "Well, Sir, if you believe two wrongs make a right, then Nixon probably made the right decision." I felt his question had no place in a New York Life training class. I think Curt sensed my aggravation and eventually backed off from encounters of that sort.

Despite my failure to sell a lot of $25,000 whole life policies, I managed to sell a lot of smaller policies—five, ten, fifteen thousand—many of them term life insurance which is similar to renting rather than owning one's home. In 1973 I qualified for New York Life's Star Club for having attained "a notable sales record." That meant Vonda and I were guests of New York Life's Star Club Seminar in Toronto, Canada. Vonda began to savor the possibilities of more financial freedom. She was not missing the heavy demands the ministry often places on clergy spouses—especially one gifted in caring for people in emotional crises as Vonda was with her Master's Degree in Guidance and Counseling.

At first I wasn't missing the ministry either. Vonda and I had transferred our church memberships to Mt. Clemens United Methodist where our four children attended church school, but I was seldom there. Most Sundays I was in a pulpit somewhere. If a nearby Methodist congregation didn't need someone, then a Congregational or Presbyterian Church would.

I enjoyed sharing my sermons with appreciative audiences—and churches that are temporarily minus a minister tend to appreciate whomever they can get. In my first two years out of the ministry I had not one funeral, sat by no beds with dying people, and had scant contact with grieving families. During my entire four years out of the pastoral ministry I delivered 260 sermons in twenty-nine different churches

Near the end of those four years I was invited back to the pulpit of First United Methodist of Mt. Clemens for one Sunday. Following the service Evelyn McHugh, their long-time organist, lingered until I'd greeted the congregation as they left. She expressed appreciation for my sermon and my speaking voice—something you might expect of an organist/choir director. I thanked her for her kind remarks. Then she sneaked up on me. "I guess right now you have all the satisfactions of the ministry, and none of the grief."

"That's about right, Evelyn."

Then she lowered her voice, looked me straight in the eye, and nailed me with, "Don, you know, and I know that you belong back in the ministry."

Shortly afterward the Almont Congregational Church asked me to take an interim pulpit ministry there because of their pastor's serious illness. I was delighted to be in that tall Gothic church with its high steeple pointing up into infinity, and its grand pipe organ played by a young man who wore jeans and Nikes under his robe. Somehow, when I stood in that second story sanctuary with its tall stained glass windows and steep pitched roof, "up" seemed higher from inside the building than the sky seemed when you were outside. The aesthetics of the sanctuary compelled an attitude of awe and reverence.   Poor health forced the Congregational pastor to retire, and shortly the church invited me to become their pastor. Something in me was desperate to accept that invitation. I was on the verge of saying, "Yes, I'd be glad to be your pastor," when I recalled the extreme kindness extended to me by my Bishop when I decided to leave the ministry four years earlier. I owed a debt of gratitude to my bishop, and my denomination. Reluctantly I passed on the invitation to Almont … but I've never put the "what if" out of my mind.

Not long afterward, while still working for New York Life, I accepted an interim pulpit ministry at a three-point parish: Utica, New Haven, and Meade on the Port Huron District. Roland Liesman—their warm and caring pastor—had become seriously ill with a heart condition. After Roland died the church board, acting on the rumor that I might be reentering the ministry, wrote Bishop Loder and requested that I be appointed as their pastor. On one hand, Utica was more theologically conservative than I, and was essentially an entry level parish. On the other hand, it would keep us close to Fraser where Vonda now taught, and Utica schools would mean quality education for our three remaining high schoolers—Lance, Lisa and Erich.

Vonda and I found ourselves in a bind. She had grown to appreciate the benefits of life outside full-time employment in the church, while a new feeling was stirring in me. I had left the ministry because it was hurting too much to stay in. With the passage of four years, I felt that significant healing had taken place. Now it was hurting more to be out of the ministry—out of those helpful relationships that are part of the privilege of being a pastor.

It was decision time again.

The Last Time I Saw Helen

Every [woman] has [her] secret sorrows
Which the world knows not;
And often times we call a [woman]
Cold when [she] is only sad.
—Henry Wadsworth Longfellow

Not everyone gets to have their picture taken by Yousef Karsh the famous Canadian portrait photographer. US Presidents? Yes. The wealthy and the famous? Sometimes. Other people? Hardly ever. Forrest Walton became a rare exception when, as a top salesman for Johnson and Johnson health care products, his company rewarded him for exceptional accomplishment with a portrait taken by Karsh.

Vonda and I were impressed when we saw the unusual black and white portrait in the Walton family room. Even untrained eyes like ours could see this was no ordinary picture. It seemed to capture things beneath the surface like strength of character, dignity and warmth, depth of intellect and that radiance of spirit which made you feel good to be around Forrest.

Forrest became chairman of the board of the Methodist mission church in Fraser during my pastorate there. We felt special warmth toward Forrest and his wife Helen. They invited us to their home on several occasions. A large white house with green shutters and impressive landscaping—first house on the left as you entered Moravian Meadows subdivision—one of the nicest in Macomb County.

Our church board hired Helen as our first church secretary when we graduated from meeting in the cafeteria of Richards Junior High, and moved into our newly completed church building.

Helen had known hard times as she grew up and was not given to superficial pleasantness. A petite white-haired spitfire—you could count on Helen's acerbic tongue to cut through the fluff and tell it like it is. She had a keen-honed sense of humor and a phenomenal sense of timing with her remarks. As a result Helen could get away with saying things the rest of us would get in trouble for and still maintain her friendships.

It was Helen who taught me something I've passed along to many others. One day in the church office I referred to my mineral collection. Helen said, "Mineral collection? What mineral collection? I've been in your home several times and I haven't seen any mineral collection. Where is it?"

"Well, right now its down in the basement packed in boxes."

"You get that collection unpacked and on display. A person's home should reflect their interests."

I did as I was told—even bought a new display cabinet at Dopp's furniture to carry out Helen's order.

Forrest and his youngest son Paul shared an interest in auto racing. Four years after Vonda and I left Fraser, Forrest and Paul headed to Indianapolis to fulfill the dream of a lifetime—attending the Indy 500 auto race. They left home with a sense of anticipation and had a great time together until, when the race was over, they headed back to the parking lot. They had nearly reached their car when Forrest was struck down and killed by a drunken driver. Now Paul, a boy of fourteen, was alone in Indianapolis with the body of his dead father.

Word of Forrest's death barely reached us from mutual friends, when Helen— sounding utterly devastated—followed with her call. "Don, have you heard about Forrest?

"Yes, Helen, Don and Mary called. We couldn't believe the news. Tell us how you're doing."

"I'm operating on sheer adrenalin. Don, I want you to have Forrest's funeral."

"I wish I could say yes, Helen, but since I'm no longer the pastor at Fraser I'm prevented from going back for funerals. Let Vonda and me just be with you as friends."

"I want *you* to have the funeral. Are you telling me you refuse?"

"Helen, I'm in an ethical bind. Chet Reynolds is your pastor now and I can't just invite myself back into his church and ask him to step aside."

"I'm not having the funeral from the church. It'll be from a funeral home in Detroit. You don't have to worry about displacing Rev. Reynolds. I'm not having him under *any* circumstances. If you don't accept you'll force me to get a complete stranger who won't be nearly so helpful to the family."

"I'm sorry, Helen, but my hands are tied."

"Are you saying it's impossible? I know ministers who came back into their former parishes!"

"It's not impossible, but former pastors usually just assist. The only way I could have Forrest's funeral is if Chet invited me to do so—and it's mighty ticklish asking him to surrender the funeral of a member of his own church."

"I'll talk to him and explain the situation. I'm not having him under any circumstance. *You get ready to come.*"

Scant time elapsed before Chet Reynolds called and graciously invited me to be the sole officiant at one of the more difficult funerals of my life. In retrospect I wonder if Chet may not have felt relieved to have been spared the task.

Helen was so distraught she seemed nearly catatonic. The entire family seemed dazed—as though there'd been an explosion and they hadn't realized what happened yet. I wasn't far behind and felt drained when the funeral and committal were over.

Helen had to adjust to a totally different life without her suddenly-gone husband. She used to smile as she referred to Forrest as "Big Daddy." He had been her rock since they first met in Youth Fellowship as teen-agers.

According to her friends, Forrest had left Helen well off. A generous estate. A large insurance settlement—most likely with double-indemnity. Unfortunately Forrest stipulated in his will that Mel, their oldest son, should be executor of the estate. After some time passed, Mel persuaded his mother to sell her home which she did. She stayed at the home of their married daughter, Caroline, until she determined where to go from there.

News came to us in bits and pieces over time. The picture we formed as a result was that, Mel—who apparently had a compulsive gambling habit unknown to his family—Mel, who fancied himself an astute investor in the stock market, began acting strangely. As Helen later found out he spent large amounts of money on himself, lost a fortune in gambling, and in the stock market. Soon Mel was nowhere to be found. All the money meant to insure her future gone with him. Going on thirty years later nobody seems to have a clue as to whether Mel is alive or dead. We may never know what happened to him.

So, Helen lost her husband, and then she lost her oldest son under unimaginable circumstances. In the end she lost her entire estate *and* the good life she had known. Like four deaths in rapid succession—not to mention the deep wound of betrayal she carried in her heart.

Helen was forced to live with her daughter and her family in their small house. That condition could not have been satisfactory to any of them. She took a low-paying job as a secretary at the Fraser school, became more and more depressed and lost weight she couldn't afford to lose. She resisted seeing her old friends, including Vonda and me, out of sheer embarrassment. Helen and I crossed paths a couple of times after that—but only briefly.

The last time I saw Helen was the bright sunshiny afternoon I conducted her funeral at the Will and Swartzkopf Funeral Home in Mt. Clemens. I watched the shadow fall across Helen's face as the funeral directors closed the lid on her casket … and felt tears sliding down my face.

Utica Years
1974 – 1980

I long to accomplish a great and noble task,
but it is my chief duty to accomplish small
tasks as if they were great and noble.

— Helen Keller

A Church Named Disco

disco, *Lat.*, to learn, get to know.

I am still learning.
—*Michelangelo's motto*

"Don ..." I recognized the voice of our Port Huron District Superintendent before he identified himself, "this is Norbert Smith. I have a favor to ask of you."

"Yes, Sir, what can I do for you?"

"I don't know if you've heard, but Roland Leisman just learned he has a serious heart problem, and has to rest up for a while. Would you be free to fill his pulpit at Disco until he recovers?"

"Oh, I'm sorry to hear that. I sure respect that man. Didn't know he had a problem. Sure. I'd be glad to cover for him."

"You're aware that the Disco parish includes the Meade church at North Avenue and Twenty Six Mile aren't you?"

"Yes, I've spoken there before." I visualized the dark red brick Meade church with its wide steps leading up to the second floor sanctuary. I could see Fran and Judy Furton, members there, who had influenced my life for the good.

"Thanks, Don, I'll count on you to be in the pulpit each Sunday until Roland's doctor gives him the okay."

After I hung up, I remembered how our family had driven by the Disco Church two or three times when I was a boy. To travel twenty miles from home back then (the late 1930s and early 1940s) was a long trip to us, and Utica was twice that far. Even then, I was struck by the Disco Church's simple beauty. It stood on the west side of Van Dyke Road under a canopy of tall maples with its white paint reflecting the sun. It had a small circular stained glass window high over two gothic windows in front. Its tapered bell tower stood out from the corner of the building, and five steps with slender rails invited you inside. Never dreamed I'd be delivering sermons in that historic church someday.

I assumed pulpit duties for Roland, and found the Disco Church family warm and welcoming. They sang hymns the way John Wesley (the father of Methodism) wanted Methodists to sing. Wesley warned his people in England to "Beware of singing as though you were half-asleep, or half-dead." The Disco Church family took singing seriously as an expression of their faith. They reached out to include others, enjoyed each other's company at church suppers and sponsored canoe camping trips that included children, parents and grandparents. They turned out for learning opportunities and, from early youth to persons of advanced age, they struck me as "live wires" and joyful people for the most part. You couldn't help but label them "one big happy family," and note that many current friends shared a long history that you seldom find in such mobile times. People with handicapping conditions and troubled lives seemed to be embraced with special warmth and compassion.

I still worked full-time for New York Life during those days, and had been providing pulpit supply for nearby churches nearly every Sunday. My four years out of the parish ministry, away from the steady flow of deaths and funerals, provided significant healing from the avalanche of deaths that led to my departure from full time ministry. I began to feel that it hurt far more to be out of the ministry than to be in.

I believed in New York Life and its products, and the good things life insurance does for people, but I sensed a greater need in the families whose homes I visited as an insurance agent. I often sensed their need for stable caring relationships in a caring community of some kind. Their need for supportive friends and a purpose for living beyond that of their occupations. Their need for someone to listen to their pain and stand by them in troubled times, and a need to extend their own caring to others. For those and other reasons, I found myself considering a return to pastoral ministry.

I covered for Roland only two or three Sundays before I learned there would be no "doctor's okay" for Roland. To the sorrow of many, this warm and caring pastor died. The district superintendent asked me to stay on at Disco until June of 1974 when Bishop Loder would appoint a new full time minister.

Two or three months passed before the congregation learned that I planned to reenter the full time ministry. Shortly afterward the Disco administrative board wrote to Bishop Loder and requested that I be assigned to Disco in June.

I wasn't sure I wanted to be there on a permanent basis. Disco was basically a fundamentalist congregation and we might not be a good match for each other. Even though I'd graduated from a conservative Christian college, I'd also graduated from a liberal seminary. I wanted the experience of contrasting traditions. I felt they both lifted up important values, that neither had a corner on the truth and neither was infallible.

The idea of going to Disco as *resident pastor* hadn't been on my radar. Vonda and I agreed that with two high school age children and a son at University of Michigan, we needed to look at the big picture, to consider our family needs.

We felt it important that Vonda maintain her teaching job in Fraser as she earned more than I. Her job represented a degree of economic security and a way for us to help our three kids go to college. I had hoped a better paying church would open up for me and so I was hesitant to agree to serve at Disco.

On the plus side, the Utica school system which included Disco, had a reputation for excellence. Another plus—Disco Church provided a parsonage in a lovely neighborhood—and it wasn't next door to the church. Yea! Living beside the church can make a pastor *too accessible.*

The invitation to serve the Disco parish is probably the closest I'll ever come to understanding the feelings of a woman who's not certain she wants to accept a proposal of marriage. On the one hand she likes her guy—on the other hand it would be nice if he were a member of a different political party, or had a higher paying job.

I shared my concern about our contrasting belief systems with the church board. I told them, "I'm not sure we'd be a comfortable match. I'd like to deliver a series of sermons to let you know where I'm coming from. Where I stand—or find it difficult to stand—on various issues. I'd prefer *not* to greet at the door on those Sundays. If it's okay with you, I'll stand where people can raise questions—or take polite exception with me—if they feel uncomfortable with my sermon content."

The next two months I delivered sermons with titles like: "Taking the Bible Seriously (not literally)," "Can Anything Good Come from Change?" "What about Religious Differences?" "Natural Evangelism," "How to Hear a Sermon" and other topics where we might be predisposed to differ. I fully expected that when the congregation

213

learned where I stood they would welcome the opportunity to withdraw their request to Bishop Loder. Much to my amazement, they responded with warm appreciation. *Had I not made myself clear?*

* * *

In June, when no other church became available within an hour's traveling distance of Vonda's school, I accepted the appointment to Disco.

Wouldn't you know it? My years at Disco United Methodist coincided exactly with the Disco Era and its disco dancing, discotheques and disco music

Early on I encountered problems with the Disco church name. Problems that had not existed the year before. I found myself in the Art-O-Craft Office Supply store in Mt. Clemens. I placed my purchase on the counter and told the clerk. "Charge that to the Disco United Methodist Church, please." He didn't want to believe me. He stood there as though petrified. He had that quit-pulling-my-leg look. I reassured him, "Yes, there really is a Disco Church. Just check your files."

Later, the ladies of our Woman's Society attended an ecumenical church gathering in Detroit. Upon hearing the "Disco Church" name an unenlightened lady said, in a loud whisper, *"Disco Church! Isn't it disgusting what some people will do to get attention?"* She assumed the name had been chosen to appeal to the contemporary generation, who were familiar with the newly-popular disco dancing and discotheques.

Of course the name had nothing to do with these new phenomena. The name went back to when there was a Latin Academy at the corner of Twenty-Four Mile Road, and Van Dyke. The academy bore the name Disco, which I was told, is Latin for "I am learning." The little unincorporated village around the academy adopted the name, as did the little Methodist Church.

The Disco name attracted multiple prank calls. A youthful voice on the phone says, "Do you have disco dancing on Friday nights? Ha, ha!" Click. My (otherwise mature) clergy friends tended to regress and call me "Disco Don" or "Disco Duck" after the song by that name which became a nationwide favorite that year. After a while it ceased to be funny, and became downright annoying to me. Their repeated

214

mocking—though not done to hurt—irked me and gave me a taste of how others might feel, when I pulled things like that on them.

It felt awkward, having always to work through the misconceptions—having to explain the honorable origins of the name Disco. Maybe the name had outlived its usefulness.

In my second year at Disco I put out feelers to individual members, and when I felt it might be safe, to the church board. "Have you ever considered the possibility of changing our church name?" You might as well expect the state of Mississippi to give up flying the Confederate Flag in 1866. I got the message. "No, nobody has *ever* thought of changing that name, and if you are, forget it." No use pushing my luck in my early years as their pastor. Later help would come from an unexpected source.

Early on I visited Martina Brown, one of the long-time members who had a strong reputation as a straight shooter. I hadn't finished my first visit in Martina's home before Martina locked eyes with me and said, "Vonda didn't want to come here did she?"

I acknowledged that Vonda had reservations. Martina told me later, "If there's one thing I can't stand it's a liar. If someone lies to me I don't want anything to do with them after that." I passed her sniff test. Vonda and I developed a warm friendship with Martina.

What Martina didn't know was that I was beginning to experience "buyer's remorse." I wondered if I were the only pastor in the United States to have an office—in the old original parsonage—with raccoons in the attic, starlings in the wall, and a skunk under the front porch.

I became acutely aware that I was back in an entry level parish less attractive than the one I started with twenty years earlier as a student pastor. Vonda earned more in nine months as a teacher, than I earned in twelve months as a pastor. Younger, less experienced, clergy than I were earning considerably more in larger churches. I know— ministers are not even supposed to think of things like that— but I did.

Martina had no way of knowing the personal struggle my ego was going through. How diminished I felt among my clergy brothers and sisters—as though my appointment to Disco were a course in Humiliation 101. After completing new church building projects in my first two parishes—and I'd never heard of *anyone* who did that—I was earning less than my peers. That's partly because, when parishioners are already doing "second-mile giving" in response to a building program, they don't have as much money available for raises. I wasn't likely to confide in Martina about this— not even in response to a direct question.

Over and over, I tried to bolster my sagging ego with a pep talk. "Buck up, Don, there's no such thing as an unimportant church. Remember that little church in Scotland where the old minister was so discouraged? He felt like a failure because membership was shrinking, and he'd only received two members all year. One was an old man, and the other was just a little boy of twelve. Remember, Don, how the whole world needed that little church in Scotland, and the world needed that discouraged old pastor—because that twelve-year-old boy's name was David Livingstone. Get out there and find your own "David Livingstone."

Sometimes I'd look at my (analog) wrist watch and tell myself, "The small gears in a watch are every bit as important as the big ones. Small churches are as important in the scheme of things as large ones. Small churches have given a lot of important people their impetus to serve on a world stage."

Other times, I remembered one of my father's favorite poems. Edward R. Sill's *Opportunity,* where Sill writes of an ancient warrior who's running away from the battle, and tells himself:

> "Had I a sword of keener steel—
> That blue blade that the king's son bears—but this
> Blunt thing!"—he snapped and flung it from his hand.
> And lowering crept away and left the field."

> "Then came the king's son, wounded, sore bestead,
> and weaponless, and saw the broken sword,
> Hilt-buried in the dry and trodden sand,
> And ran and snatched it, and with battle-shout
> Lifted afresh he hewed his enemy down,
> and saved a great cause that heroic day."

You'd think that might guilt me into feeling bold and courageous. It didn't. Nothing seemed to dispel my feelings of being ignored and overlooked. I wasn't feeling the least heroic when a startling event diverted my attention from my pity party. There's nothing like a threat to redirect your thinking.

216

When Bishop Loder appointed me to serve Disco in 1974, our country was in the midst of a hot war in Viet Nam and a Cold War with Russia. Insulated by distance from those titanic struggles, the little Disco Church stood by the side of Van Dyke Highway like an island of peace. People often told me how picturesque the building was—how it reminded them of a photo on a calendar, or a Christmas card.

I discovered that our church sat on a fault line emanating from those wars. An unwanted situation began to develop after our church women invited Laura Benson, a Registered Nurse and mission-minded leader from downtown Detroit, to present a slide program about her three-weeks in Mainland China. Our ladies thought it important that everyone be invited to hear her story on a Wednesday evening. About forty five persons, both men and women, came.

Laura told us up front, "I'm no expert on China, and I'll be talking about my *limited* experiences based on only three weeks in China." She said, "I went to China, because, as a Christian, I'm deeply concerned about our global tensions. China has a population of nine hundred million people. If we don't start building bridges of friendship, the weapons we have aimed at each other are likely to start another war. I want to be part of the bridge building process."

Laura's slides centered on women, children, the Chinese countryside, and included medical services, and education in the New China. Halfway through her presentation, she told us a story that was hard for us to swallow.

She said, "We had been on a shopping trip in the city. Afterward, we had time to go to another point of interest, but we didn't know what to do with our packages. Our tour guide told us, 'Not a problem. We'll just leave them here on the sidewalk, in front of the department store and pick them up when we get back.'"

"We couldn't believe our ears, and asked if he was joking. He assured us, 'It's okay. We do it all the time. It's safe. You'll see.'" Reluctantly, Laura's group left their packages. They couldn't believe they'd be there when they got back—but they were. Laura said, "That's something you'd probably never see in the U.S." Then, with exquisite timing, she added: "Later, we learned that the penalty for theft in China was to have your hand cut off."

Curt Spangler, a retired army Major, seemed to feel that Laura was painting too rosy a picture of life in China. He challenged her.

"Are you saying there is no crime in China?"

She said, "No, I'm not. The crime in China is the government but, because the government is so harsh and repressive, travelers like those in our group experienced something unheard of in the United States."

Laura continued her presentation, and fielded a few more questions. When time was up, her audience applauded. That was the end of it—until two weeks later when we heard from another military member of our congregation. Ed Akers, a Colonel in the Air Force Active Reserve flying out of nearby Selfridge Air Force Base became suspicious. Ed heard about the program from his wife Sandy, and contacted the FBI. I assumed he had special clearance. He inquired about *The US-China Friendship Association of Detroit* under whose auspices Laura had taken her trip with $2,000 travel assistance from Methodists of the Detroit Annual Conference. Ed was told the group was a Communist front organization and was under surveillance by the FBI.

Nobody relayed this information to me, nor did I know Ed shared his information with a handful of others. They had begun holding meetings to determine what steps they could take to oppose this "Communist threat"—this *treason*. One member of the group shared her concerns with me as though she wondered about a bit of hearsay. At first I responded on a private and personal basis. I expressed my complete confidence in Laura, our Bishop and officers of the Detroit Annual Conference. Later, I learned there were about a dozen persons who had met and were about to demand explanations. I knew then, it had to be dealt with publicly.

I called the FBI in Mt. Clemens and Detroit, and the Department of Justice in Detroit. They were not, or could not be, forthcoming. The FBI told me, "Our employees are forbidden by law to characterize any individual or group as being Communist or under investigation"—which an agent had apparently done in this case. When I inquired about President Nixon's widely publicized "enemies list," the agent said, "All former enemy lists have been abolished by President Nixon's Executive Order 11785 which prohibits the use or dissemination of such lists."

I called the Department of Justice in Detroit to see if they could shed any light on our situation. I was referred to "a person who would know." He said, "Let me check my list. Humm … humm, no I don't see that group anywhere on my list." That call proved some sort of list was alive and well in at least two places.

We requested that the FBI send a representative to a specially called meeting to address our concerns. They declined. That left us facing an issue that threatened to tear our congregation apart. Attendance and financial support dropped about fifteen percent as a result. A McCarthy era lynching mood swirled around us. Accusations of criminal activity don't get much more serious than treason. The heated rhetoric of this small group made me wonder, *why are we using a flame-thrower when a flashlight would do?*

I recalled the letter Bishop F. Gerald Ensley sent me when I was a student pastor. A member had sent hate literature subscriptions to me and several members of our church board. The material turned my stomach. It condemned blacks, Jews, religious hierarchies and seminaries—even President Eisenhower—for involvement in Communist conspiracies and treason. This member, whom I had considered a friend, continued to agitate within the membership. I sent Bishop Ensley a *"Help!-what-do-I-do-now?"* letter. He wrote, "Donald … unless you are adept at fighting hornets I would stay out of the fray. You are not going to reason people out of positions they were not reasoned into in the first place."

I believed that to be true. Still, I felt helpless and responsible that our Disco congregation might be about to go under on my watch. Where could I turn?

In early June 1975 I tried reaching the Director of the FBI in Detroit by phone. Definitely outside my comfort zone. What possible leverage did I have with an experienced man in his office? To make matters worse he was in a surly mood.

His first words were a gruff, "How'd you get through to me?"

"Well, Sir, I just identified myself and said why I'm calling and the receptionist put me through."

"You're not supposed to be talking to me except at my invitation. Why are you calling me?"

"I'm calling because an FBI agent apparently made statements that are causing serious problems for our congregation. We've lost members and income as a result."

He responded with a dismissive, "Sounds like an in-house problem to me. You'll have to iron that out yourself," he said. "You interrupted me in a meeting. I've got to get back."

"I'm sorry if I upset your schedule, Sir, but that FBI agent's statement could put us out of existence. Our little church could disappear without a ripple, but you should know that our Bishop has been following this issue closely. He's concerned about what this portends for the United Methodist Church as a denomination."

His tone became more conciliatory. "Hmmm...well, I'd appreciate it if you'd keep the lid on this for a while until we see what we can do."

"I can't do that, Sir. It's out of my hands. I'm going to Annual Conference in Adrian next week, and, if the issue comes up, you're dealing with 230,000 Michigan Methodists."

Late the next morning two FBI agents, Paul Chenault and John Pizzotti appeared at my door and insisted on taking me to lunch—a lunch that lasted two hours. They spoke to me of the absolute confidentiality of all FBI files and private communications. They said, "We are duty-bound neither to confirm nor deny Col. Aker's remarks, nor any call which may have come to us from him. Any remarks he may have made did not have the approval of the FBI. They are his subjective judgment alone."

They downplayed the issue, "It's no big deal. The Communist Party is legal in the US. Our country still operates on the principle of innocent until proven guilty, and there's no need for you to be concerned."

I said, "I want our membership to feel reassured. Would you please send me a brief letter covering the main points of our conversation? I'd like for them to hear it from you rather than me."

They declined. "Sorry, we can't do that."

After we parted I felt frustrated that an FBI agent apparently got us into this mess, but the FBI could or would do nothing to repair the damage within our congregation.

I decided to send the two FBI agents a registered letter that summarized my take on our conversation and asked them "to correct me if, in any respect, I am mistaken." I distributed copies of my letter to our congregation in the hope that it would serve almost as well as a letter on an FBI letterhead.

Meantime our church board prepared for a congregational meeting to respond to questions anyone in the church wanted answered—a meeting to which the FBI would send no spokesperson.

Bishop Loder sent his assistant, Dr. Royal Synwolt, a gentle, knowledgeable man skilled in conflict resolution. His purpose was to draw out, and respond to all questions at issue. Rev. Patton Zimmerman, chair of the Board of Christian Social Concerns also came as a resource person. We had gathered, printed and circulated all questions in advance. As Dr. Synwolt opened the meeting he solicited any further questions that were not on the list. Someone seated in the rear whispered loudly, "See! That's how the Communists operate—divide and conquer."

That struck me as a strange statement. Soliciting *all* questions and promising to respond to them—even of it took more meetings? That approach impressed me as an exercise of democracy, openness and facing the truth wherever it led.

While it seemed the agitated conversation might go on and on, it eventually wound down. I could tell by the occasional nodding of heads, the more relaxed atmosphere and a growing number of smiles that most of the folks in attendance were convinced the charges ware baseless.

Royal and Patton amazed me with the breadth of their knowledge, their patience and gentleness in responding to questions. They impressed me with their ability to restate a questioner's concern more clearly than the questioner had in the first place.

They were not out to *destroy* anybody's arguments and make them feel like enemies. They came to resolve differences within a church family and bring healing.

No matter how hard we try, we don't always succeed in healing differences. We all tend to cling to our own version of the truth—in spite of evidence to the contrary sometimes. Disco church lost several couples who remained convinced that the Methodist church was in league with the devil. I felt sad that we lost them; they had been an important part of our fellowship. It's sort of like marriage. You like to see a couple remain in love and harmony. However, we know there are such things as irreconcilable differences where remaining together is destructive.

Our congregation survived the threat, closed ranks, picked up the pieces and continued with the work of the church. During the eighteenth century, John Wesley, the "father of the Methodist Church," said, "The world is my parish." We believe it still is our parish, and that securing peace and justice are ways of loving the world and its people.

* * *

About this time, those who favored changing the Disco church name got a boost from an unexpected source. A stranger stopped in front of our church, took a close-up photo of our church sign and sent it to the National Lampoon magazine. They published the picture. If the National Lampoon thought it was hilarious enough to print in their magazine, they must have felt their readers would get a hoot out of seeing it.

I circulated copies of the Lampoon photo to the congregation. From then on our name change was pretty much assured. I traced the photographer's name in our local phone book, and sent him a sincere letter of thanks.

Words and meanings change over time. Attitudes change. Former church members die or move away. Newcomers with no strong attachment to *the way things have always been* soften resistance to change.

I could identify with those who resisted the name change. Some felt a genuine affection for the Disco name, and held active memories of its past and the devoted souls the Disco church had gathered. Of course they were likely to feel that any change was a sacrilege—a violation of their past. One or two may have resisted out of sheer cussedness or ignorance—as though they were members of the Flat Earth Society.

Nellie Speegle let me know she was irritated that I had introduced the idea of a name change. She said to me at a preliminary meeting about the name change, "I don't know why *you* should have any say about it. *You* may not even be here in another year or two."

Old Josh Hobgood thought it a bit incongruous for Nellie to suggest that *I* wouldn't be there—given *her* age, and health problems. Josh spoke right up and said, "Well, you might not be here either, Nellie." He couldn't resist a little chuckle over what he'd just said. Then, aware of how he might have come across, he added, "Maybe none of us will be here."

As it turned out, Nellie was recalled by her maker a few months later.

Well, the vote carried. Disco was given the new name *Hope United Methodist*—to the dismay of a few and the relief of most members. No longer would the church bear a name that conveyed an unwanted impression.

A new church building now stands where the old 1890s church once stood. I know some of the old timers feel sad, even though they know it's for the best. I feel sad along with them as I remember my few childhood trips past that lovely place that seemed to radiate a sense of Divine Presence to my child mind.

I think of the early generations of people who knelt at the altar of that little church and gave their hearts to the Lord—a few of whom felt that was the *only* way a person could come to God. I think of the hearts made kind and generous and caring as a result of that church building's being there.

Despite the occasional pain and frustration of being a pastor there, I'm glad to have been a part of Disco's history. It provided a raft of friends, both youth and adult, for our children. Time and again church members gave the church and our family the gift of their labors, and their affection—their skills in carpentry and plumbing, of recreation and music. Their gifts of fresh fruit and vegetables from their gardens...the gift of laughter and togetherness around meal tables in their homes. They gave themselves with a magnificent prodigality, and some of our closest friends today are those we met when our lives overlapped and meshed at Disco.

Old Josh Hobgood was right when he referred to a day "when none of us will be here." Generations of families come into this world and pass on. Clothes and church buildings wear out or become too small. But in the midst of change, and with the knowledge that our days are numbered, it is a great thing just to be alive. Just *to know* we belong to each other in a fellowship of caring. Yes, the world is a classroom, and you can get *to know* a lot from a little country church. I have come *to know* you can.

The old Disco church is gone from the place it occupied for over a century, but it lives on. It has a new life as the "Disco Chapel." You can see it in the Civic Center at Utica, Michigan where it has been moved to become part of a historic village complex—a place where it continues to serve as a wedding chapel and meeting place.

223

Harper Woods Years
1980 – 1988

To love and lose is a tragedy, but it's not the
end of our life. It's part of the journey.
—*Source unknown*

Laughter and Tears

Fun is good.
—*Dr. Seuss*

Life is not easy for any of us. But it is a continual
challenge, and it is up to us to be cheerful and to be
strong, so that those who depend on us may draw
strength from our example.
—*Rose Kennedy*

I stood in the pulpit of Redeemer United Methodist Church in Harper Woods for the first time in mid-June of 1980. I liked what I saw. The A-frame building was well-kept, clean and spacious with a strong sense of openness, loft and light. Geometric patterned stained glass windows—combined with clear glass—leant warmth and brightness. It had the look of a building that was loved and cared for. It felt like sacred space.

I looked out at the congregation as they gathered for worship. They appeared generous with their smiles as they greeted others and settled in their pews—always a good sign. I sensed warmth in their greetings with each other and with me after the worship hour. They spoke freely about their sadness in losing Rev. Chuck Jacobs, my predecessor. It's an interesting dynamic that one of a new pastor's first responsibilities is to be sensitive to the grief people feel in loosing their previous pastor. At the same time a new pastor is experiencing a similar kind of loss in being separated from parishioners in his previous congregation. I took those feelings as a positive indicator that when I left they would feel the same affection for me as they now felt for Chuck.

The character of the congregation became apparent early on. Monday morning found me emptying many boxes full of my books and placing them on the shelves in my new office. Vera Staperfenne, a petite middle-aged lady, went by the office and noted all the empty liquor boxes in the hall. (I've always found liquor stores a good source of packing boxes the right size for books and other things.) Vera stepped inside the open door, and said, "Wow that must have been some party you had when you left your other church."

227

As I began my second week, I crossed paths with Vera in the church parking lot. She was wearing her *Built Like a Mack Truck* t-shirt (a gift from her husband who worked for Mack.) She stood with arms folded—one foot on the driveway and the other on the curb—and spoke to me ex-cathedra: "I don't suppose you've had a chance to read all the small print in your contract yet, but we expect our minister and his wife to take the Youth Fellowship to downtown Detroit for the 4th of July fireworks. It's almost that time.

Methodist ministers don't have written contracts—though there is a three page list of *Responsibilities and Duties of a Pastor* in *The Book of Discipline*. Vera was referring to unwritten expectations—of which there are always more than a pastor knows and which a pastor usually learns *after failing* to meet those expectations.

I didn't want to appear easily manipulated so I responded, "It sounds like you've been reading *Winning through Intimidation*."

"Hah! Read it? I wrote it," she said. Vera was typical of the majority of folks in the congregation. Always a friendly smile. Always an amusing comment that made you feel better for the encounter.

A short time later, Jean Bricker served cake at a church function in her home. She handed me a piece, with plate, fork and napkin, as I stood talking with a new friend. She said—in a *louder* voice than necessary—"This is called 'Better than Sex Cake'—that's its real name. Let me know how you like it."

Now how was I to respond to that? She had set me up with some sort of gastronomic Rorschach test. No matter how I responded I was going to have to reveal something about my sex life.

When we crossed paths later on, Jean stood squarely in front of me. "Well," she prolonged the word, plainly signaling a double entendre, "how did you like the 'Better than Sex Cake'?"

I said, "Jean, the cake is scrumdillyicious but it's vastly over-rated." That seemed to satisfy her without my being too revelatory.

Vonda's birthday rolled around in April. Once you know Vonda was born on April first it's hard to forget she's an April fool's day baby from then on. The mischievous triumvirate of Jean Bricker, Vera Staperfenne and Nancy Hathaway worked behind the scenes drawing up plans for Vonda's birthday which fell on Sunday that year.

April first arrived. An announcement in the church bulletin invited everyone to the fellowship hall after worship for punch and cake in celebration of Vonda's birthday. Vonda and I joined the line of happy, laughing people going downstairs. These people seemed to latch on to anything as a good excuse to party and enjoy each other.

Nancy Hathaway directed Vonda to the cake table which held a large sheet cake for general consumption. Then, to personalize the occasion, she presented Vonda with a beautifully decorated cake about four inches high and fourteen inches square—attractively presented on white doilies. The frosting was a work of art with fancy curlicues and red rose blossoms and green leaves. Birthday candles blazed while a large fire extinguisher sat conspicuously nearby. Vonda reveled in the show of affection as the group sang a rousing "Happy Birthday." She blew out the candles—all but the trick candle she couldn't blow out. As Vonda removed the candles, Jean Bricker handed her a long knife and a stack of dessert plates so she could start the cutting and serving.

No stranger to this sort of thing, Vonda took the knife confidently in hand and took a bead on where the first cut should be. She placed the knife gently on the surface so as not to disturb the artistic frosting and began a gentle back and forth motion. Nothing happened. People stood waiting for their cake. Vonda applied more pressure. Still the cake resisted being cut. She thought to herself how embarrassed the church member who baked that tough cake was going to feel. She applied more pressure until she began to hear snickers in the crowd. She'd been set up! A sideways scrape of the frosting revealed that she was not trying to cut cake but a large cellulose sponge frosted as though it were a real cake.

These were the beginnings of a long string of happy times and laughing times which Vonda and I enjoyed during our eight years at Redeemer church. What impressed me about this church family is the way they took their work as seriously as their play—and their play as seriously as their work. If smiles and laughter weren't happening all around you—you probably weren't with Redeemer people.

Harper Woods was surrounded by East Detroit (now Eastpointe) and St. Clair Shores on the north, by Grosse Point Woods on the east and by Detroit on the south and west. Redeemer Church operated a popular thrift shop in their original white wooden church next door. It filled the entire church and part of the basement. A number of volunteers, both women and men, gave time each week to help make used clothing, furniture and household goods available to struggling families nearby. The profits were split between mission projects and areas of special need within the church.

I visited the thrift shop at least once each day when I could. You could depend on those volunteers to be chatting and laughing. It gave me a pick-me-up to be part of the laughter when many of my responsibilities immersed me in sadness. I seldom left without chuckling to myself—like the day when we discussed how to pronounce a new person's last name. Mary Lou Hess, a long-retired school teacher said, "You don't pronounce the h. It's silent, like the p in swimming." It took me a minute to catch on. But here I am remembering twenty-five years later and smiling as I remember Mary Lou.

Later on, Lori Kall and I sat in the surgical lounge for six hours as Mary Lou was operated on for a brain tumor. Mary Lou had no family but her Redeemer Church family. Lori and I recalled how Mary Lou had invited our Senior Citizens group (the Verniers, after the road our church was on) to her cottage north of Port Sanilac on Lake Huron. It's one of my special happy memories to see that group of young hearted people—fifteen or twenty of them, all in their seventies and eighties—wading in Lake Huron. They behaved as though they were small children delighted to find a shell or a pretty stone, or a Petoskey stone—the state stone and fossil of Michigan.

When Mary Lou died, there was sadness at her funeral of course, but just underneath, and ready to break out at any moment was the laughter which Mary Lou triggered wherever she went with her wild sense of humor. Again, laughter trumped tears in the Redeemer church family.

When Detroit's auto industry dipped and people were laid off our church family made it possible for dozens of families to receive boxes of food during their time of crisis. We helped everyone we could, either with direct help or referral to other agencies.

I remember the afternoon Harvey Moore, a jobless father of four, sat in my office and sobbed because he could not meet his rent, nor keep enough food on the table. His deep feeling of despair blotted out the bright sunshine outside. Harvey gave serious thought to suicide, thinking his insurance would help his family when he couldn't.

Thanks in part to Redeemer Church folks, Harvey lived to laugh again.

Three months after my arrival I was asked to officiate at the funeral of a fifteen year old boy (not a church member) who was accidentally shot to death by a friend while hunting. I remember how difficult it was to be in the funeral home when the boy who had done the shooting appeared at the funeral home despite the grieving family's request that he not come. Much of a minister's time is taken up by requests for help outside the church membership. Situations the congregation is likely never to know.

Russell and Marie Hough were retired when I met them. When some boisterous merriment or laughter broke out at a church gathering they were likely to be in the middle of it. Marie earned the nickname "Sassy" because she was always ready with her repartee.

When Russ died, Marie chose the Harris Funeral Home in Detroit. Two things stood out about Russ's funeral. First, the way tears flowed so freely and unselfconsciously from both men and women. Second, the way laughter broke out again and again as people talked during visitation, and during the funeral service itself. I remarked while delivering his funeral mediation, "I've never taken part in a funeral visitation where so many tears flowed and so much laughter rose from friends as they did as they recalled Russ's life." Laughter and tears—mixed together—and I think the laughter won out in the end.

A pastor doesn't have to be in a new church for long before he becomes a frequent listener to private struggles, pains, problems, and fears that beset all humans. Redeemer was no exception, despite the misleading outward appearance that many of its people didn't have a problem in the world and lived in a cloud free environment.

I am remembering an old English story about hell:

"A man who was careless about spiritual things died and went to hell. And he was much missed on earth by his old friends. His business manager went down to the gates of hell to see if there was a chance of bringing him back. But, though he pleaded for the gates to be opened, the iron bars never yielded. His cricket captain went also and besought Satan to let him out just for the remainder of the season. But there was no response. His minister went also and argued, saying, 'He wasn't altogether bad. Let him have another chance. Let him out just this once.' Many other friends of his went also and pleaded with

Satan saying, Let him out. Let him out. Let him out. But when his *mother* came she spoke no word of his release. Quietly, and with a strange catch in her voice, she said to Satan, '*Let me in.*' And immediately the great doors swung open upon their hinges. For love goes down through the gates of hell and there redeems the damned." (Source unknown)

Redeemer Church, it seemed to me, was well named for again and again I became aware of members who entered other people's hells. Hells of betrayal, painful terminal illnesses, hells of alcoholism and other addictions, lonely old age, of run-away children, and hells of overwhelming grief.

The laughing, party-loving people at Redeemer were capable of great seriousness and deep caring for people who were hurting. I had every reason to be glad they were that kind of people. Our family was about to go through the most hellish nightmare experience of our lives and we would need all the help we could get.

The Day We Went Down to
The Water Six and Came Back Five

There is a strange foreboding in the sea,
it crashes hard on our hearts, and wakens
memories of shipwrecked dreams.
—Eileen Lynch

I hear the sound of water and my heart leans to the North. Instantly, in memory, I am standing on the shore of Lake Huron at Port Sanilac. It is the day our family went down to the Lake six and came back five.

I hear the sound of water and I think of the day his mother's water broke. Colin, our firstborn, is cradled in his mother's right arm beside her in bed at the DeWitt, Iowa hospital when I see him for the first time. Tears brim in Vonda's eyes as we both marvel at his intricate little fingers and nails. Vonda says, "Oh, Honey, isn't he beautiful?"

Unable to see past the deep red wrinkles of his puffy face I shade my response, "Well, he's got possibilities." And what vast possibilities they were.

I hear the sound of water, laughter and splashing. Our toddler splatters water every which way in our old bathtub with its claw feet and scarred white porcelain. Squeals of delight echo in our ears from the hard surfaces of the bathroom. I hear him again even now. Still see his face alive with joy.

I hear the sound of water and again our family of six is canoeing on the Titabawassee River—vacation adventures at our family cottage up north in Michigan. Colin's first solo trip in our canoe—what pride he took in his accomplishment. New wonders open to us as we paddle in the backwaters of the river: churning swarms of baby bullheads ... the shy Great Blue Heron taking flight...large carp startled as our canoe silently glides over them and the water boils as they flee leaving a trail of mud and bubbles ... turtles sunning on logs ... deer coming down to the water to drink ... beaver dams—those marvels of engineering ... and deep water on the outside bends of the river inviting contemplation.

233

I hear the sound of water. Colin has launched upon his voyage of education. Not quite a brilliant mind perhaps—but determined, tenacious, thirsty for knowledge and willing to pay the price to become a learned person—long grueling hours of study and research. It's now his senior year in high school. He's president of the student body, of his senior class, of the Key Club, and the National Honor Society. He is editor of his Mt. Clemens High School paper, "The Mirror."

"Colin, you're working too hard. You're taking on too much," I say to him as he works past two in the morning.

"It's OK, Dad. The more I have on my resume, the more likely I'll be accepted at Harvard. Then I can cut back on my involvements." Colin almost made it to Harvard, but has now finished his second year at University of Michigan. Entirely on his own, he plans a year's overseas study at University of Leeds in England. Vonda and I watch his huge jet thunder skyward from the runway of Metropolitan Airport in Detroit. Our throats tighten and our eyes fill with hot tears as his plane becomes a speck in the far distance. Now a thin vapor trail is the only evidence of his flight to the other side of the Atlantic.

He crosses the ocean again coming home after a long lonely year, but he pulls it off as he always seems to when he makes up his mind. He squeezes in a trip to the mainland of Europe, visits Paris, mountain climbs near the Matterhorn and comes back with photographs he took which reveal his own unique perspective on things. He comes back somehow different. A bit distant? Not taking his usual delight in life? Maybe it's only our imagination. We miss his frequent laughter—his eager sharing of his experiences with us. A year passes. He graduates from University of Michigan. Is he drifting away from us, from his friends, from his plans for law school? The difference is becoming more pronounced. We still can't define it.

Colin crosses the Atlantic a third time. This time, to our utter amazement, as a member of the U.S. Army. Our son, the Viet Nam War Protester, has done the unthinkable and enlisted for military service. We wonder how he got past the military entrance exams as the difference in him has become more obvious. Our wondering is not to last long. His stint in Germany is cut short by hospitalization there and in the Psych Ward of Walter Reed Army Hospital in Washington, D.C. The army doctors have a label for it—schizophrenia.

The waters of his life become more disturbed—more ominous. After months of treatment and hospitalization at Walter Reed, Colin receives his medical discharge from the army. He seems remote ... detached. Through the good offices of a friend he is able to take on a responsible job with General Motors in Warren. He does well for a while. But then he has several relapses, hospitalizations, and episodes of multiple personalities at home. Our lives are all centered on his illness.

We schedule an appointment with his Harvard educated psychiatrist. "Dr. Day, we need for you to level with us. Is there any hope for Colin? What's his prognosis?"

"Do you really *want* to know?" she asks.

We nod.

"Of young men who have this syndrome 80%, plus or minus, wind up taking their own lives. The other 20%, plus or minus, wind up as loners—sleeping under bridges, eating out of garbage cans, in and out of trouble with the law, in and out of hospitals. No exceptions!"

Not the answer we hoped for. It's hard to believe it could be true in Colin's case. He'd not seemed depressed in our presence or about to give up in his struggle against the schizophrenia.

Weeks pass. Colin returns to our home from the hospital when his Blue Cross medical insurance runs out. Each week I drive him to Glen Eden Psychiatric Hospital in Warren for outpatient counseling. Then, without warning, without a word being spoken, it happens.

We're driving home on the Ford Expressway. I'd just looked at the speedometer. We're traveling just over 50 miles an hour near the Ten Mile Road Exit when Colin suddenly opens the door and rolls out onto the highway.

It's like a nightmare in slow motion. I look in the rear-view mirror and see his body bouncing over and over on the pavement. Cars swerve to miss him like water bugs scattering on a pond. I pull to the shoulder about 50 yards further south, unable to believe this is for real—trying to steel myself against what I might be about to see. Colin is slumped near the base of a freeway sign—dazed, but conscious. I cannot believe it but he stands as I come near. I put my arms around him gently—certain he's sustained fatal internal injuries. All I can manage is a foolish, "Colin, why did you do that?"

He tells his Aunt Lorna later, "The voices told me to do it."

"Colin, what happened? What were you doing?" the doctor at St. John's Hospital in Detroit asks.

"I was doing studies of bodies in motion," is his reply.

"His only injuries are abrasions on his buttocks and shoulder," the doctor tells us in a consultation room. "We can't keep him here in the hospital. He's an adult. As long as he denies trying to suicide, we have no basis for keeping him. We could be sued!"

Later, during a quiet moment alone, his mother says, "Colin, I hope you never do anything like that again,"

"I don't think I will but I'm not making any promises," he says.

It is about three weeks later now. I hear the sound of water. Colin is showering, "Getting ready to visit a friend, go to my apartment, and take care of some business," he tells us. As he strides out the back door and down the sidewalk dressed in jeans and a blue dress shirt with cuffs rolled up, Vonda says, "Isn't he handsome, Honey?" Where had I heard that before? My mind goes back to day one of his life.

Colin does not return that night. No response to our calls to his apartment. Another sleepless night for Vonda, fitful sleep for me. I get up early. I'm in my office when the call comes from the Macomb County Sheriffs Department. "Mr. Lichtenfelt?"

"Yes."

"Are you Colin's father?"

"Yes."

"We have Colin. Could you please come in and talk with us?"

"Is he dead?"

"Yes."

"Oh, my God! What happened?"

"We'll tell you about it when you come. He didn't suffer."

I hear the waves of Lake Huron swooshing far up on the shore and rattling pebbles as they retreat. Vonda and I and Colin's sister Lisa and brothers Lance and Erich are at the marina in Port Sanilac— on the east coast of Michigan's "thumb." It is mid-October, 1981. Most of the pleasure boats are dry-docked for the winter. The owner of the charter fishing boat *Miss Port Sanilac* just got out of the hospital but he kindly agrees to fire up her dormant engine and take us out on the water to scatter Colin's ashes as Colin had requested in the note he left behind. Vonda carries the shiny canister holding all that is left of our firstborn. The sky is dark gray, but it's not raining.

Lake Huron waves crashing near Lexington, Michigan

The wind groans in a low monotone. Lake Huron heaves with heavy swells as *Miss Port Sanilac* leaves the shelter of the harbor and enters open water. Shortly the pilot shouts over the wind, "Is this okay?"

I shout back, "A little further, please!"

As we travel the bottom of a trough we can scarcely see the buildings on shore. When we rise on the crest of a swell it feels like we are about to be launched skyward.

Another shout over the groaning wind, "This okay?"

"Yes, fine!"

The five of us—parents and siblings—huddle near the stern. We kneel together holding tight to a roof pillar for support in the tossing boat. I say a prayer of thanks for Colin's life and share some lines from Longfellow for whatever comfort they may give. We unseal the silver-colored canister holding Colin's ashes. Erich, Lisa and I take turns, each scattering a portion. Then Lance and the rest of us drop flowers from the spray on Colin's casket on the sullen water. The floating blooms of yellow, bronze and orange mums toss in sharp

237

contrast to the gray water and gray gloomy sky. Lisa shouts through her tears, "Good-by, Colin!"

We keep silence as we head back to the harbor. The heavy thrumming of the engine laboring against the enormous force of the water, and the moaning of the wind combine to drone a slow mournful lament for Colin and for the day we went down to the water six ... and came back five.

In the Presence of Absence

Life is full of suffering. It is also
full of the overcoming of suffering.
— *Helen Keller*

The colored maple leaves have nearly all fallen to the ground now. Only a few still flutter on bare branches. Our family has returned from the harbor at Port Sanilac, where at Colin's written request—his "In the event of my death" note—we have scattered his ashes on Lake Huron from the stern of the charter fishing boat *Miss Port Sanilac*. We took turns scattering his ashes on the water—at the same time scattering the high hopes we held for Colin. His sister, Lisa, speaks for us all above the wailing wind: "Goodbye Colin." His brothers, Lance and Erich, watch silently with unfocused eyes. Constriction pains our throats with its stranglehold as we return to the harbor—our eyes full of burning tears.

I'm remembering the words of Samuel Beckett, "I can't go on. I can't go on. I'll go on." The calls for a pastor's services continue. I have to go on. Today I'm driving to Bon Secours Hospital in Grosse Pointe to visit an at-risk parishioner. I pass by Mack Avenue and go east to the more beautiful Lakeshore Drive, and follow it south along the edge of Lake St. Clair. It makes me feel closer to Colin. By now some of his ashes may have passed under the beautiful Blue Water Bridge at Port Huron linking Michigan with Canada, south on the St. Clair River, to Lake St. Clair. Eventually the water may take some of his ashes down the Detroit River to Lake Erie, down the Niagara River and over the roaring Niagara Falls. On through Lake Ontario, up the mighty St. Lawrence River and into the cold North Atlantic. There's a sort of beauty and omnipresence about the whole panorama that opens me up to Infinity. I remember the words of Kahlil Gibran, "Life and death are one, even as the river and the sea are one." I like that.

Grief does strange things to people—our minds are still playing tricks on us. We see Colin in stores—full six foot three inches—smiling, striding toward us, but no, it's not Colin. It's someone else's son. Colin died. Remember? *Oh, get the phone. Maybe it's Colin.* I

239

forgot again. He died. *Next time I see Colin I'll have to tell him....* Why can't I get it through my head? He's dead. Grief makes grown men and women cry. Makes a father angry. Makes a mother not want to live. Takes away your sleep. Your appetite. Your sex drive—when your tears flow at the memory that this bonding was how his life began. Makes you feel like a broken strand of beads with parts of you scattering every which way. Vonda sees Black-Eyed Susans blooming in a yard—instantly her tears gush as she remembers the last bouquet Colin brought her were Black-Eyed Susans he picked for her from the lot behind his apartment. Will we ever get ourselves together again?

Judi Quatrain told us after she saw us standing together in front of Colin's casket in the funeral home, "It made me think of you standing in front of Colin's crib looking at your newborn child." We ask ourselves why the crib and the casket have to be so close to each other. Our lives are all jumbled up. Children are supposed to bury their parents.

I officiate at the wedding of a young couple. Of course the groom is tall with brown eyes and brown hair like Colin's. I try to maintain a professional composure. Try to keep my mind on the wedding and off Colin. It becomes doubly difficult when the bride's father sings his baritone solo, *Sunrise, Sunset*," from *Fiddler on the Roof.* That song nearly undoes me on a good day, but now I nearly disintegrate. My atoms are coming apart as the father sings of childhood and youth and fatherly affection. I'm thinking *this could be Colin. He should be the one getting married.* But no, he'll never know the softness of a wife. Never hold his children on his lap and hug them and laugh with them. He'll never hold the office he trained for. Never see another autumn with leaves in flame and bonfire skies. Never watch fluffy white snowflakes swirling around black tree trunks in winter.

Vonda and I review the sympathy cards and letters sent by family and friends with their welcome written messages. One says, "The world has lost a special person." That says what we're feeling. Another card says, "Grief is not forever—love is." Right now grief has a forever feel to it. We hope it changes.

It doesn't help that the "happy" holidays are just around the corner: Thanksgiving, Christmas, New Year's Day—days we usually associate with joy and celebration but following a death they only intensify the pain, and become difficult to bear.

Still, it's not like we have to bear them alone. Unlike some lonely grievers, we have reinforcements—angels, agents of God's love and healing in the form of caring parishioners and friends. Those who came to the memorial service and reminded us again of the power of a touch, a hug, of clasped hands, a look and smiles accompanied by tears.

We feel we're walking in a strength not our own—strength originating in the many acts of kindness and compassion from family and friends. We need, and are grateful for, every sympathy card and letter—every hug and every word of appreciation for how Colin's life touched another for good. We're grateful for people who asked questions and let us talk—for every person who signed the register at the funeral home and Colin's memorial service. Vonda said she never realized how much just a person's signature on a line could mean—even if we hadn't seen them or talked with them. She determined to remember that when other families had losses.

Jean Dezur's husband Don died the same night as Colin. I was with her that night and came home to learn of Colin's death early the next morning. She attended her husband's funeral on Saturday and Colin's on Sunday. That's love and caring support.

We had Joyce Ross who spent two days with us addressing, and mailing out acknowledgements to people for their kindness. We had jobs to go back to that helped take our minds off the pain. We were surrounded by people who, at this time in our lives, had an uncanny sense of when to stand by us and when to give us space for private grieving. We had the great hymns of the church, two of which we sang together at Colin's memorial service: "How Firm a Foundation," and "Be Still My Soul." We had the healing power of poetry and prayers.

We had Colin's friends telling us that he often spoke of how much his family meant to him. And his friend Mark Brewer whose efforts established a scholarship for aspiring writers in Colin's name.

We had many helpful books by people who had walked this valley before us: *The Bereaved Parent*, by Harriet Sarnoff Schiff whom we heard in person...*After Suicide*, by John Hewett...and *When Bad Things Happen to Good People,* by Rabbi Harold Kushner. Later I heard Kushner speak at Temple Beth El in Southfield. I pressed my way up to see him following his presentation. I had to thank this man who had suffered the early loss of his son to progeria (premature aging) for what his book had meant to me. He gripped my hand, looked me straight in the eyes and said, "Thank you. I'm sorry you needed it."

So many good things happened to us. Royal Synwolt, assistant to the bishop, and his wife Margaret took us to Topinka's Restaurant in Farmington during the holidays. He just said, "Tell us how the two of you are doing." And he let us talk without any effort to "make it right." And that helped make it right.

And early on the morning of August 18, Vonda got a call from Bill Quick, pastor of Metropolitan United Methodist in Detroit. "Vonda, this is Bill Quick. How are you doing?"

"Frankly, Bill, this is not one of my better days. Today is Colin's birthday, and I'm having a rough go of it."

"I know. That's why I called." Bill listened while Vonda poured out her pain. His call gave her permission to tell her friends, "You know, the nicest thing happened this morning. Bill Quick called and…." His call was the scalpel that lanced the boil of that day's pain, allowing it to drain and healing to follow."

If you could have read my thoughts during those days you'd know I was feeling uncertain about my role in the ministry. Do I belong any more? Do I have the heart for it? How could people put confidence in a minister who couldn't prevent the suicide of his own son?

I remember how I got up early on the morning after Colin's funeral—couldn't sleep anyway. I went into the family room in my pajamas, sat down on the white sofa and had a good cry—and I swore I wasn't going to let his death put me down for the count. Somehow I'd find a way to turn this loss into a plus for others. There's a thin line between sacrifice and waste. I didn't want Colin's death to be a waste.

To my surprise, rather than shying away, people began to open up to me. "You know, Don, I seldom talk about it, but my father took his own life when I was nine." "You know, my brother wasn't right when he came home from the war, and one day he went into his bedroom and put a bullet in his head." "When I was little my dad lined us kids up in the kitchen, held a gun to our heads and said, 'Which one of you wants to be the first to die?' Then he swallowed poison and died a miserable death right in front of us kids." "We never had a clue anything was wrong until our son hanged himself in the basement. He never left a note so we still don't understand."

What I thought would be a barrier to my usefulness became an opportunity for me to listen to others spill out their bottled up pain—to enter their grief without having to have an answer. Early on I attended a meeting of The Compassionate Friends in Saginaw. I was impressed with the effectiveness of this self-help organization for bereaved parents. I shared my story in a small group session, and was invited to lead a session at a state-wide meeting in Ann Arbor. From there I was invited to lead a seminar at a regional meeting in Columbus, Ohio where I was one of the lesser lights in a program featuring Dr. Elizabeth Kubler-Ross, author of the classic *On Death and Dying*, and popularizer of the five stages of grief.

Back home in Harper Woods I began to realize there were hurting people by the hundreds all around us. I proposed to our Grosse Pointe Ministerial Association that we sponsor an annual grief seminar especially for those who had recently lost a family member, or close friend. They embraced the idea. We secured a well-known grief counselor to address the first seminar. People turned out and shared their raw pain with each other, and appeared to leave with a degree of comfort. Almost without my knowing it a door was opening wide for me to put my own grief to good use.

October 15, 1982—the first anniversary of Colin's death. We are not just *thinking* about it, we are *reliving* the experience. About now we received word of his death from the Sheriff's Department. About now we were shown his body in the morgue. About now we would be reading his suicide note. Now we would have been scattering his ashes in Lake Huron and throwing those bronze, orange and yellow mums on the water.

One thoughtful friend made it a point to send a simple handwritten note: "Though these days have a meaning you alone can understand, someone else remembers and wants to let you know." How could we not feel cared for?

Each anniversary of Colin's birth and death still bring memories and tears. We still live with our questions. We don't know as many things for sure as we once thought we did. But we got through that most difficult of all times—thanks, in large part, to the love, concern and support of our church family and other caring people who surrounded us, held us up, and never let us down. That—insofar as we can tell—is the way God works: through the loving kindness of caring people for each other.

243

August, 1982

Life must go on.
I forget just why.
—*Edna St. Vincent Millay*

It's mid-afternoon, August 1982—nearly ten months after our son Colin's death by suicide. We're still feeling the shock and depression. Vonda is only now beginning to let go of the thought that she doesn't want to go on living without Colin. I'm still feeling angry that one so gifted, so full of promise fell prey to schizophrenia and too-early death.

I'm finding it painful trying to be a clergyman in these circumstances—trying to feel compassion for the grief and sorrows of others while my own is dominant. I'm not here in the church office because I want to be.

I'm sitting here in an oak swivel chair at a big roll-top desk and staring at mounds of things I should be tending to but can't bring myself to care about. I feel like I'm fading into the gauzy light coming through the sheer curtains. Numbing out. Don't want to think about anything. Don't feel like doing any thing. Wish I didn't have responsibility for anything or anyone. Life hurts too much. Got to numb the pain. No, that doesn't work. Got to face the pain. Deal with it. Work through it. Got to keep busy. Can't give up. Do something. Anything. Just keep busy. Start with something easy. But what?

My eyes scan untidy stacks of papers on the large desk. Where to start? Annual Conference reports? Last thing in the world I want to do right now. Pastor's report to the Administrative Board? Can't stand the thought of it. Here's a note on a wrinkled scrap of paper—been sitting there for days. "Call Beth Miller about nursery school." OK, start there. That's easy enough. No big deal.

I scan the M section of my Rolodex for Miller's number. Here it is—Miller, Thomas, "Tom," 10907 Nottingham, Detroit. I dial their number with limited enthusiasm and get ready to use my professional happy voice. Several rings, then an unfamiliar voice answers, "Miller's."

"Hello. This is Don Lichtenfelt, pastor of Redeemer Church. May I speak with Beth, please?"

"Just a minute. I'll get her." I hear hurried footsteps clicking on a hard floor, a door creaking open, and a muted, "Beth. Telephone. It's your minister."

More footsteps and a husky, "Hello, Don."

"Beth, you sound out of breath."

"Don, Tom had a heart attack. EMS just left. I was getting in the car to go to the hospital."

"I won't hold you up. What hospital?"

"Holy Cross in Detroit."

"Okay, I'll see you there. I'm on my way."

I get in our white Buick and head west on Eight Mile Road cheating on pink lights when I can. Now south on Van Dyke to where you can see Holy Cross sitting way back on the left. I hang a left on Outer Drive just beating the red light. Two short blocks and another left into the hospital parking lot. I pull into the best available parking space. The sign says, "No Visitors." I pull out my "Clergy Emergency" card and put in on the dash. Now I'm moving up on the elevator to the Cardiac floor. The door glides open and I see Beth sitting alone in the lounge, eyes brimming with tears—soggy handkerchief in her hand. I sit down beside her and give her a long hug.

"I don't know if he's going to make it. It looks pretty bad," she moans.

"Do the kids know yet?"

"No. It was so sudden—there wasn't time."

A tearful neighbor gets off the elevator and joins us. I get the Miller children's numbers from Beth and head for the pay phone. The neighbor and Beth embrace each other and don't let go. They are still gripping each other's hands when I return.

"Okay, I got through to Phil. He'll call the others. They'll be here as soon as they can."

An unsmiling nurse comes through the Cardiac Care door. "Mrs. Miller?" Beth stands up—a stricken look on her face. Her body stiffens as though to fend off unwanted news. The nurse rests her hand on Beth's arm and looks at her with soft eyes. "Mrs. Miller, we're working with your husband. He's still alive, but we're not getting much response. We'll keep you posted." She gives Beth's hand a long squeeze and turns and walks briskly through the same door.

We sit down. Beth breaks the silence giving voice to her slow meandering thoughts. "I can't believe this is happening to us. He's only sixty-one. No sign he had a heart problem. Just keeled over in the bathroom and hit his head on the tub. Big cut over his eye. Ambulance got there right away though. Guess we won't be going to Minnesota next week like we planned. Hope the kids get here soon."

The three of us pass half an hour in sparse and tense conversation between us. Waiting. Waiting. Waiting. Finally the door opens again. More slowly this time. The nurse walks in our direction. We know by the droop of her head and shoulders that it's over. "Mrs. Miller, I'm sorry. He didn't make it. It was massive and nothing we did could pull him through. If you want to see him you can, but I have to warn you it isn't pretty. You know he has that big cut over his eye and there are still tubes in his nose and throat."

Beth wants to see Tom for herself. She asks me to go with her. The nurse leaves us alone beside his gurney. The nurse was right—not pretty. Strange medicinal odors mingle with the stench of vomit. There's a stained and crumpled sheet over Tom's hips. The rest of his body is bare. His skin is a light blue-gray. His head tilts back at an awkward angle. Eyes half-open. Congealed in a final stare. A large plastic tube dangles helplessly from his open, slightly bloody mouth—as though admitting failure.

Beth touches Tom's arm lightly. A far off look in her eyes. Tears flowing slowly down both cheeks. This is what is left of her husband of thirty-nine years—the man who short minutes ago was moving around their house ... talking...laughing...planning their vacation in Minnesota.

We leave Holy Cross each in our own cars. Beth—devastated—along with her children who arrived too late to see their father alive. I am alone with my thoughts. I'm wondering why I chose that precise moment to call her after I'd put the call off for days. Seconds later and she would have been out her drive and I wouldn't have been at her side.

I know one thing for sure today—I'm not the only one hurting. You find hurting people everywhere. The hurt doesn't always show. But it's there. It may be deep within. But it's there. You can count on it.

God Bless This Mess

There is delight in disorder.
—*Emily Dickinson*

One of the advantages of being disorderly is that
one is constantly making exciting discoveries.
—*A.A. Milne*

I catch a lot of good natured flak about the constant clutter on my desk here at Harper Woods United Methodist. One concerned member donated a "God Bless This Mess" sign which only mildly shamed me. Jean Bricker proved more empathetic. She promised to give me another sign she'd seen that says, "If a cluttered desk indicates a cluttered mind, what does an empty desk indicate?" I like that a lot.

Another member, whose name I will not deign to mention, gave me a cartoon with two desks in a room. A secretary sat at the neat desk and was answering the phone. The other desk was piled so high with clutter you couldn't see if anyone was seated there. The secretary was saying to the person on the other end of the line, "I don't know if he's here or not. Let me check." Now that's definitely over the top. It borders on insult.

Joyce Ross, our former church secretary in Utica, was a radical neat nick. Once she walked into my office with a stack of mimeograph copies she'd just printed. She looked at the cluttered surface of my four by six foot desk top. "Where do you want me to put this?" she asked...and snickered.

For revenge I went out and bought her a Lucy (of *Peanuts* cartoon fame) poster with the caption, "A clean desk is a sign of a sick mind." I posted it directly over Joyce's desk in the hope that it would bring her back to the real world.

As I survey the mounds of clutter on my desk I know my old scoutmaster would weep for me after all the times I recited "A scout is (amongst other things) neat!" It's just as well that I'm not a card carrying scout anymore.

Mine is not a prestige desk with which to impress the public. It's a working desk. It's my work shop and workbench all in one. There sits the postal scales. We send out dozens of personal letters nearly every week to affirm people who have done nice things for others, to the bereaved, to those celebrating birthdays and anniversaries and those who are to be congratulated for their accomplishments. Next to the scales is a package of two hundred envelopes for an upcoming special offering for people with mentally handicapping conditions.

Here are two phones. One carries a lot of interpersonal conversations concerning problem situations. The other carries a daily recorded *Dial a Prayer* message to those who find it gives them a boost for living. Some have reported it helped pull them through tough times.

There are three piles of books. I read some to nourish my own mind and heart, others are loan books for people they may help, and others for sermon preparation. Preparing a sermon each week is a lot like turning out a weekly term paper—and you know how much clutter term papers generate.

Here's my clipboard with memos from funeral homes, items about people with problems not unlike my own, and from various organizations—usually soliciting our help. Much of it is "sad but necessary to deal with" stuff.

There in the middle you can see a corner of the *Michigan Christian Advocate*. It's our Michigan United Methodist newspaper. It reminds our congregation and me that there's far more to our church than what goes on here at Vernier Road and the Ford Expressway, and that the sun never sets on the work of the church. The sometimes sharp-toned letters to the editor remind me we're a pluralistic church with many points of view. Sometimes I wish truth were simpler—but it's not.

Here are bills for our treasurer and a letter to our Youth Fellowship reminding them of their CROP (Christian Rural Overseas Program) Walk-a-thon. Here's another letter from a lady asking me to take communion to a shut-in friend and one to the six of us that will be attending the Congress on Stewardship in Flint shortly.

In addition there are cassette tapes, magazines and brochures I take to hospitals or insert in letters and a pocket prayer book I dip into when I'm "standing in the need of prayer." Here are memos about births and baptisms, deaths and funerals, problems and joys. And, o yes, photos of the five new members who joined recently. I was supposed to post them on the bulletin board and haven't yet. I'd better get them up before they're lost in the kerfuffle. Sometimes I feel like T.S. Eliot had me in mind when he wrote about being "distracted from distraction by distraction."

Here's a portfolio on *Suicide, Helplessness and Despair* from a seminar I attended at St. Joseph's Hospital in Mt. Clemens last week and materials on "Alternatives to Prison" I picked up after an informative program on the theme at the Grosse Pointe Ministerial Association yesterday.

What some would call the "mess" on my desk—in their more charitable moments—is "creative clutter" to me. It says a lot about what I do—as well as what I don't get done. It speaks of what Redeemer Church family is and does.

No, it's not a neat desk and it's not a prestige desk. I can't always find the material you ask for right away—even though I know it's there somewhere. But I like it, and I feel comfortable amidst this clutter because it's about my life and my work as a pastor.

I know the "God Bless This Mess" plaque wasn't given me as a compliment. More likely it hangs there as an earnest prayer from the donor. I accept that and I hope Jean Bricker delivers that other plaque right away—the one that asks "If a cluttered desk indicates a cluttered mind, what does an empty desk indicate?" I think those two plaques belong together.

The Return of the Memories

The past is not dead.
In fact, it's not even past.
—*William Faulkner*

The holiest of all holidays are those
kept by ourselves in silence and apart;
the secret anniversaries of the heart.
—*Henry Wadsworth Longfellow*

There is no overlooking the time of year our son, Colin, died. It happened in mid-October when maple leaves turned to flame and did their pirouettes in the autumn air on their return to the cool earth. There is no hiding that his death was a suicide. For practical reasons Vonda and I concealed his schizophrenia as best we could while he was alive.

Since his death in 1981, this season—which has always been my favorite—remains the annual reminder of our son's death. The intervening years have not erased the memories of that morning—though sometimes I wish they could.

As surely as the leaves fall each October—so the memories come unbidden every year. Every year a different assortment, but the memories come back—randomly—in an ever shifting collage.

I can still hear the soft voice of the officer who called: "Mr. Lichtenfelt, this is the Macomb County Sheriff's Department. Are you Colin's father?"

"Yes."

"We have Colin. Can you come in and talk with us?"

"Is he dead?"

"Yes."

"My God, what happened?"

"We'll talk about it when you come in. He didn't suffer."

The Sheriff's Department had called our home first and asked for me. Vonda ran the short distance from our house to the church office. As I hung up she came into my office—her face distorted in pain. "Is it about Colin?"

* * *

250

We began to stumble our way into our new role as bereaved parents. At first we felt total shock and numbness—as though our world had exploded and we just stood, uncomprehending, in a dream state. Not knowing what to do. We drove to the Sheriff's Department in Mt. Clemens as though anesthetized. There two investigators led us into an office and told us how Colin had attached a vacuum cleaner hose to the exhaust of his silver AMC Pacer and fed it inside the car through the rear hatch.

We told them what led to this day, about Colin's high achievements as a scholar and leader in high school and his studies at University of Michigan. His serious focus on learning and his year of study at University of Leeds in England. The strange personality changes before graduation from University of Michigan. How Colin—the Vietnam war protester—veered off course, enlisted in the army and found himself in Germany where his mind failed him and the army returned him to the psychiatric ward at Walter Reed Army Hospital in Washington D.C., with a diagnosis of schizophrenia. His medical discharge. About his new job at General Motors where he seemed to do well for a while. His relapse and treatment in Glen Eden—a private psychiatric hospital. His attempt at suicide two weeks earlier when he threw himself from the car I was driving on the Ford Expressway—having just slowed down to fifty miles an hour for the Ten Mile Road Exit. How I saw him in the rear view mirror tumbling over and over on the highway like a rag doll. The cars swerving back and forth like water beetles to avoid hitting him. How doctors released him from St. John's Hospital in Detroit suffering only abrasions on his buttocks and shoulders…unable to keep him because he would not acknowledge his action as a suicide attempt and because, as an adult, Colin could sue them if they kept him.

I remember with gratitude how the investigators questioned us with extreme gentleness and kindness and then released us to walk across to the morgue where Colin's body was being kept. It had to be a dream—the attendant pulling open the large drawer holding the lifeless body of our firstborn—his face reddened by carbon monoxide

We drove to his apartment to see if Colin left a note. There a sense of his absence clung to everything like an echo without a voice. I opened the center drawer of the old roll top desk I'd refinished and loaned to him. I picked up and read the salutation of a full page letter written on college ruled note paper. It began, "Hello, it's me." Foolish old father, I thought, *Nobody begins a suicide note that way*. It would be "Dear Mom and Dad." I set it aside not knowing it was what we were looking for and did not read it until the day after his funeral.

I'd never read a suicide note before and I hope I never read another even though there was a haunting beauty about it. Colin began, "Everything is in order," and he wrote about how beautiful a thing life is and how he'd experienced so many wonderful things in his twenty five years.

His second paragraph began "Everything is in disorder." He wrote about the pain, humiliation and rejection he'd suffered because of schizophrenia—the close friends who now avoided him...and how he'd lost the will to fight.

I remembered feeling I'd betrayed Colin the day I drove him from Pontiac General Hospital to the Pontiac State Mental Hospital and hugged him goodbye in a ward where a group of patients were wailing like banshees as they ran through the hall swinging their arms over our heads and nearly striking us. Colin put his hand on my shoulder and said, "It's okay, Dad, it was worse than this at Walter Reed Army Hospital."

I remembered how Dr. Ruth Day, his Harvard educated psychiatrist, described Colin's plight—his difficulty in sorting out perceptions. She said, "His mind is like a TV set receiving six or seven channels at once and they're all rolling." If I had been in Colin's situation I might have made the same choice as he did—only sooner.

Our muddle continued with hasty funeral preparations and shared hugs and tears at the Harris Funeral Home in Detroit where I looked down into Colin's casket as though in a mirror and viewed the wreck of the son I once regarded as a new and improved version of myself. I felt like a wrecked father.

I remember how when we left the funeral home and saw all the cars flowing along Eight Mile Road and crowds of people shopping at Eastland Mall, I wanted to put my flashers on, lay on the horn and get out and hold my hands out and scream, "Stop! Stop everything! Don't you know our son died?"

I remember how I drove the car Colin died in to the home of a friend who graciously offered to clean it up for sale...and thinking as I drove, *this is exactly where Colin sat when he died. Part of me died here too.*

I remembered standing in my grandmother's attic after her death some years earlier. So many dead flies lay on the windowsills and wondering *in the end...are we any different from flies?* I'm wondering those same thoughts again.

* * *

An overflow crowd of friends and relatives came to Colin's memorial service to be of support and to place this incredible event in the context of our religious faith—a faith I decided needed some revision and less certainty. I take comfort in the words of the clergywoman who said, "The opposite of faith is not doubt. The opposite of faith is certainty."

We found comfort in the fact that even though our family circle and our circle of friendships had been broken by death, they were still circles and they still included Colin—though in a different way.

I will always remember the Edwardian bouquet Dr. and Mrs. Bob Ward (pastor of Grosse Pointe First United Methodist) sent to our home with the note, "The pain you bear is not yours alone but is shared by those who know and love you." We placed the bouquet in the center of our dining room table where it could grab out attention. I read that note several times a day for the nearly two weeks the bouquet lasted.

I can still hear Colin's friend Cathy Yarbro singing "Morning Has Broken" at the memorial service with tears in her eyes and in her voice. Ken Bricker, another of Colin's friends, playing piano accompaniment—both of them about to lose their composure. Colin would have liked their gift of love for sure. He played Cat Steven's recording of that song on a regular basis. Loved it. We all loved it. Still do.

I recall our three clergy friends who shared in Colin's memorial service: Ken Harden who baptized Colin in Iowa and befriended him over his lifetime and Jack Harnish our closest clergy neighbor as well as family friend and Colin's Uncle Ray. We felt our pain softened when we learned that after the service they gave way to their feelings and sobbed together in the church office. A grief shared may not be a grief halved but it is a grief somewhat reduced.

* * *

So each year during late autumn the memories return like falling leaves. Some have already composted and become part of the soil of our lives. Some have not been assimilated. Those memories make me the doubting believer I am and I go on believing that faith is an "in spite of" sort of thing and that when we touch hands in fellowship and love we discover the miracle of living.

We make it with the help of our friends.

Silence at the Seminar on Suicide

Silence is a statement that is open
to gross misinterpretation.
—*Craig Bruce*

There is more in my silence
than in my words.
—*Kahlil Gibran*

The phone rang late one evening just as we were going to bed. "Gotta be trouble," I said to Vonda as I picked up the receiver. It was trouble. Stan Cooper, a parishioner and career army man from a previous parish, got right to the point, "Don, I want you to talk with me. I'm thinking of taking my own life tonight and I have the means to do it on the table in front of me."

I waved Vonda on to bed without me, knowing this will be a long conversation *if all goes right.*

During the next hour or so I half expected to hear a pistol shot and Stan's body thump against the floor. I did the best job of listening and reflecting I could so late at night. I hoped Stan would feel relieved after pouring out his story and would put his gun back where it belonged.

Sleep eluded me much of that night and in the days ahead I knew Stan was still high risk. Would I get belated word he had taken his own life at his new home in Virginia? No word came. He did not provide me with his phone number or address.

Suicide concerns me both as a pastor and as a person. Thoughts of suicide were my constant companion for an extended time in my early childhood. I drew up a serious plan. I'd overdose on medication, climb in the bathtub, slit my wrists and pull the radio into the water with me. More than once I went into my father's bedroom to find his .38 revolver under his stack of handkerchiefs, put its cool snout to my temple, snug the trigger and wonder what it would be like not to be. Years passed before those urges left me.

My mother shared some secret information with me when I became a late teen-ager—my older sister Clarice (according to Mother, Clarice was more of a mother to me than Mom was) had made two attempts on her life. Once with rope. Once with poison. Mother went into no further detail. Given our family's penchant for secrecy I'm surprised she shared that much. But that helped me understand her anxiety when I talked of suicide.

During my pastoral ministry I've conducted funeral services for around two dozen persons who took their own lives. To my great sorrow my ninety-one-year-old grandfather and our twenty-five-year-old son also took their own lives.

I took a risk when I attended a seminar on *Suicide, Hopelessness and Despair* about fifteen months after our son Colin's death by suicide but I was eager to understand all I could in my own need and I wanted to help those survivors of suicide who sought me out when they learned of my experience.

St. Joseph's Hospital East in Mt. Clemens sponsored the event for the benefit of doctors, clergy of all faiths, social workers, and nurses. Forty-some of us gathered to hear Dr. Kamal Hanna, head of psychiatry at St. Joe's, and a handful of other speakers. Dr. Hanna's opening bothered me. He smiled what seemed to me an inappropriate grin and said, "Now suicide is a very interesting *phenomenon*." He seemed amused by the thought. His continuous smile told me that—initially at least—he was taking a strictly clinical approach and I might have to adjust to that as one whose recent experience of suicide had been anything but clinical.

Dr. Hanna's overview of suicide touched upon many aspects of the "phenomenon:" Estimates of the large numbers of people who attempt suicide each year compared with the numbers who succeed. (More actual suicides *each year* than were killed in the entire Vietnam War—if you take into account the many single car accidents by teen-agers that experts believe *weren't accidents*.) How more women than men attempt suicide but more men than women actually kill themselves. How men usually choose the messier and more certain methods. How attempted suicide is often a disguised cry for help rather than an actual desire to die. How members of certain professions, including medicine, are more likely to suicide than others. The obvious symptoms that a person may be considering suicide and Dr. Hanna's flat-out statement that *all depressed persons are potential suicides.*

Dr. Hanna took pains to point out that all suicides were by no means alike—some caused by mental illness—often schizophrenia, as our son Colin's was. Other deaths were due to intentional drug abuse, some the result of extreme rage and some for revenge against a person who would have to bear the onus of the suicide's death for the rest of their lives. Still others due to sheer ego—as when one person gets a promotion or an award that another person felt belonged to them.

"Then," he said, "There are those 'mystery suicides' where everything seems to be going well in a person's life and they kill themselves without leaving a note or a clue. These, he said, are especially difficult for family and friends who are tormented by their 'whys' for as long as they live." This was the first indication I saw that Dr. Hanna might be departing from *statistics* to deal with the *feelings* of the survivors of suicide.

Yes, I had to agree with Dr. Hanna. *"Suicide is a very interesting phenomenon"*—so long as you can discuss it clinically. Yes, I need to have empathy for persons whose profession keeps them immersed in the hopelessness and despair and the constant threat of a client's completing suicide—after all I'm one of them. But there was one phrase that came up again and again in every speaker's lecture and it bothered me. The phrase *"committed suicide," "committed suicide," "committed suicide"* echoed like a refrain in every speech. It felt to me like an accusation, a judgment.

I am not one who often stands up and challenges the "prevailing wind" but I had to speak up. When the time came for questions and comments I stood up with my heart in my throat and on the verge of tears. I said, "Several months ago I would be talking just as others here today. I would not say "suicide" without saying "committed" first. But today is different—today I'm the father of a son who took his own life and the words *committed suicide* feel harsh and judgmental to me. I know it's perfectly correct English but the word *committed* is almost always used with crime. We say someone committed rape, or murder, or arson, or war crimes."

"I would like to see us, as members of helping professions, use language that sounds less accusatory and more gentle to those in grief—maybe *completed suicide*, or just *suicided*, or *took his own life* and not add to the pain that survivors of suicide are already feeling.

The convener thanked me for my remarks and said, "Perhaps we all do well to reflect on how we use words and the impact they may have on others".

257

Following further questions and remarks we were released to visit the washrooms and come back for a tasty lunch provided by St. Joseph's. During the entire lunch break and the afternoon session nobody said anything to me about my remarks—not a word like, "Sorry to hear about your son. How old was he?" Or, "I appreciate your sharing with us as you did." Or, "Are you comfortable if I ask about your son?" I felt like a man who'd just lost an arm—and nobody mentioned it because they thought I wouldn't notice it so long as nobody talked about it.

Their silence puzzled me and began to pain me. Had I said something foolish and inappropriate to the situation? Had I unintentionally given offense? Is their silence a sign of anger? Was it simply a non-issue to them? Several times that afternoon speakers stumbled over the word *committed* or used a gentler word.

Then I tried to put myself in their situation. I thought of situations where I'd kept quiet for fear of saying the wrong thing and making things worse. That's something I do more often than I care to admit.

I thought of the time I did a perfectly okay thing for a pastor. I drew upon an ancient church prayer to the Holy Spirit just before delivering a Sunday sermon. It begins, "Come, Holy Spirit, come. Come as the fire and burn. Come as the wind and purify. Come as the light and illuminate…." I got no further than the word "burn" when I regretted choosing that prayer because seated in the congregation was a member whose 18 month old daughter died from a scalding accident earlier that month. My words may have struck her like the crack of a bull-whip but I couldn't take them back. I didn't have the courage to apologize for how those words *may have hurt* because *I didn't want to risk adding to her pain.*

What did the silence of those men and women in "helping professions" mean that day? I don't know for sure but I did what I'd want them to do if the situation were reversed. I gave them the benefit of the doubt. I accepted their silence as not wanting to make things worse for a grieving father. And I hoped those with whom I'd been silent in the past would take my silence in similar fashion.

Saying Goodbye

Penultimate! Was it in fifth grade that word was first dropped on me? Anyway, I was impressed with this new polysyllabic puzzler. Didn't have the slightest idea what it meant. (At that point Mary Poppin's "supercalifragilisticexpialidocious" would have left me spastic.) Now that I'm fifty-five, I finally have a chance to validate the wisdom of my fifth grade teacher by using this hardly-ever-used word.

Penultimate means "next to the last." This is my penultimate month in my penultimate pastorate.

One beloved woman who really likes me, but usually pretends to be my thorn in the flesh said, "Good riddance! We're not going to miss you at all." Another said, "I hear you're leaving us. I hope you don't feel good about it." Somewhere in between, I suspect—at least, I hope—is where most of the church family find themselves.

My wife is the nearest to a basket case I've seen her in our nearly thirty-five years of marriage. These eight years in Harper Woods are the longest she's ever lived in one place in her life. Sometimes she cries when we talk about leaving. She'd rather stay here until retirement. Using my worst counseling technique I've tried to override her tears using reason, ridicule, lectures and other equally futile methods.

I, on the other hand, attempt a calm, dispassionate, professional attitude toward moving to another parish. "Like a ripe apple on the end of a branch," is how I describe my feelings. Yet, the tears are always near when I recall how this church family accepted us with such warmth, and stood by us when our son died, when Vonda had her operations for cancer, and the three operations which saved me from certain blindness in both eyes. I wish Redeemer Church were easier to leave. And sometimes I wonder what happens to the "apple" when it "falls off the branch."

The saying, "Every goodbye is like a little death" holds truth. It hurts. But "penultimate" applies to goodbyes too. They are not the end, but transition.

Good memories, and good friendships are a paradise we cannot be driven from … and as the old German proverb puts it, "Those who live in the Lord never see each other for the last time."

Note: This article appeared in the *Redeemer Church Review*, and was printed in the *Michigan Christian Advocate* on May 23, 1988

Royal Oak Years

1988 – 1994

The life of faith is a continually renewed victory over doubt, a continually renewed grasp of meaning in the midst of meaninglessness.
—*Leslie Newbegin*

Not My Usual Self

Love is how you stay alive,
even after you are gone.
— *Morrie Schwartz*

When you are sorrowful look again in your heart,
and you shall see that in truth you are weeping
for that which has been your delight.
— *Kahlil Gibran*

What was happening to me? This had never happened before. This stuttering and stammering. This being filled with emotion which interfered with my ability to speak during a funeral. These long involuntary pauses and biting my lip and wondering if I'd be able to continue without public tears. It took me completely by surprise.

I had conducted several hundred funerals after forty years as a minister—including my mother's and several relatives. Many of those earlier funerals were pretty sad and I've done my share of crying. After Diane Burmeister was killed in a freak farm accident at age four when her daddy was giving her a ride on the tractor I kept my composure until after I got alone following the funeral. Then I sobbed. Likewise after her father was crushed by a truck on his way to Chicago just months later. It's far more difficult to conduct a funeral when you're there as a griever as well as a pastor.

Our family cared for little Julie Wilson several times in our home about the time she learned to walk. Our kids treated her with wonder and awe—as though she were their new little sister. Weeks later she suffered scalding over much of her body. I spent a lot of hurting time in the hospital during those days as she whimpered her just-begun life away. One day I entered her room and found her pediatrician standing by her bed with tears flowing unchecked down his face knowing he could not save her.

Despite my tears before and after Julie's funeral I put on my best professional face, insulated myself from my feelings and conducted the service with hardly a hitch in my voice. That's why, after forty years of this sort of thing I was surprised how full of emotion I was at Bertha Elliott's funeral. I stalled out six or eight times and wasn't sure

I could get a grip on my composure and go on. I did, but with more difficulty than usual.

Some people sneak up on us and take over our hearts before we know what happened and Bertie was such a person to me. She topped out at about five feet two inches and looked like a second cousin to a marshmallow. She wore a nearly perpetual smile which accentuated her prominent dimples. Her freckles matched the reddish tones in her hair and her general look of mischief.

Bertie was one of those delightful persons whose sense of humor and irony canceled out a lot of the downright distasteful things a minister has to put up with. It's a wonder Bertie had any sense of humor when you consider that she was about nine when her father lined up his four kids against the wall in the family kitchen and threatened to kill them all. He put the cold snout of his pistol against Bertie's temple and asked her if she wanted to be first to die. Then he proceeded to consume poison and died a miserable death before his children's eyes. It's beyond my comprehension how she turned out to be the happy laughing lady she became.

People loved being around Bertie. She kept everyone in stitches with her clever sense of humor. Her rapid-fire repartee. Pomposity didn't stand a chance around her. She was as irrepressible as a cork released under water. As a close friend of Marsha, our church secretary, she often dropped in to Marsha's office to chat. If nobody was in my office with me she'd stick her head in and say something like, "It's about time you came in to work," or "There's our under-worked and overpaid pastor sitting there trying to look busy." I felt her words came from a place near her heart and I felt affirmed and warmed by her banter.

I never met Bertie's husband but they say she landed a good man and they had a special relationship until his death thirty some years later. Bertie donated a water-fountain to the church in his memory. I thought of them often when I drank at that fountain with the little memorial plaque in his memory. I found refreshment at that fountain but even more in Bertie's warm friendship and wild sense of humor.

Bertie's two young grandsons lived on Edmund Avenue about ten doors from our home. It was a delight to see her out in the yard wearing a baseball glove and playing catch with the boys or shooting baskets through the hoop mounted on the front of their garage. She was still a dynamo in her early seventies. What must she have been like when she was younger? Following church one Sunday, a relative snapped her photo just as she squared off for mock combat with her brother. Looked like pretty good boxing form to me. Like she could hold her own if she needed to.

Once she sent me a birthday card with an ugly witch on a broomstick on the cover. It read, "I've come to remind you that you're a year older." Inside it said, "It's a nasty job but I sort of enjoy it." Bertie signed it *Broom Hilda* after the cartoon witch with whom she shared a slight resemblance. In jest I began to call her *Attila the Hen* which delighted her—and especially her sister who shared our wacky style of humor.

Bertie always enjoyed verbal sparring but when Reo DuBey died two weeks after offering me some constructive criticism, Bertie warned people, "Whatever you do, don't criticize the minister. Look what happened to Reo."

On my fifty-ninth birthday Bertie and Marcia, our church secretary, took me to lunch at Bill Knapp's Restaurant. The three of us ate and bantered and laughed. As we waited for desert Bertie pulled a small gift package from her purse and slid it toward me on the table. She grinned as she waited for my response upon opening it. She had written, typed and framed a poem for me—a deliberately clumsy parody on Joyce Kilmer's *Trees* which she entitled *A Sentimental Tribute*. It read:

> I think that I shall never see
> Another Preacher quite like thee.
> Thou pickest on me it is true
> So why in heck do I like you?
> Because thou worketh night and day
> To keepeth us from going astray.
> Thou teacheth us what's right and wrong
> Both in scripture and in song.
> But that won't get thee off the hook,
> I still regard thee as a Schnook.
>   (signed) —Broom Hilda

I felt delighted to be immortalized by her poem but sadly Bertie disappeared from our lives almost as quickly as we came to know her. She had delayed visiting her doctor about some unusual stomach problems. I think she had an inkling it was cancer and that it was terminal. If so, she was right on both counts.

Vonda and I visited her several times at Beaumont Hospital. The end came in short weeks. Bertie's only comment to us about her terminal illness, just a day or two before she died, was a tongue in cheek, "Life can be beautiful."

I had officiated at hundreds of funerals prior to Bertie's. Many of them gut-wrenching in their tragedy and sorrow. Almost without exception I was able to set aside my personal feelings and conduct myself in a professional manner—though I sometimes had a good cry in private. I had no idea how full of emotion I was when I began Bertie's funeral until I stalled out the first of six or seven attempts and had to bite my lip and fight back tears until I regained my composure.

Bertie left us in August of 1991 just three years after we met her. Every so often I look up on my office wall where I've hung her oddball poem and a snapshot of the two of us standing beside the church. I chuckle as I read her mock insulting poem and remember her gift of laughter and I'm grateful that Bertie is still a special part of my life.

Confessions of a Letter Thief

Plagiarism is the sincerest
form of flattery.
— *D. J. Taylor*

Plagiarism is the sincerest
form of theft.
— *Source Unknown*

I didn't plan to become a letter thief. The practice sort of grew on me by barely perceptible degrees...and then it snowballed and became a habit.

Most boys don't feel the need for much letter writing until they take a typing class or fall in love with a girl from out of town. Of course a good mother makes sure her children learn how to send prompt thank you notes but long letters don't usually enter the picture for a boy until a girl lights up his life. Someone once said, "With love letters the longer the lovelier. With business letters the briefer the better." Once you've married that girl from out of town the need for long letters is pretty much a thing of the past.

Some people amaze me with the way they say so much so well with so few words. I began to collect such jewels for my own files. It may have started in the hallway of my older brother R.J.'s home. R.J. was fond of framing and displaying pictures and other treasured items. One framed congratulatory note was from Dr. Charles Anspauch, then president of Central Michigan College. It said simply, "One of the finest privileges of friendship is to share the happiness of a friend on a special occasion. Marie and I join you in celebrating the well-deserved honor you've just received." Impressed, I jotted it down for future use. I've used adaptations of that note hundreds of times over my 40 years in pastoral ministry.

Carol Pence sent me a keeper shortly after my mother's death. "Dear Don, Our hearts join yours in sadness at the death of your mother ... but are also with you in rejoicing that she has gained new-found freedom and peace." Hundreds of grieving people have received Carol's note over my name. When I told her years later, she didn't remember having dashed that note off, but she was glad her words could have a ripple-effect in so many other lives.

Partway through my years as an active pastor I stole a sign-off phrase from Steve Piper. He had signed one of his letters, "Smiles and rainbows, Steve." I latched on to it. One lady said, "Smiles and rainbows—how wonderful! Do you mind if I use it?" Confession gives my conscience relief when I acknowledge I stole the phrase from Steve and tell others they're welcome to be my partner in theft.

Early in my life as a clergyman I made it my business to learn the birthday, wedding anniversary and fresh anniversaries of family deaths of all our parishioners. I tried always to send them a brief note on those special days along with a couple of helpful printed items — often one serious and one humorous—a joke, poem or cartoon.

I've lived long enough to know a lot of people are fragile, vulnerable, and in need of support—even when they *appear* to be coping well. Often those who try to right a wrong or champion an unpopular cause are opposed and rejected. That's why I've tried to acknowledge the good others do ... especially if it has involved public rejection and/or loss of income. There have been a few times when I've felt all alone on a limb and have been glad for any reassurance my efforts were appreciated—if only by a few people.

Once while serving in Fraser, I sent a thank you note to Charles Swartzkopf, a devout Lutheran layman and president of the State Bank of Fraser. Charles took me completely off guard by his brief and heartwarming response. "Dear Pastor Lichtenfelt, It was thoughtful of you to take time out from a busy schedule to write me. I am deeply grateful and appreciate your good wishes particularly as coming from one whom I hold in special regard." Do you think I may have kept that letter? Do you think I may have used his words more than a few times on other occasions?

I find myself scanning greeting cards I've received with an eye to recycling their message. I do the same with greeting cards I've purchased. I type the message on four by six-inch file cards. I file them according to topic and enter the names of people I've sent that greeting to in order to avoid duplication within the same family—or in successive years.

You're feeling alone and lonely and get a note that says, "Bet you thought I forgot you. Guess again." Or, "You're getting a note for no reason at all. If that doesn't mean you're special I don't know what does!" Or, "When I like someone I like to tell them so. Consider yourself told!" Doesn't that give you a pick-me-up?

You're recovering from surgery and you get a note that says, "Glad to hear you're improving. That really surprises me. I thought you were already as nice as anyone could be." Is that good medicine or what?

It's your birthday and you get a note saying, "Happy birthday to a friend who is the epitome of manly strength and fortitude (or feminine pulchritude and sagacity) ... but otherwise not bad." Can you read that and not smile? Or your birthday is past and you wonder why you haven't heard from a friend who then writes a brief, abrupt, and unsigned note that says "May I be struck speechless if ever I forget your birthd ... ." Can you suppress a laugh? (Of course the return address on your mailing envelope identifies you as the sender.)

You're about to move and a friend sends you a simple note: "Your moving is going to make a lot of people happy—the people where you're going!" Or you get to your new location and someone writes, "I don't miss you half as much as I thought I would. I miss you twice as much!" Could a long letter say it any better?

In my forty years as a clergyman I've never done anything that took as little effort and met with more appreciation than notes timed to arrive a day or two before the anniversary of a death. So often bereaved people aren't just *thinking* about their loved one's death— they are *reliving* it in painful fashion. For years I've been sending a little note that says, "Though these days have a meaning you alone can understand, someone else remembers and wants to let you know." I've sent it with two or three relevant enclosures. Responses run something like, "I was feeling so alone in my grief until I got your note" or "You were the only one who remembered."

Others may have *remembered* but it's the *note* that brings comfort.

In the last half of my pastoral ministry our church secretaries and I sent out two or three dozen assorted notes a week. I count sending these brief notes (with enclosures) amongst the most supportive things I could be doing and it involves little time or cost.

Yes, my card file is packed with many "borrowed" letters. If this kind of "theft" is against the law then I'm in deep trouble. But, it's my hope that when the Great Postmaster comes to mark against my name, She will look upon my intention to give people a lift and grant me a pardon.

269

Goodbye, Lake Huron

Where there is sorrow
there is holy ground.
— *Oscar Wilde*

O world invisible, we view thee,
O world intangible, we touch thee,
O world unknowable, we know thee.
— *Francis Thompson*

Lake Huron is calm now. Yesterday she was thrashing about wildly. She crashed and foamed and roared, as a strong northeast wind shredded the crests of her waves.

Now, Vonda and I stand together on Lake Huron's high banks. We look down on quiet water with its slow gentle swirls. The water has the look of molten gold under the glare of the morning sun.

This land, and the house with its tall oak trees, dense pines and its over-view of the water, has been ours for eleven years now. It served as our mental health retreat as we recovered from our son Colin's death. Now, with retirement and moving to Kentucky just around the corner, the time has come to sell. After today, it is no longer ours.

Hand in hand we descend the fifty-five railroad-ties that curve down to the shore. Today we walk the beach without concern that a sudden wave will soak our shoes. We walk the waters edge stepping on sunlit pebbles resembling jewels in their moistened state. We are almost ready to apologize for trampling on such beauty.

We've come down to say goodbye to Lake Huron. It's our long-standing custom before we go back to the city. For eleven years we have left our tracks in this moist sand—for miles along her shore. We walk as far as we can with the time that is ours. Reluctantly, we turn around and head back.

Lake Huron is an eraser. She has erased our coming-out tracks. Over long periods of time she has erased stones and stumps along her shore. She has erased people who were careless with her power. She has eroded and erased high sandy banks along her shores. Lake Huron has a way of erasing time and making you think of eternity. The eternity it took for glaciers to carve out her bed—the eternity it took to tumble large jagged rocks until they were smooth and hot to our touch in the bright sunshine.

Lake Huron is a mirror reflecting the flight of hungry gulls over her waves...reflecting the hulls of muscular boats hauling iron ore from Duluth...reflecting the white fluffy clouds floating overhead and the advance of white sails on the Port Huron to Mackinaw racing boats. Night-time and she reflects a contorted moon sprawling out to sleep. Lake Huron is a mirror.

Lake Huron is a repository for thousands of wrecked ships— some located, many not. Some hold gold in the remains of their cargo. A historic plaque in the state park tells about the great storm of November 9, 1913 with its forty foot waves. Ten ships sank that day, more than twenty were driven ashore and 235 seamen drowned in the Great Lakes. All in one day! You begin to appreciate why she is called one of the most dangerous waterways in the world.

Among the sunken treasures beneath her surface are the ashes of our first-born son. The lake is a repository of things important to us.

Lake Huron is music. The steady drumbeat of heavy surf combines with the discordant whine of the wind, and the deep bass of thunder. The sudden crash of lightning is like giant cymbals in unseen hands.

There are days when you hear the music of many hands clapping, days when you hear the sound of only one hand clapping and the andante of waves whispering to the sand. There are days when your body cannot help but relax to the gentle swish and gurgle of indecisive waves just muddling on the shore. The lake is full of music. Full of emotion. One day her waves are laughing, another sobbing, another howling and shrieking. Through it all, flows the sense of a Presence and a strong note of yearning for the Undiscovered, the Indescribable, and the Mysterious.

We say goodbye to Lake Huron as we would to any friend. We thank her for her gifts of beauty, her music, her sometimes moody but life-giving water, her touch of mystery, her whispers of Infinity. Not least, we thank her because she holds our son in her bosom and gently rocks him. We leave Colin in her care.

The Stone that Spoke

"Night is drawing nigh"
—For all that has been—Thanks !
To all that shall be—Yes!
— *Dag Hammarskjold*

Most of us would like to end our lives feeling both
that we had a good time and that we left the world
a little better than we found it.
— *Philip Slater*

I can't tell you how many times I've felt the urge to drive down
Deanville Road to see what might be left of the tiny town of
Deanville—but something always thwarted my intention of doing
that.

Back in the late 1960s my grandfather gave me a copy of the little
book *The Waites of Deanville* written by his cousin Roy Waite, a
former professor of agriculture at Maryland State College. Roy wrote
of his experiences as the son of some of the earliest white settlers in
the thumb of Michigan, and listed family trees which included my
maternal ancestors, including my own family. I felt I needed to take
this trip. I wanted to see where those early ancestors had lived.

Last spring when I finally had time to myself I drove north on
busy Van Dyke Highway which stretches straight north from Detroit
through Michigan's Thumb to Port Austin. I crested a tall glacial hill
and turned east onto Deanville Road where I had the smooth asphalt
all to myself. I dropped my speed to ten miles an hour. Rolled my
window down and listened to the wind song. Smelled the moist earth
and the delicate scent of blossoms—many kinds intermingling as one
fragrance.

I couldn't help but think of the glaciers—two miles high—that
deposited those high sand and gravel hills over 12,000 years earlier
and how, according to geologists, the land is still rebounding from
their enormous weight. Couldn't help but think of the White Pine
Forests which covered most of Michigan before it became a state—
not a one left to see in this area—and how Michigan was so full of
swamps that many people wrote the area off as worthless. How the

272

earliest settlers, including my ancestors, faced tangled thickets with little more than axes and oxen and fire to clear the land by slow, tedious degrees.

I drank in the many shades of greens in field and fencerow and forest and felt amazed at the three giant gravel pits that opened up on the south side of the road—like huge craters on the moon. Their enormous basins had to have yielded hundreds of thousands of truckloads of sand and gravel for the building of roads and homes and factories in eastern Michigan. Once these huge cavities had been glacial terminal moraines pushing 300 feet tall—now they were yawning pits, the results of man's rearranging of nature.

My smooth ride ended just past the entrance to the third pit and I found myself on a steep descent on a now gravel road—uneven and loose surfaced. The roadsides were crowded with dense brush and the slope leveled off to more of the same. Here and there I drove by a house that echoed antiquity, along with a light sprinkling of newer but inelegant homes. If only those old decrepit homes, weathered by many a hot summer and severe winter, could tell their stories.

I continued east over flat land for about five or six miles and seeing few farms and nothing that remotely resembled a town—not even an old foundation here or there—I turned around and traveled the opposite direction. Near the intersection with Brown City Road I spotted a couple working in a field in front of a small greenhouse. A teen-aged girl was working inside the doorway. I pulled in the lane, parked on the trampled grass and walked to where they stood near a display of potted flowers. "Excuse me, I'm a stranger to these parts. Could you tell me where the town of Deanville was located or if anything remains of it?"

The man looked at me with an amused smile and opened his arms in a wide arc. "Right here—you're in it." He pointed over his left shoulder, "That building over there on the next road used to be the Deanville School House but it's been made over into a home. And if you look straight west—see up on that little rise? That's the Deanville cemetery. That's all that's left. When the railroad didn't go through here like they expected, people moved their houses from Deanville to Brown City and that was the end of it."

"Wow, hard to believe that everything's gone. I was expecting to see a foundation or two at the least." I explained how my grandfather's cousin had written a book about the early settlers here titled, *The Waites of Deanville.*

"Oh, yes, I've heard of the book and the Waite family, but they're all gone now. Been gone a looong time."

I thanked him for his time and the information and was about to return to my car, when almost as an afterthought I said, "I'm sorry, I didn't introduce myself. I'm Don Lichtenfelt from Lexington, Kentucky. I used to live north of here in Marlette.

He brightened and said, "Hi, Don, I'm Eugene Wilcox and this is my wife Carol." Then he scared up a memory. "Lichtenfelt. Lichtenfelt. We had a Mrs. Lichtenfelt here once. She was my first grade teacher in Brown City."

"Really? That would have been my mother."

"Well, I want to tell you, Mrs. Lichtenfelt was a **teacher**-teacher. Not like the ones we have today. When you got through her classes you knew what you were supposed to learn—or she'd hold you out of recess until you did. As a matter of fact, my cousin, Larry, had a rough time in school. He was flunking first grade, but Mrs. Lichtenfelt said, 'I think Larry could make it to second grade okay with a little help. If you could bring him to my house in Marlette I could work with him.' So they took him there to work with her and Larry made it just fine after that. My family always appreciated that she took the extra time with him."

"Well, I never heard about that. It's nice to hear good things about your family. You know, it's a strange thing—our meeting like this out in a field—and if you had my mother as a teacher that means I have a class picture of you in my home in Mom's scrapbook. Isn't that incredible? I'm sure glad we met."

I thanked them again for their time and information and drove off, turning south to drive by the old Deanville School which had been converted to a small home. It appeared shabby and uncared for—hardly recognizable as a school anymore. A man bent over working amidst the clutter of his front yard. He looked up puzzled at my going by so slowly, obviously giving his property a once over. I wondered about the school. How long it had been there, how many pupils had attended there over the years and how many were still around. *No, use your head, Donald, they're all scattered far and wide like leaves on the wind. They're all in cemeteries someplace.*

I doubled back taking a long last look at the only remaining building of Deanville and headed toward the little cemetery Mr. Wilcox had pointed out to me. The plot was about fifty yards wide and a hundred yards deep. Level near the road and gradually rising to the high point of the slope. The bulk of the weather-beaten old marble grave markers were at the top. The newer granite tombstones were near the road. I wondered about this arrangement. Had there been a church there at one time with the cemetery in the rear? Had the earliest graves been near the road—perhaps marked with only wooden markers? Who knows?

I wandered about the small cemetery, stopped at the wire fence on the east side and looked down the long slope. I watched a farmer driving an old tractor—the kind with metal wheels and wedge-shaped lugs. He chugged across the field with his engine making a high-pitched metallic pinging as he dragged the rich brown loam for planting. I wondered if he might be the descendant of somebody in the cemetery—if he saw me looking down and wondered who I was—what I was doing there—if I might be a distant relative of his—if we might enjoy talking with each other if he were to stop and come up the hill. I regret not talking with him though, since plowing a big field is a lonely business, he may have welcomed the interruption.

I followed the fence to the rear left corner—the highest point in the little plot. There, in the midst of a small rock pile of weathered granite rocks left by the glaciers—were several soiled and weathered fragments of old marble tombstones. I picked up a small rectangular piece about the size of a bar of Ivory soap—hackly on five sides, smoother on one. I held it in my hand and wondered whose marker it had been. Someone's child? An elderly grandparent? Someone's spouse or parent? Someone who didn't live long enough to marry? Whomever the stone belonged to, I felt sure it had been cried over, visited and revisited, caressed, and the name engraved on it had been traced by the finger of at least one survivor.

I thought, *Talk to me stone. Tell me about yourself.* Of course it didn't—not in an audible voice. Yet in a way it did speak as the words of an old epitaph came to my mind, "As you are now, I once was. As I am now, so you will be."

It spoke to me as the words of Longfellow's *Evangeline* came rushing into my mind: "Where is the thatch-roofed village, the home of Acadian farmers / Men whose lives glided on like rivers that water

275

the woodlands / Darkened by shadows of earth, but reflecting an image of heaven?"

It spoke to me as I recalled the words of Isaac Watt's hymn, *O God, Our Help in Ages Past*: "Time, like an ever rolling stream bears all who breathe away; they fly forgotten, as a dream dies at the opening day."

The stone spoke to me. I decided I'd take it home, clean it up and polish one side on my diamond polishing wheel. It now rests on my desk—on top of *The Waites of Deanville*. I pick it up every now and then. Hold it gently in my hand. Feel its hackly sides and the one smooth side. I wait for it to speak to me again. Letting it remind me, in the silence, of the little town of Deanville—the town that was and her people now gone—my ancestors, my fellow humans, whom I shall soon follow.

Lake Huron, view from our home, north of Lexington, Michigan

Epilogue

Where Memory Lives

Memory is the diary that we all
carry about with us.
— *Oscar Wilde*

And who is to say that, in some crucial
sense, the life that we remember is not
the life we lived?
— *Deborah Tall*

I will not be buried in the Marlette Cemetery with my parents, my father's father and my half-sister, Virginia. My ashes are to be scattered on the blue water of Lake Huron near Port Sanilac with our son Colin's.

Still, my home town cemetery holds an endless fascination for me. Whenever I'm near Marlette I feel an overwhelming urge to return. Once there, I pick up a double-dip butter pecan cone at Moore's Dairy Bar—still there after more than 60 years in business—and drive around town remembering people and places—reliving events and feelings. Then, on to the south edge of town for a long walk through the cemetery.

Look at the back of your left hand. (We Michiganians use our hands as a map.) Place your right index finger on the middle bone of your thumb. That's Marlette—halfway between Lake Huron and the end of Saginaw Bay. Our town cemetery lies on rolling hills of gravel left by glaciers tens of thousands of years ago. Seems to me all cemeteries should be like that—gentle hills with winding gravel roads insisting on the way. And tall trees in the oldest sections: maple and elm, ash and oak, hemlock and pine and flowering shrubs to soften the hardness of stone—a place where it's impossible to be in a hurry.

I park near the entrance and walk to the first curve. Already I'm aware this is more than a burial ground. It's a powerful memory jogger. On the right is a raised earthen platform, three feet high, with a tall flag pole in the middle. Its slopes are covered solid with smooth granite rocks the size of your head. I can still see the Memorial Day services there during World War II—still hear the high school marching band playing Sousa marches in their smart red and white uniforms. See the members of the American Legion and Veterans of Foreign Wars in their varied uniforms—still hear the solemn tones of the speaker and the soft flapping of many small red, white and blue flags on ever so many graves of veterans—the pledge of allegiance— and the solemn hush that fell on us as a bugler played taps. Taps always gives me a painful knot in my throat—more so on this day because I feel the absence of my three older brothers in military service. Today they are serving our country in far away places: Europe, India, and the Pacific.

From here the road bends left. I see that gray headstone with "Weldon A. Gift, M.D." He's the doctor who brought me into the world—tended my childhood illnesses and injuries and presided over the births and deaths of so many in Marlette.

Now the road sways right and dips low. Right here I had a pivotal experience when I was four and a half years old. My parents and I were walking up to my grandfather Fred's grave site to see his newly installed red granite marker. Right here in the gravel, I spied a strange stone and picked it up. It was brown like a Hershey bar and looked like a little curved animal horn. Dad said it was some sort of fossil— that it had been a living thing thousands of years ago. I learned later he was off about 350 million years but finding that horn coral was the beginning of my life-long hobby of collecting fossils, gems and minerals.

Now I come to the hill where my mother and father are buried. Here's where I indulge in a little ritual. When they're in season, I always pick a blue chicory blossom for Dad's grave (because blue was his favorite color) and a dandelion for mother's (because I tried to say my first "I love yous" with dandelions.) Then I kneel on the grass in front of their reddish grave markers. I reach out my hands and feel the smooth cool granite of the polished portion and then the hackly unpolished sides. I run the tips of my fingers over their names. Then, I find a twig and scrape out the algae and lichens that like to grow in the engraved portions. I always feel a twinge of regret knowing we were not as close as some families I've known...and I don't even know why not.

Up here there's usually a good breeze. There's always a good view. Walk in any direction and I'll come across people I chatted with when I was a clerk in my father's I.G.A. store. Their names are always on the breeze up here: Thompson, Burkholder, Barnes and Gould. There are those I was with two hours every Sunday morning at the Methodist Church—their names are music: Schlichter and Hobson and Caister and Cripps. Classmates and friends at high school whose names murmur like a deep river Gerstenberger, Kukovich, McLaren, DesJardens, and Alonzo. Boys I went to Scout Camp with and boxed with—whose names whisper through the hemlocks: Maxam, Elliott, McKinnon, and Cochrane. Over there, to the north, is the fresh grave of Don Marshall, my sparring partner. Didn't know Don was gone until my last visit up here. Not far from Don you see the grave of Marian Caister—our church choir director and my piano teacher. I must have been one of her greatest disappointments—loving piano music as I do but never getting beyond that *John Thompson Third Grade Piano Lessons* manual.

Here you'll find dozens of people I delivered the Port Huron Times Herald to sixty-some years ago. In my mind's eyes and ears, they still greet me with smiles and call me by name: the Westovers, Heines, Benedicts, McCreas, Stevensons, and Sanchezs. All these people were part of my growing years—neighbors and friends who helped shape my view of things.

I'm always amazed at the peace I feel up here and how those old audio-visual tapes run through my mind in color and how—in my mind's ear—the familiar voices of those long dead come back to me—live again. No, my body will not be buried here, but this is where part of my heart is. The other part is in Lake Huron.

Let the Mist Rise

Let the mist of early evening
  whiten the air in low places
  and rising, envelop the field.

Let the frogs begin their nocturne
  as lilacs perfume the night with involuntary fragrance. Let the mist rise.

Let droplets moisten the untouched door knob
  on the guest house. Let stars spangle the sky
  and the moon display her curved sword.

Let the swallow settle soft in her nest
  let breathing slow…rest. Let the fog
  blend all as one. Let the mist rise.

To the lost ball in the grass, to the fork
  in the hay, the blown-out candle
  let the mist rise.

Let it rise. Let it rise, and feel
  no alarm. God gives treasures
  of darkness, so let the mist rise.

— Don Lichtenfelt
After Jane Kenyon's
"Let Evening Come"

Author's Notes

Memory is notoriously unreliable and sometimes plays tricks on us. At times we recall situations accurately, at other times we mess up no matter how we strive for accuracy. At times we find ourselves influenced by how we felt (emotional memory) at the time. I've tried to tell these stories as close to fact as I can get them and any departures are unintentional. Clearly I've been swayed by my emotional truth at times.

Of the six parishes I've served under appointment of my six bishops, three have been single churches, two have been paired, and one has been a three point parish. In my book divisions (based on years spent in each parish) I've listed only the church where the parsonage was located and by which the parish was known. No prejudice is intended toward any outpoints—some of which varied during the time of my appointment.

Early on I refer to my denomination as The Methodist Church, later as The United Methodist Church. The name change is due to our merger with the Evangelical United Brethren Church in 1968.

Some names and circumstances have been changed to mask the identity of persons or places. Many close friends and family have not been included, though I hold them close in my heart. I've omitted lengthy reference to some powerful life-changing experiences—including Vonda's scary encounters with cancer resulting in her double mastectomy, and our son Lance's encephalitis at age two which resulted in brain damage—and his living with us all the years of his life to date.

About the Author

Don Lichtenfelt is the grandson of a German immigrant. His father was born in a log cabin and had no formal education beyond the eighth grade though he read on a daily basis. Don was born during the early years of the Great Depression in Marlette, Michigan—the eighth child of his father and the first of his mother's three children. According to *The Birth Order Book,* the spacing of his family makes him "an only child in a family of ten children."

As a young man, Don would "rather box than eat," and fantasized about becoming a professional fighter. Instead, he chose the Christian ministry. (Long ago his wife asked him, "Isn't that a bit incongruous?")

He attended Central Michigan College, and graduated from Asbury College and Garrett Theological Seminary. He served as a United Methodist minister for forty years in Iowa and Michigan, during which time he was involved in the completion of four church building programs.

He has been a mineral collector since he was four years old and is a former vice president of the Michigan Mineralogical Society, and the Bluegrass Gem and Mineral Club. In retirement, he has focused on writing his memoir and gardening.

His articles have been printed in the *Grosse Pointe News*, the *Michigan Christian Advocate*, and he was awarded the Carole Petit Legacies Creative Writing Medallion at the Carnegie Center for Literacy and Learning in Lexington, Kentucky.

Don and his wife Vonda are the parents of four adult children: Colin (deceased), Lance, Lisa (Mrs. Michael Gribbin) and Erich. They make their home in Lexington, Kentucky.

CPSIA information can be obtained at www.ICGtesting.com
Printed in the USA
LVOW11s2245221013

358152LV00002B/2/P

9 781936 138630